HEARING THINGS

HEARING

THINGS ✤

Voice and Method in the Writing of Stanley Cavell

TIMOTHY GOULD

The University of Chicago Press ✱ *Chicago and London*

Timothy Gould is chairman of the Department of Philosophy at the Metropolitan State College of Denver.

The University of Chicago Press, Chicago 60637
The University of Chicago Press, Ltd., London
© 1998 by The University of Chicago
All rights reserved. Published 1998
07 06 05 04 03 02 01 00 99 98   1 2 3 4 5
ISBN: 0-226-30562-7 (cloth)
ISBN: 0-226-30563-5 (paper)

Library of Congress cataloging-in-publication Data

Gould, Timothy.
    Hearing things : voice and method in the writing of Stanley Cavell
/ Timothy Gould.
        p.   cm.
    Includes bibliographical references and index.
    ISBN 0-226-30562-7 (cloth : alk. paper). — ISBN 0-226-30563-5
(pbk. : alk. paper)
    1. Cavell, Stanley, 1926–   . 2. Language and languages—
Philosophy.   3. Methodology.   I. Title.
    B945.C274G68   1998
    191—dc21   98-23109
                                                                        CIP

∞The paper used in this publication meets the minimum requirements of the American National Standard for Information Sciences—Permanence of Paper for Printed Library Materials, ANSI Z39.48-1992.

To my mother, Toni Stern Gould

and

to my father, David Gould

Problems are solved (difficulties removed), not a problem. There is not a method in philosophy, though there are indeed methods—like different therapies.
—Ludwig Wittgenstein

Listening not to me, but to the account.
—Heraclitus

Bene ascolta qui la nota.
—Dante

Contents

Preface and Acknowledgments

Underneath the accounts of voice and method that I provide in this book lie two plain facts about the human capacity for speech and meaningfulness. What we say to one another depends on a common fund of language. And when we speak, we speak in a particular voice. Initially, this says nothing more mysterious than that we generally speak in a particular *tone* of voice, whether harsh or soothing, assertive or seductive, confident or desperate, anxious or relaxed. But we also seem to know what it means to say that, whatever the particular tone we take on a given occasion, we are normally speaking in our own voice. The police and the FBI may prefer fingerprints or dental records for purposes of identification. But most of the time it is our voices that harbor our idiosyncrasies and (along with our faces) hold the key to our sense of singularity and, perhaps, identity.

So much seems obvious enough. You do not need to be a philosopher to appreciate such familiar human matters. In fact, it is in our more ordinary exchanges that we are likely to use these features of our speech as idioms or symbols of communication and expression. To say that we "speak the same language" is to suggest that we are in a state of intimate accord and need not waste time on unnecessary explanations. And the voice is commonly used as a symbol of the human need to express something unique about ourselves. Even more frequently, the inability or refusal to hear a voice is used to symbolize the denial of the human need for recognition. By now, such ideas of speaking in your own voice and of learning to listen to different voices have become so pervasive that we are hardly aware of using figures of speech. They provide natural ways in which to talk about the issue of who is speaking and who is getting heard. Such ways of talking have found a home in contemporary cultural and political discourse.

Not even a philosopher would just set out to deny such familiar features of our language or to deprive us of the happy idioms that we have constructed from these features. And yet the study of philosophy often leads us to want something *more* from language, something it seems incapable of giving. For instance, the words we are supposed to work with can suddenly seem unbearably vague and imprecise, scarcely fit for serious intellectual endeavors. Or certain words can come to seem too personal, too loaded with idiosyncratic associations: it seems impossible to get a meaning across in such a fashion and working with such crude materials. Again, when we are trying to think about a philosophical issue or text, we sometimes find it objectionable that the meaning of an utterance can change depending on who utters it and on the circumstances in which it is uttered. In the grip of the question of how words can conceivably mean the same for you as they do for me, we will not want to dwell on the painfully obvious fact that the same words may strike us quite differently or that I myself may be affected differently on different occasions. And— as Wittgenstein sees fit to remind us—words can be hard to say.

At some stage in our efforts to pursue a thought philosophically, it is almost inevitable that we arrive at the sense that ordinary words are too crude for our purposes. But this is not the only way we become conscious of our words when we are engaged in philosophy. We may find ourselves thinking that the difficulty in saying what we mean derives less from the poverty of language and more from the difficulty of seeing, and saying, the obvious. Here the difficulty is perhaps better thought of as stemming not from the crudeness of words but from their obtrusiveness. We can at times be overtaken by a sense of being obtrusive in speaking or writing *at all*, as if we are in danger of betraying a kind of perpetual clumsiness in the face of the objects and events we are trying to understand.

Wittgenstein entered my education as the philosopher who made our entanglement with words into part of the texture of philosophy. A little later, Stanley Cavell provided me with an access to Wittgenstein's *Investigations* that placed its obsessions with language in the midst of the problems of self-knowledge and human culture. Cavell's readings of *King Lear*, Beckett, Fellini, and Schönberg were not separate from his depiction of contemporary philosophers—or anyone in a philosophical frame of mind—as picking apart the web of connections that binds the human being to everyday life. Like other mortals, we analyze not to destroy but to evade.

On Cavell's account, Wittgenstein's gaudy yet painstaking modes of writing have everything to do with the difficulty—but also the triumph and the pleasure—of seeing the obvious. What Cavell characterized as philosophy's typical alternation between obscurity and obviousness was also one of the ways he was teaching us to move between the philosophy of ordinary language and the work of a writer like Samuel Beckett. For Cavell, as for Wittgenstein, how you go about giving an account of the obvious is as much of an issue as how you go about seeing the obvious in the first place. Such questions have been for the most part ignored or covered over in recent years.

One primary motive for the writing of this book has been to reawaken the question of the obvious, along with other issues of the ordinary and the everyday. Within the question of how we are to put the obvious into words there is a further question of the power of the obvious and of everyday things themselves. Wittgenstein writes:

> The aspects of things that are most important for us are hidden because of their simplicity and their everydayness. (One is unable to notice something—because it is always before one's eyes.) The real foundations of his enquiry do not strike a human being at all. Unless *that* fact has once struck him.—And this means: we fail to be struck by what, once seen, is the most striking and the most powerful. [*Philosophical Investigations*, #129; I have modified the Anscombe translation in several places.]

Many commentators have recognized that Wittgenstein is making an issue out of the difficulty of seeing the obvious and the everyday. I translate *Alltäglichkeit* in the first sentence more literally as "everydayness" rather than as Anscombe's "familiarity." This helps to emphasize that for Wittgenstein it is everydayness itself that we have to overcome in order to allow ourselves to be struck by the importance of the everyday.

I also want us to hear the undercurrent of strength in *die Stärkste*, which is at least as relevant as the idea of the "most powerful." Once we let the everyday and the obvious become *striking*, we also become aware of their strength and even their sturdiness. It is their strength, more than their power, that lets them serve as foundations. However we translate the word, Wittgenstein is insisting on the everyday character of our words as precisely what supports our enquiries into them. Moreover, this everydayness is a stronger foundation for our enquiries than the various substitutes and supplements that we are likely to come up with. Wittgenstein is also reminding us that this strength of the everyday is something that has to be recognized to be accepted. And it has to be accepted in order for its strength to become effective.

It seems to me that this sense of Wittgenstein is not widely shared, at least by English-speaking philosophers, and it is not shared by some very devoted readers of Wittgenstein. A philosopher might, for instance, suppose that once the grammar of what we say has become clear to us there is no *special* philosophical problem about how to make this grammar clear to a reader. Nor is there a special problem about achieving in a piece of writing the strikingness and effectiveness of the everyday. Here the danger is that you will succeed in calling attention not to the ordinary and the everyday matters that you were pointing toward but rather to the language you are using to direct the audience's attention. For the more familiar responses to Wittgenstein, on the other hand, a "perspicuous representation" of our utterances is just a way of describing them clearly enough to show that what we thought was a philosophical perplexity was really based on a misunderstanding of our grammar.

In Cavell's reading of Wittgenstein, the ways that we find to put the obvious into words are part of what makes the writing of philosophy both distinctive and difficult. To put it more sharply: The demand that we show, in words, how the obvious can be obvious (and therefore how it can have remained obscure) is part of what makes philosophy philosophy. And these ways are also part of what makes philosophy into a form of *writing,* or at any rate, part of what makes the writing of philosophy so essential to its achievement. The discovery of this question of how to register the obviousness of the ordinary world in words was part of what drew me to Wittgenstein and Cavell and, later, to Heidegger. But it also drew me, for instance, to Wordsworth, Hölderlin, Whitman, and George Eliot. From early on in my education, I felt called on to say something about what gives this issue about writing and the everyday a distinctively philosophical form. And there were, at that time, not only no obvious answers to such a question but no obvious direction in which the question might even be pursued.

I would not, for instance, have thought of the voice as anything that might provide a philosophical form to the issues that I was thinking about. And I certainly would not have thought of *Cavell's* voice as relevant to how something becomes a philosophical issue. On the contrary, my goal would have been to keep Cavell's voice and, more generally, his style from becoming the wrong kind of issue—something that threatened to drown out his distinctive contribution to philosophy. Before any of us could learn to think of the voice as something worth studying philosophically, we had to be able to understand the voice as something that the dominant versions of philosophy were denying or repressing.

But philosophy's traditional lack of interest in something as undependable and as mundane as the voice seemed much too casual to regard as a symptom of something as momentous as intellectual repression. No one would have simply *denied* such facts as that a human utterance normally makes the most sense when we understand it as uttered by a particular human, with a particular voice. And we all know that human beings are sometimes called upon to give voice to some condition or feeling or thought. More steps had to be taken to get us from a sense that philosophers had little use for the voice in thinking about human meaningfulness to the idea that they were engaged in wholesale acts of repressing and banishing the voice from the terrain of philosophy.

Cavell took these steps in his reading of Wittgenstein: The pervasiveness of the need to give voice to our utterances is the other side of the pervasiveness of the shared criteria in our use of the words that convey our communications. Our awareness of Wittgensteinian criteria seems to come about only when something about our ordinary capacity for successful speech has been challenged. It is from within Cavell's efforts to characterize the threat to our mutual attunement in criteria—our attunement in words and in speech—that he first produced an explicit, positive conception of the voice. Consequently, the suppression of criteria can be seen as deriving, in part, from the philosopher's wish to suppress the requirement that a human being actually be thought of as *uttering* the remarks that evince those criteria. And this in turn could well be construed as the suppression of the voice, considered as the medium by which we give voice to our utterances.

This is the way of understanding Wittgenstein and Austin that Cavell was then developing. But these developments did not happen overnight. That this understanding of the voice took a while to develop is, I think, the single most crucial fact in the genesis of the present book. On the one hand, I learned to hear the question of the voice as epitomizing an entire region of questions about the means by which human beings express themselves and the depth of our need for such expression. And then I began to understand that the actual development had occurred much more slowly than it would later appear. In fact, Cavell's idea of the voice developed inexorably, but at first quite unmethodically, in the course of at least twenty years of work. Not until *after* the work represented in *The Claim of Reason* was completed did Cavell arrive at a position where he could explicitly name and characterize the voice as one of the central issues of his work.

It began to occur to me that Cavell's work could be presented in the different terms and stages of its development. Moreover, if the chance for this kind of account of his work were missed, then something crucial would remain inaudible. Since Cavell himself had employed the appeals to ordinary speech without explicitly recognizing them as appeals to the voice, then others might also find themselves in that position. Then there was a step to be isolated and accounted for, a step *between* the appeals to the ordinary and the recognition of the voice within those appeals. It dawned on me slowly that this step was not to be taken once and for all: To understand Cavell's work—along with that of Wittgenstein and Austin—you have to be willing to go back over that step and to take it on your own.

Tracing the development of this recognition of the voice in Cavell's work became part of my effort to come to terms with my own relation to ordinary language philosophy and to the voices that emerge out of that mode of philosophizing. As I worked out the terms of my account of that recognition, I discerned a connection between Cavell's emerging conception of the voice and the gradual transformation of his philosophical practices and, most especially, the philosophical practices of reading. Finally, it began to seem clear that the gradual emergence of the idea of the voice within Cavell's philosophical methods was a kind of enactment of the lifting of the repression of the voice. Once again, the deepest recognitions of the ways in which philosophy defends itself against an unwelcome thought or phenomenon are found in those who are best able to recognize these mechanisms in themselves.

In finding out these things about the voice and about the developments in Cavell's understanding and invocation of the voice, I was also finding out how to tell a story about these things. Telling a story is a good way to treat of certain kinds of developments in a thinker's position. It is also a good way to help sort out the confusions that Cavell's readers are exposed to when different phases of his development are collapsed into each other. When the subject is the voice, then the story has perhaps an even greater scope. And my story has a kind of natural shape—or plot outline—involving philosophy's initial suppression and loss of the voice and its subsequent recovery in Wittgenstein, Austin, and Cavell.

Perhaps only a philosopher would think it worthwhile to attempt to recover something so obvious as the human voice from something so unobvious as philosophical discourse. It is a strange business, requiring first that we find the places where philosophy has denied the obvious, and then that we attempt to undo those very denials. How strange to think that one could rescue our everyday words and rehabilitate the human need to give voice to our thoughts from the very philosophical discourse that seems so distant and so alienated from that ordinary world. But for various reasons, I was drawn to depict just this scene of banishment and eventual return.

I also wanted to remain subjected to various tugs from the direction of poetry and literary theory. I still want there to be a region in the humanities where these issues can be entertained and explored. For me, it would have to be a place where Wordsworth could be understood as placing demands on language as exorbitant as any analytic philosopher's or deconstructionist's.

> . . . Oh! why hath not the Mind
> Some element to stamp her image on
> In nature somewhat nearer to her own?
> Why, gifted with such powers to send abroad
> Her spirit, must it lodge in shrines so frail?[1]

Unlike the philosopher who finds words to be vague, or perhaps clumsy, Wordsworth is here finding them frail. He is afraid that mere words in mere books will not be able to sustain and protect the mind's power to communicate itself.

The poet's anxiety about language is not separate from his anxiety about the power of the imagination.

> Imagination—here the Power so called
> Through sad incompetence of human speech,
> That awful power rose from the mind's abyss
> Like an unfathered vapor that enwraps,
> at once, some lonely traveller. I was lost;
> Halted without an effort to break through . . . [Book 6, lines 592–97.]

Philosophers have typically worried that the imagination will subvert the power of language to render accurately the facts of the world or the verdicts of reason. Wordsworth worries that language will not be up to the burden of communicating and preserving the mind's highest knowledge of the world and itself. He turns to nature not so much for relief from these anxieties but for a confirmation that within nature the mind can still rise to the occasion. Instead of an immediate confirmation he gets something like the same anxieties writ large. Left to its own devices, the mind does not seem to know the difference between up and down, or anyway between the upward and the downward path. Wordsworth knows he is lost not because of the weight of custom or the pressure of city life: he is lost in part because of the very power of the imagination that he looks to for his guidance and his vocation.

And as he retraces his steps, a voice emerges from within the disorder of nature: "Black dizzying crags that spake by the wayside/ As if a voice were in them . . ." (book 6, lines 631–32). The voice the poet hears in the waterfalls corresponds to Wordsworth's wish to speak directly to the presences of nature. The voice of nature talks back to the voice of the poet and responds to the demands on nature that voices like the poet's are inclined to make. The Romantic willingness to listen for a more than human voice in nature is equally a yearning for a more than human form of writing. The surrounding sublimity of the trees ("woods decaying, never to be decayed") and the power and repetition of the water shooting through the rocky passages of the waterfall yields a sense of the "workings of one mind":

> . . . the features
> Of the same face, blossoms upon one tree;
> Characters of the great Apocalypse,
> The types and symbols of Eternity,
> Of first, and last, and midst, and without end.
> [Ibid., lines 636–40.]

For all my sense of the power and passiveness of those Romantic voices— with their own scenes of loss and recovery—it was after all something like philosophy that kept drawing me on. But my path to the question of how to make the voice audible within philosophy began to diverge some- what from the path of Cavell's solutions. For in telling the story of his development, I often found myself doubling back: I wanted to get back to the originary texts of Austin and Wittgenstein and to get behind Cavell's first efforts to characterize the methods of ordinary language philosophy. I believe this doubling back to be a necessary movement for staying on the track of a writer like Cavell. I think it is especially useful for under- standing the various ways in which Cavell was able to make a kind of beginning or an opening for philosophy. And his ways of beginning to think continue to shape the various fields in which his work shows up.

But this sort of return to the point of origin is not the same journey as when Cavell in his later writings revisits Austin's work and his own ear- liest essays. Some of the differences will emerge in what follows. And some of those differences derive from the fact that, in telling this story, I am also putting forward something of my own account of the realm of the ordinary and of the voices that inhabit that realm. The story I am telling is a story of a kind of development, and this suggests that our relation to the ordinary is not static. (Perhaps, indeed, we might say that our relation to the ordinary is not itself describable purely in terms of the ordinary. But that would be to get ahead of the story.)

I am implicitly giving an account in this book of how I came to be in a position to tell just this particular story of Cavell's recovery of the voice. I am also putting forward, somewhat more explicitly, the idea that this story contains an element of method. Obviously, most of the steps I am characterizing as intended to be taken by others were first put forward by Cavell or inherited by him from Wittgenstein and Austin. But the effort to sort out the different steps taken by different thinkers and to sort out the different stages of development is largely mine. And if that effort sometimes proposes methodological caution, it is also meant to provide methodological opportunity. There are steps of thinking and reading laid out in this book that others can follow and verify for themselves. Indeed, I trust that there are places where others can stand while they figure out still further steps for us to take.

A book about voices is likely to sustain itself on conversations, both real and imagined. Among the local sources of intelligibility were Naomi Reshotko and David Sullivan. They kept the climate of Denver closer to its promise of green. Rick Doepke showed his collegiality in more ways than one, not least by his example and by his willingness to run interference. Still within Colorado, Jane Kneller, Marian Keane, Allan Franklin, and Luc Bovens each made it possible—and also reasonable— to go public with work that was still in progress. Kevin O'Neill mingled computer advice with discussions of Preston Sturges and Samuel Beckett. Southward in the same time zone, Gus Blaisdell provided sanctuary and critique. The philosophy department of the University of New Mexico, and most especially Russell Goodman, provided an audience for both the earliest and the latest stages of this work. Michael Fischer was often present on those occasions, and his book on Cavell was on my mind more often than I make explicit.

Jon Kamholtz and Josh Wilner have sounded enough notes of encouragement to last me for several ages more. They have tried to keep me honest, as well as critical, and they tutored my capacities for listening. Eve Sedgwick—and several liquor boxes worth of e-mail—walked me through some very dull regions of my brain and somehow reflected back to me the very brightest pictures of possibility. It was her invitation to the English Institute that produced the impetus to write "The Unhappy Performative."[2] This was my first chance to think publicly about the contrast between J. L. Austin's reception in literary theory and his reception in Cavell's work and mine. One of the instructive pleasures of her idea for that occasion was that I should share the panel with Judith Butler.

Garrett Stewart, Nataša Ďurovičová, and Stephen Melville have provided support and direction for some of my physical as well as my metaphysical wanderings. Just outside the gates of philosophy, they offered me the best of reinforcements and the most perceptive of readings. Susan

Howe, Barbara Packer, and Christina Zwarg have made me think about the voices and conversations within American writing. And Dick Moran always seemed to know when I needed a phone call to keep me at it.

Friends who go back to the beginning of my efforts to write philosophy provided responses and comments at crucial moments. Paul Guyer, Barbara Herman, Chris Korsgaard, and Mickey Morgan each found something philosophical to like in my work, hence something for me to pursue. Ted Cohen and Stanley Bates were among the first to read the whole manuscript, enduring much typographical menace. They appear within this book as the joint authors of one of the earliest—and best—pieces of work ever done on Cavell. But they have been pushing me, and pulling me, out of rough spots for longer than that.

People have been trying for years to find adequate words in which to thank Stanley Cavell. And for almost as long, I have been maintaining that saying "thank you" is not as difficult as it sometimes appears. It is admittedly not always easy to be clear about the difference between the fruitfulness of the books and the empirical generosity of the man who gives his name—and, no doubt, a local habitation—to those books. Getting clearer about this difference between the man and his books, and hence about their ultimate connection, was one of my private motives for beginning to write about Cavell. It is, however, plain enough that in at least one of his more significant aspects, Stanley Cavell is the very literal sine qua non of this book. And he had a lot to do with the actual writing of it. I am happy to be able to say so.

This is a good place to note the obvious: the errors and infelicities contained in this book are mine. But here the claims of indebtedness and of responsibility pull more strikingly in different directions. Part of the claim embedded in this disclaimer is that there is enough independence at work in this book to *make* the errors mine. It is almost a consolation.

It was helpful to read Steven Affeldt's dissertation, especially his chapter on Stephen Mulhall on Cavell. A couple of dozen conversations with him have made this a better book. Nancy Bauer gave me some of the perspective I needed to think that I had something useful to say on these subjects, and Alice Crary's notes on the first draft provided an early focus for my revisions. James Conant's helpfulness is approaching legendary proportions, but it is nonetheless worth being grateful for. William Day sent me detailed comments on increasingly large pieces of manuscript. And Randall Havas, Richard Fleming, and Martin Stone each said things that allowed me to figure out something crucial. Ed Minar—especially in his response to my paper, "This Skeptical Life"—confirmed my sense of my claims and offered me a chance to sharpen my formulation of them.

William Rothman comes in for some criticism in this book. But nothing that I say detracts from the power of his critical insights or from his continuing meditation on the nature of film. I have been learning from him about film and philosophy since the early 1970s. There is not much in the realm of the humanities that approaches Rothman's ability to unleash the world of a movie from the reading of a sequence of frames.

It sometimes surprises me to remember how many of my former students have chosen to earn their living as teachers. But they are not the only ones who taught me something, or wrote me something, that I am not likely to forget. I am happy to acknowledge the benefit of having worked with (in chronological order) Brom Anderson at Harvard; Rick Eldridge, Jeff Wieand, Susan Carlisle, and Jon Petrik at Middlebury; Dick Liebendorfer, Isaac Nevo, and Kirk Ludwig at U.C.–Santa Barbara; Robert Gamboa at the University of Nevada–Reno; and Sara Gadeken, Frank Kusumoto, Julie Liggett, and Tina Rogol at the Metropolitan State College of Denver. Chris Devlin, another former student, read the entire manuscript with the care of an editor and the "No" of a more tactful Socratic *daimon*. Her intervention—along with that of Steven Affeldt— is visible on almost every page.

Institutional alienation should leave room for the exceptions: Larry Johnson and Joan Foster—both as deans and as friends—managed to let me know in practical ways that they approved of my activities. The National Endowment for the Humanities supported work of mine on Kant and Romanticism, which cleared at least enough of the deck for the present project. Mark Rhine, Denise Griffey, Ed Hoskins, Barry Seldin, Norm Lackey, and Deborah Deeg each took care of some aspect of the inner and outer circumstances of this book's production. Toward the end of the project, David Brent demonstrated in detail his practical and heartening conviction that the circumstances of inner and outer production were ready to come together. Salena Krug contributed a series of congenial editorial suggestions, along with the encouragement needed to implement them.

Gordon Gould provided me with the means to supplement a sabbatical leave in two successive fall semesters. He offered me the continuing reassurance of family support and a glimpse of civility in the mountains of Colorado. At the same altitude, Marilyn Appel managed to put together a kind of salon, where music and conversation about music seemed once again welcome. Michael Linville, Don Wilkinson, Steve Wiseman, and Ann Lillya were part of the music of those occasions, and Emile and Barrie Chi were part of the magic.

My parents, to whom this book is dedicated, gave me the support that got me started toward a life of intellectual work. And they also gave me something to work with. My father's gift for music has provided me with some of my earliest memories. And I am glad to find something of my mother's relation to German poetry and culture at work in my most immediate concerns. Kathryn Gould and Jeffrey Gould have each seen me through difficult stretches. They offered not only the support of a sister and a brother but also the kind of friendship that is, as Emerson says, a gift of nature. And my brother's advice about books—especially about how to get them off your desk—has been both timely and expert. Chris Flink was, formally speaking, my stepson when I began to think about this project. He continues to make it clear that he was along for more than the ride. And I like to think that our paths will continue to cross.

Katherine Campbell, my frontier lawyer, has provided consultation of incalculable worth. She has also provided me with the latest opportunity to exercise my talents as a basketball coach, in the person of Timothy Madison Campbell.

1

A PRELUDE TO THE STUDY OF VOICE AND METHOD

In this book, I tell a story about a fundamental shift in the philosophical methods and procedures of Stanley Cavell. I focus first on three of the routes by which the voice emerges as an issue in Cavell's work: (1) The voice is a condition of human expression and meaning to be recovered from its philosophical neglect. (2) The voice is a way of conceiving the medium and the goal of the philosophical method of appealing to ordinary language. (3) The sound of Cavell's voice as a writer is an inescapable feature of his presence in his work.

Each of these paths to the human voice is at issue in Cavell's work, and especially in the account that he gives of the relation of his writing to the enterprises of modern philosophy. It is one of the principal virtues of Cavell's work to have rendered the contested character of the voice a comprehensible feature of the history of philosophy since Descartes. For instance, we ought now to be able to discern a tension between the steps we try to take methodically as philosophers and the voices in which we speak our minds or express our perceptions. In this book, I attempt to bring the tensions between voice and method more distinctly and centrally under the lamp of investigation. I intend to present this issue as something at once comprehensible in the terms proposed by Cavell's work and, at the same time, usable by those who wish to understand that tension in terms that are applicable to other philosophers.

But here a central irony in Cavell's writing emerges. Cavell's very insistence on the human voice might have been heard as an effort to make the struggles concerning the voice into a theme for philosophy. Instead, Cavell's writing is heard as his insistence on his own particular voice. That insistence is in turn generally taken to be a matter of Cavell's preoccupation with a certain style of writing. And his writing is perceived as given over to a kind of self-involvement that goes beyond the more decorous forms of self-expression. In a further twisting of the concepts, the fact that Cavell's writing presents itself as committed to a certain style is often characterized as its being produced by his personal voice.

The interlocking network of these concepts of voice, style, and personal manner has tended to confine the discussion of Cavell's writing within a series of sterile controversies. Only rarely has the discussion moved on to include even a rudimentary account of the issues Cavell raises about philosophical method. Only rarely do such discussions display even the crudest awareness of the categories of literary or rhetorical analysis. And rarer still is any discussion of Cavell's work that moves on to include the issue of method.

The way the issues of style and voice get raised about Cavell's writing has tended to guarantee that the issues of personality and self-expression will be paramount. Thus one fate of his writing is to raise issues and controversies about itself that obscure precisely the original issues that the writing was intended to raise. I will argue that only when we get past this surface level of controversy surrounding Cavell's voice and the way he writes can a deeper set of issues about voice and method start to get the attention they deserve. But of course the picture is not so simple as this preliminary account might suggest. The controversies were not created from nothing, and I cannot simply bypass them and move directly to what I take to be the more substantial issues in Cavell's writing.

Despite my claim that Cavell's manner of writing and his emphasis on the voice are designed to raise the philosophical issue of the voice, I am not denying that his style makes a very particular and often problematic impression. His writing presents itself to many as a unified field of force, insinuating and domineering by turns. I think it is crucial to an adequate understanding of Cavell's work to hear it as containing more than one voice. But we have to be aware of the impression of singleness and, indeed, of self-absorption that Cavell's voice makes on so many of his readers. What we can learn about the source of this impression has something to teach us about the positive contribution of Cavell's writing to the study of philosophical method. For the writing creates the impressions it does—both good and bad—in large part because of the kinds of demands it places on the reader's attention.

When we start to appreciate the demands that are being made on us, we will be in a better position to know exactly at what stage of our own philosophical preparation we are prepared to meet those demands. Then we are better able to see how Cavell's work enacts the steps by which voices are allowed to emerge from their seclusion and within which the elements of a kind of conversation can begin to be heard. The fact that Cavell's singular voice has called forth clouds of controversy—blotting out the issues that he is trying to raise—need not be the end of the story. Unfortunately, the controversy about his writing and his voice has not progressed beyond the crudest and most obvious terms.

Even some friendly commentators seem to have accepted the idea that the singularity of Cavell's voice is the principal issue to be dealt with. At that stage the questions can be easily predicted: Is the dominant presence of Cavell's voice a sign of the shallowness of aesthetic self-absorption or the depths of a merely personal confusion, masquerading as a call to think? Or, as some have now started to maintain, as if in reaction to the fixated criticisms, is Cavell's voice rather a sign that he has reached some new height of philosophical expressiveness and accomplishment?

My business in this book has been to balk at these first impressions of Cavell's writing, whether they are favorable or unfavorable. My aim is to resist—and to resist *methodically*—the various ways in which the impressions of Cavell's work have dictated the terms in which it is generally discussed. Among other things, the aim of this book is to dislodge at least some of the misleading and superficial ways of posing the issue of philosophical style and substance, hoping to replace them with a problematic of voice and method. I side with those who hear Cavell's voice as an aspect of a philosophical project. But while others have spoken of the relation between Cavell's voice and the philosophical methods he inherits and discovers, not much has been done to chart this difficult territory.

Without some accurate map of these routes, the reader is likely to lose sight of the basic philosophical steps Cavell is taking, lost in the swirl of his critical insights and in the complexity of his style. Hence, a great deal of what follows presents itself as a kind of commentary, following out a particular set of issues about voice and method as they emerge in a crucial set of Cavell's texts. But this book keeps within the limits of a regular philosophical commentary no more than Cavell keeps within the limits of regular philosophy.

This question of the limits of the regular in philosophy goes beyond what are perhaps the more immediate questions about academic philosophy and its decorum. The question about decorum might be put like this: Why does Cavell keep writing in ways that seem to flout the normal tone and mode of addressing an audience in academic philosophy? This can lead to a further question: Can anyone who has not sometimes been at home in these rules and conventions get much intellectual satisfaction out of breaking them?

Behind such questions lies a still more difficult region of worry: Why, when a philosopher is raising the question of the limits of philosophy and its modes of expression, does it seem necessary to enact the transgression of those limits? Why can't the limits of philosophy or of the mind or of language be discussed in some more appropriate fashion? Why give the impression that you are seeking to provoke the very offense that is likely to be forthcoming anyway? In short, why take all this trouble about *writing* philosophy, or about something called achieving a voice in philosophy? What does this have to do with the methods and the sense of possible progress that brought you to such issues in the first place?

These and similar questions recur throughout this book, framing a kind of conversation with Cavell's work. This book looks to the course of his development not merely for the sake of telling the history. Tracing the various ways in which Cavell's writing develops and forms itself around issues of voice and method is itself a way of posing and answering some of these questions.

First and foremost, this book tells a story about the emergence of the voice as a theme for philosophy and as an aspect of a philosophical method. But as the voice emerges within Cavell's work, there is a fundamental and to some extent countervailing *shift* in Cavell's methods and procedures. I characterize a metamorphosis within Cavell's work from a model of philosophical method that invokes our most ordinary grasp and use of words to a model anchored in the idea and practices of reading. The first model is inherited, with differing inflections, from the work of J. L. Austin and Ludwig Wittgenstein. The model of philosophy as a kind of reading derives, most explicitly, from Cavell's encounters with Emerson and Thoreau. But the force of the model was fed by his explorations of Shakespeare and film and Cavell's increasingly less subterranean conversation with Freud's writing and with various ideas and methods of therapy. Cavell's relation to both the model of ordinary language and the model of reading thus raises a further set of issues: How is a philosophical method to be inherited, and how is it then to be possessed and transmitted?

This book argues that these changes in Cavell's methods, and in his various depictions of those methods, form a vector of his development as a philosopher that should not be neglected in any accurate computation of the direction and force of his writings. To understand the nature and the depth of this metamorphosis does not, by itself, suffice to command a complete view of the breadth and depth of Cavell's philosophical accomplishment. This book is meant rather to offer a series of perspectives on the progressions and variations of Cavell's voice as a writer, as conjoined with the evolution of his methods as a philosopher. I do not mean to make a schematic division between the way Cavell writes and the methods that he is following. But my sense is that there is a tension between the methods that his writing enacts and the voice that his writing contains and releases. It is difficult to grasp this tension, and it is even more difficult to understand how Cavell made something productive out of it. Without some such understanding of the interconnections between voice and method, readers will tend to overlook the very existence of Cavell's methods, let alone the possibility that they are philosophically effective in his work. Other readers have tended to assume that Cavell's goal was to achieve a kind of perfect harmony of voice and method, and that his stylistic achievement of voice was meant to carry the burden of philosophical method.

As I suggested, there are those who regard Cavell as following no particular method. According to them, he has gone even further than Wittgenstein is supposed to have gone in allowing his intuition to dictate the contents and manner of his writing. For at least some of these readers, it might be said that the presence of Cavell's voice distracts attention away from *any* question of his method. The sense of Cavell's self-conscious presence on the page has allowed some readers to treat the voice of the author as a kind of artifact of his personality and of his need for self-expression.

It is hardly surprising that those who disdain Cavell's work should have acquired such a view of his manner of writing. What is, to my mind, much more surprising is that readers who take themselves to be sympathetic to Cavell's enterprises have come to harbor an impression of his voice that is structurally analogous to that of his detractors. Such readers seem to share, in particular, the perception that the point of Cavell's achievement of a voice is, essentially and ceaselessly, to voice himself. This tendency in such a reader takes the impression of Cavell's voice to be almost the whole story of his work. Cavell's voice emerges as a kind of emblem and expression of the self in the field of philosophy. And since philosophy is, in this view, characterized as a field that has made itself barren of selves and selfhood, Cavell's achievement is thought to consist precisely in some such reassertion of the self.

It is when I began to realize that the power and range of Cavell's voice had become a kind of problem for some of his most interested readers that this book began to take its present shape. I began to understand that to rest content with one's reaction to Cavell's admittedly impressive voice, whether that reaction was hostile or devoted (or both by turns), was precisely to miss the questions of method that inhabit that voice. These questions are scarcely hidden in Cavell's work: one might almost say that this voice was called into existence in order to ask precisely these questions, and they lie on the surface of almost everything he writes. So pervasive is the intertwining of questions of method and questions of voice that even readers who have gotten beyond the poles of sheer rejection and sheer acceptance may have trouble unraveling them.

Only if we possess a more usable account of Cavell's methods and only if we allow ourselves to do the philosophical work that the methods call for can we provide a useful criticism of the modes of writing in which these methods are proposed. Only then are we likely to appreciate the tension and the interaction between the methods that Cavell proposes to inherit and the voice that inhabits those proposals and those methods. And only then can we hear Cavell's voice as other than a token or an icon of a particularly fascinating (or particularly self-absorbed) human being. Then we might hear it as it was intended to be heard, as making a contribution to the subject of philosophy. Thus Cavell discharges a debt to the methods of philosophy that enabled him to find his voice in the first place.

I n the remainder of this chapter, I want first to suggest a little more of the overarching shape of the story that I am telling, and then to locate my work within the still relatively small anthology of approaches to Cavell's work that are now available. In the process of thus situating my account, I also want to guard against a couple of misunderstandings and to say at least something about the audience I take myself to be addressing. I hope these clarifications and warnings will work to sharpen some of these issues about method and the inheritance of method. In the hands of the right reader, these preliminary remarks might point beyond the issues of this account to further fields of work.

My account of this shift in Cavell's methods will exhaust neither the intricacies of Cavell's relationship to philosophy nor the persistence of the self-questioning of philosophy that Cavell insists upon. The methods that I have focused on—the methods of ordinary language and of reading— are not intended to represent either the completed edifice of Cavell's work or its foundations. But they do provide a series of compass readings from which one might take one's bearings.

My account will not be convincing apart from the details of Cavell's work that it marshals and organizes. Indeed, conviction must await the perception of patterns and the sense of textual detail that readers will have to produce out of their own experience of reading Cavell. Only if my story reaches into the folds of such reading and such criticism, and only if the claims of my commentary help to elucidate specific perplexities, can these claims achieve the kind of confirmation they are after.

The goal here is not to provide some single key to unlock the secret of why Cavell writes like that. It is rather to help the reader struggle past the difficulties on the surface of the prose and get deeper into the territory of Cavell's projects. But the surface of his prose is anything but irrelevant to those projects. Although I certainly hope I have cleared up some of these difficulties and allowed the reader a clearer perspective on Cavell's texts, it seems to me that a good many of the difficulties are intrinsic to the problems and issues that he is addressing. The reader must expect that further difficulties will emerge as we proceed. What this suggests is that the question of my own procedures is already bound up in my sense of what a reader might find obvious or obscure. I will come back to this connection between a philosopher's sense of what the problem, at some given moment, is supposed to be and the philosopher's sense of the audience that he or she is addressing.

The reader may find it useful to have a map of the territory that I will be exploring in more detail in the later chapters. Roughly the first half of my story is the emergence of the human voice in Cavell's writing, both as a medium for philosophy and as one of its primary subjects. My initial claim is that the steps by which Cavell arrived at these emerging ideas of voice were anything but obvious. Later on—and only after the work of *The Claim of Reason* is completed—Cavell will describe himself as encountering the appeal to the voice in the procedures of Austin and Wittgenstein. This characterization of the appeals to ordinary language as appeals to the voice is not an obvious interpretation of Austin and Wittgenstein. It is also not an obvious interpretation of the first twenty-five years' worth of Cavell's engagements with Austin and Wittgenstein.

Of course, one might say that this question of the voice has *become* obvious. It is hard to imagine, at this stage of reading Cavell, that a reader would simply dispense with the idea of the voice as one of the primary keys to the significance of his writing. But then the fact that the presence of the voice became obvious has a certain claim on our attention. After all, Cavell characterizes one of Wittgenstein's contributions to philosophy as a method of studying the oscillation between the obscure and the obvious. Thus the fact that Cavell's first approaches to the voice were not obviously moving in that direction is itself of interest to me. Indeed, that one could trace the emergence of the ideas and practices of the voice was part of what caught and held my attention in the writing of this book.

My claim goes further than the possibility of tracing the emergence of the voice from Cavell's encounters with the appeal to ordinary language into his later works. My claim is that there is something of philosophical importance to be learned from tracing the progress of this emergence.

Here, there is also some precedent in Cavell's own acts of reenvisioning and reinterpreting his prior understanding and prior progress with these appeals to ordinary speech. It took further acts of interpreting his own progress, and investigations of the appeal to what we say, for Cavell to arrive at his understanding of these appeals as related to the recovery of the voice.

But Cavell's acts of understanding and appropriating his own development are only part of the story. His returning to the earlier stages of his work is almost always in the service of a search for what is still usable in that past. Such searches may obscure as much as they reveal, if only because they make the path from the past to the present much straighter than it was. The story I am telling in this book attempts to reopen certain paths that may have fallen into obscurity. And thus, like other narratives about the development of a philosophical position, my story has one foot in historical actuality and one foot in philosophical possibility. In retracing the steps by which Cavell discovered what was philosophically available at a given moment of his work, we learn how to discover our own philosophical options.

The appeal to ordinary language requires us to recall or to produce instances of what we would say when in a given set of circumstances. We imagine surroundings in which our utterances are naturally called for. For instance, when would it be natural to say that someone had inadvertently spilled the cream? Or, given something that is commonly said, such as "He inadvertently knocked over the pitcher of cream," we try to produce cases in which the phrase seems to be a natural description or response. For example, "He was reaching for the gravy boat when his son's question about the car keys distracted him and he inadvertently knocked over the cream." Already in his first essay on Austin, Cavell insists that the appeal to ordinary language may start from the words we use to invoke the world and its circumstances, or it may start with the cases that call (or seem to call) for the words we are inclined to use. In either direction, we are searching for the moments in which we grasp the mutual illumination between the utterances we make and the circumstances in which we naturally make them.

Cavell has spent a great deal of philosophical effort trying to characterize this relation between the circumstances in which we are prepared to say that something was done "by mistake" and the circumstances that constitute a mistake. The question was always easier to ask than to investigate. And so sometimes it was easier for the practitioners of ordinary language philosophy to go on charting the specific examples in which it made sense to say, for instance, that "She did it inadvertently" (or "by accident," "thoughtlessly," "voluntarily"; "willingly," "reluctantly," "wholeheartedly"). On the other hand, we somehow knew that we were, at the same time, investigating the circumstances that constitute *the fact that* something was actually done inadvertently (or by accident, thoughtlessly, voluntarily, willingly, reluctantly, or wholeheartedly). The question of the relation of our utterances to the part of the world that they purport to be uttering used to be quite widely discussed by Anglo-American philosophers. These days such questions seem again to have been supplanted by some version of the older questions: about the relation of the word to the thing that it refers to, and about the relation of a proposition (or something very like a proposition) to the state of affairs that it is meant to record.

"Aesthetic Problems of Modern Philosophy" contains one of Cavell's earliest and most developed discussions of method. Toward the end of the essay, he sums up one direction of his reflections:

> Such facts perhaps only amount to saying that the philosophy of ordinary language is not about language, anyway not in any sense in which it is not also about the world. Ordinary language philosophy is about whatever ordinary language is about. [*Must We Mean What We Say?* 95.]

This was a good place to get to, in which a great deal of previous work could be epitomized and consolidated and some new routes of investigation could be planned. But it was not meant to be the last stop on his methodological journey.

In recent years, Cavell has spoken of the "internality" of the relation of our utterances to the world that they are meant to utter. This is only one of a series of provisional efforts to characterize such a relation, and it should not be taken as final. Indeed, rejecting finality here is not a matter of mere intellectual caution. Following Wittgenstein, Cavell has consistently maintained that there is no single spot, no ultimate resting place, from which to characterize this "internality." There is no way to arrive at a purification of the medium, at least none that is not already a full-blown use of it.

This stricture does not mean that the method of appealing to ordinary circumstances is condemned to a mere reproduction of the circumstances of the world as it now is. Nor does it mean that the philosopher of ordinary language is condemned to incessant flights of self-revision. It does mean that the methods of ordinary language must always come on the scene in medias res. More problematically, it suggests that the achievement of usable results in appealing to the ordinary may come to seem indispensable to our ability to perceive the existence of the methods at all. Mill's methods of scientific reasoning, Descartes' method of doubt, and Plato's method of division may be discussed even while they are derided, and even when no one thinks there is much to be gained by employing them. But unless we are actually feeling the exemplary power of Austin's successes, we may come to doubt if there is anything like a method present at all. And this doubt may afflict those who were once quite absorbed in the world of ordinary language philosophy.

Faced with these and with other circumstances, Cavell has probed both the appeal to ordinary language and the world of ordinary things and events toward which that appeal is directed. At the same time, Cavell's version of these methods urges attention to the ways in which our words get *away* from us, forced or twisted just beyond our reach. Cavell develops and revises Wittgenstein's specific characterizations of how our words get away from us, and he works out of Wittgenstein's methods for bringing our words back from the emptiness and distances of metaphysical assertion to the forms of life in which they are once again alive. Even beyond Wittgenstein's particular sense and depiction of how our words get away from us and are returned to us, Cavell sharpens our awareness of philosophy as the medium of a particular alienation from our words. Cavell reads Wittgenstein as offering ways and methods of knowing that the drive to *reflect* on a given situation has urged our words beyond our ordinary ability to say them and mean them, in that very situation.

We may not know at the outset whether such reflection occurs because some human concern has taken the shape of a philosophical problem: it is possible, of course, that we are trying to bring a situation within the bounds of our queries, perhaps to freeze or fix a situation for further analysis. We may also come to understand that the philosophical form of the problem is a cover for a more human worry. Even Wittgenstein's characterization of a philosophical problem as having the form "I don't know my way about" does not make his work immune from these evasions. Admitting to one kind of lostness may well be a way of avoiding a more ordinary or a more terrifying region of disorientation.

If you appreciate this sort of spiritual risk as intrinsic to the study of philosophy—and presumably of the humanities in general—then perhaps you will be prepared to recognize that the reverse is also possible: the apparently more immediately human response to a situation may be an evasion of a thought that we needed to take up. Both of these dilemmas are worth attending to: you can hide from your problems inside philosophy, and you can hide from your tendency to think by taking refuge in the world of everyday concerns. (Hume's tactic of playing billiards as a relief from the melancholy of reflection and skepticism is a relatively un-sophisticated strategy, compared to some that I know of.)

Both of these forms of intellectual scrupulousness are capable of main-taining a provisional boundary between a philosophical problem and the human anxiety it may be connected to. But both also tend to make this boundary more permeable than most philosophers would like. In any event, Cavell uses Wittgenstein's work to further permeate the bounda-ries between what counts as a properly philosophical issue and what lies "outside" philosophy.

These paths are worth sketching in, if only to suggest the range of de-velopment, interpretation, and revision that Cavell takes away from his inheritance of the philosophy of ordinary language. Perhaps most decisively, however, he also begins to draw out the range of ideas and concepts associated with the phenomena of the voice. These voices are precisely meant to inhabit the realm of the ordinary and to be located primarily within the ordinary utterances of that realm. But the idea of voice, once unleashed, is so powerful and works in so many registers at once that the presence of a voice tends to undercut the very ordinariness of the appeals by which the voice is to be recovered.

Thus, on my account, it is a quite fateful step in his intellectual career when Cavell comes to interpret the appeals to ordinary language in Aus-tin and also in Wittgenstein as appeals to the voice. From now on the philosopher who ignores the appeal to ordinary speech and its potential for illuminating certain regions of the world will be characterized as de-nying, more or less actively, those very appeals. In thus denying them and their potentiality, such a philosopher can be taken as suppressing the voice that lies within the appeals and within the region of the world to-ward which the appeals are being made.

Cavell can therefore go on to interpret the philosopher's wish to speak "outside language-games" (as Wittgenstein put it) as a wish to banish the voices that inhabit the speech of our everyday lives. In turn, the wish to banish the voices of our ordinary world is characterized as perhaps the most visible edge of the wish to suppress altogether our need of the hu-man voice, and to banish the world as such.

In reconceiving the methods of Austin and Wittgenstein as already invoking the voice and already related to the skeptic's desires, Cavell comes to treat the voice as, so to speak, both subject and object of the procedures of philosophy. In chapters 2 and 3, I track this emergence of the voice, primarily as it occurred in the work that is enacted and rep-resented in *The Claim of Reason*. The discovery that functions as the guiding thread of my interpretation is this: It was only after Cavell completed this work of reconceptualizing the appeals to the ordinary as the recovery of the voice for philosophy that he was able to characterize this work in precisely those terms. In chapter 4, I characterize this deferral in naming the work of recovering the voice as itself part of the development and metamorphosis that it enables.

C avell's reconception of the methods of ordinary language as appeals to the voice prepares the way for his transition to what I call the model of philosophy as a kind of reading. I track this transition in chapter 4 as a response to a kind of methodological crisis or overload. In chapter 5, I trace it back to some of the acts of reading (especially in Emerson and Thoreau) out of which the model emerged. And I point forward to some issues about Cavell's increasing use of psychoanalytic therapy as a companion—or even competing—source of elements for this model.

The model of philosophy as a kind of reading is harder to discern than the model of ordinary language. Once discerned, it is even more difficult to bear in mind as a guide to practice. (One motive for this book is certainly to make it easier to put this model of reading to work, in philosophy and in literary criticism.) In chapter 4, I characterize Cavell's idea of reading as containing a series of representative exchanges: between the philosopher and the text to be read, between the philosopher and the (actual, empirical) reader, and between the active and passive aspects of the actual enterprises of reading. I try to characterize the philosophical possibility—which presents itself as a kind of requirement—that these exchanges be *representative*. This possibility of representativeness is certainly related to Cavell's practices as a critic and reader of literature and film in ways that are not that difficult to chart—though they are sufficiently difficult to imitate. The issue of the representativeness of a critical reading comes up at the beginning of his early essays on Beckett and *Lear*, and it remains a crucial point of exchange between those essays and his more explicitly epistemological work. Already in chapter 1 there are issues about reading and representativeness. In later chapters, I develop these issues in relation to the texts of Wittgenstein, Emerson, and Thoreau. But the bulk of Cavell's specific critical claims about Shakespeare and film lie just beyond the scope of this book.[1]

I claim that Cavell's version of these exchanges and his way of meeting the demand of representativeness are best characterized by what I call the reversals of reading. This is not to say merely that the model composed of these reversals is a good model for critical reading and interpretation. I am claiming that his later ideas and practices of reading can be construed as an actual, working model of philosophical method and investigation. Of course, this claim also implies a much closer connection than has so far been publicly formulated between Cavell's philosophical practices, strictly speaking, and his critical efforts.

I want to make it clear from the outset that this transition to a new model of philosophical method does not constitute an abandonment of the methods of ordinary language. It would be more accurate to say that this transition represents a radicalization and a metamorphosis of those methods. The methods of appealing to the ordinary are not relinquished, but they become harder to keep track of. The very success of the appeals in facilitating the recovery of the voice makes it somewhat harder, in a given text of Cavell's, to locate their exact point of application.

Most often, Cavell pursues this radicalization of the appeal to the ordinary by way of his idea that Emerson and Thoreau are engaged in the "underwriting" of the work of Austin and Wittgenstein. Whatever else "underwriting" refers to (and the word is surely chosen with some degree of irony), it is precisely *not* going to supply us with anything like a foundation for the appeals to ordinary language. Cavell is not searching for something as permanent as what philosophy thinks of as "foundations." He is searching rather for the transitional resting place, which allows us the insights and the satisfactions of a temporary intimacy between the world and what he starts to call our wording of the world. This search points back to the intimacy between our ability to recall the circumstances in which we would, in general, speak of someone's "inadvertently knocking over the cream" (perhaps while reaching for the gravy) and our ability to recognize (and accept) that someone, in a given situation, has inadvertently knocked over the cream.

This momentary intimacy of words and the world is revealed as a way of characterizing the achievement of the appeal to the ordinary. The perpetuated possibility of this intimacy is revealed as something like the ground of those appeals, or at any rate, the only ground that we can bargain for. In relation to Emerson, Cavell is more inclined to characterize the ground as a kind of step. The issue becomes for Cavell one of finding oneself on a step, and of finding that one is able to take the next step. He intertwines the issues of finding and of taking steps with the question of how we came to afflict our ideas of founding something with a certain picture of foundations.

This single issue of underwriting therefore points toward some issues about reading, since it is all but axiomatic for Emerson and Thoreau that the writer must display in his writing the steps he has taken as a reader. But this also becomes an issue of method because of the issue of taking steps—and of showing oneself to be taking steps. In chapter 4, I locate these issues about methods and steps in the region of reading, regarded first of all as a means of taking responsibility for one's words. The intimacy of our words with the world shows the implications of our saying something, at a particular time, in particular circumstances. And these implications are found to reach far more deeply into the conditions of our language than those more strictly characterized as "logical."

This sketch of the transformation in Cavell's philosophical methods ought to suggest that its effects will extend into every corner of his work. Whatever else he invites us to think about, the question of his procedures as a writer will sooner or later be on the table. However particular his readings of Shakespeare, film, and opera can get to be, the question of philosophy—and therefore of philosophical method—continues to be among the central questions of his work. Taking on the self-conception of Cavell's work will require that we trace the weaving of intimacy and antagonism that constitutes an essential element of his relationship to philosophy.

Part of what makes these topics difficult is also part of what makes them interesting: Cavell inherits a tradition of philosophy that refuses to separate the assessment of the results of thinking from the assessment of the steps by which those results are reached.[2] The refusal to separate a stage of judgment and assessment goes with the wish to reattach or reconnect the content of a thought to the forms that the thought takes and the circumstances in which it has formed.

Both the refusal of separateness and the wish for reconnection are among the goals of reading. This is true not only of the goals that may guide our actual acts of reading but also of the goals that are built into Cavell's model of philosophy as a kind of reading. Most immediately, however, the refusal to take separation (and in that sense analysis) as the criterion of philosophical understanding links Cavell's methods to those he inherited from Wittgenstein.

In Austin, there is a greater disparity, or perhaps a greater willingness for a tension, between the drive of his methods of producing the circumstances within which we would ordinarily say something and the surface decorum of the writing in which he sometimes reports and sometimes reenacts his discoveries. But in Austin also there is a quite specific refusal to take the results of "analyzing" a form of words as the desired outcome of our investigation. We are not to take the result of "analysis" to be a form of expression that can simply be *substituted* for the utterance that is being analyzed. This tendency gets one of its most sophisticated expressions in "Ifs and Cans," where Austin finds a number of ways to deny that you can substitute the philosophers' still-cherished "could have if I had chosen" for the plain old English "could have."[3] (This denial that analysis reaches the logical structure that it is aiming at is the kind of thing that leads Cavell to suggest that Austin is not an "analytic" philosopher.)

Cavell refuses to acquiesce in the separation of the content of a thought either from the circumstances in which the thought has formed or from the formal "architecture" in which it comes to be housed. This refusal is a common thread running from Cavell's inheritance of Wittgenstein to his later use of reading as a model and a medium of thinking. As I shall try to make clear, accepting the burden of such enactments and accepting the consequent burden of describing the precise forms that a thought may take are preconditions for any useful idea of philosophy as a kind of therapy.

There are, of course, a number of regions of our intellectual and academic culture in which such procedures for the evaluation and assessment of thought are scarcely controversial, at least in theory. Perhaps such ideas are more common in literary studies, and in those portions of philosophy most affected by recent currents in literary theory. But even in philosophy narrowly construed, such a tradition can be regarded as reaching back to Plato's invention of the philosophical conversation. Perhaps related issues of reattaching the thought to its point of origin are to be found among the motives for Wittgenstein's darker and less conversational modes of dialogue.

But along with his efforts to claim his kinship with other traditions of reflection and critique, Cavell is also at some pains to keep his work in touch with English-speaking academic or what we can still call "analytic" philosophy. This is certainly one region of our intellectual culture in which there exists no such tradition of assessing the relation between the content of a thought and the form or context of that thought. Whether this is fortunate or unfortunate is hard to say, since the refusal of such assessment seems to be one of the founding pedagogical gestures of analytic philosophy. It seems to be a crucial aspect of the philosophical training in this field that one learn to detach the results or theses of a philosophical position from the various processes of thinking that gave rise to those results. This movement of separation or detachment is one of the last practices of analytic philosophy that still receives widespread agreement. It is perhaps harder to characterize than the movements of thought loosely grouped under the idea of "analysis"—of the breaking down of expressions into their fundamental units of meaningfulness. But the general habit of separating issues from their wider cultural context seems no less crucial than the methods of analysis in characterizing the legacy of analytic philosophy.

Cavell does not suggest that we simply give up those practices and habits of intellectual analysis. Indeed, sometimes he seems to place entire strands of "analytic" thought into a kind of quasi-Austinian context. At least once he explicitly urges that we place the philosopher's utterance in the context of the philosopher's own motives for speech. Cavell describes this as the "grant[ing] to philosophers of the ordinary rights of language" that Austin grants to ordinary speakers.[4] But these "rights" of speech— and above all the right to have one's utterance treated as the expression of a wish to make sense—are precisely what philosophers of language have wished to give up. No doubt they wish to give up the human motives of speech only for the sake of a greater clarity about what is getting said. But this is the moment—as Cavell will later characterize it—in which the philosopher almost casually shows his willingness to trade the human voice for something more orderly and easier to transcribe.

Cavell's work thus sometimes—even often—requires the counter-pressure of the analytic tradition that he is working free of. It is one of the themes of this book that Cavell's work frequently performs this double gesture of inheriting the tradition he is criticizing, and of criticizing what he inherits. To understand his relation to such traditions is necessarily to become involved in both the acts of criticism and the acts of inheritance.

Cavell often works to reinsert the utterance of a thought into the context in which it has its most legitimate claim to making sense. Without the counterpressure supplied by our sense of the thought's legitimacy, a great deal of Cavell's critique of the thought in question will lose its point. Often the counterpressure derives from Cavell's ability to activate a tendency that in turn derives from at least the spirit of analytical philosophy. Another goal of this book is to recover enough of this current of analytic thought to demonstrate precisely this aspect of Cavell's methods.

We can experience what Cavell calls the recovery of the voice only when we have experienced its exclusion and repression by philosophical means. In practice, this tends to mean that we have experienced a certain strand or spirit of Anglo-American analysis, and moreover experienced the *validity* of some of the work that is done within this strand of thought. To speak usefully of the repression of the voice in philosophy requires experiencing in some sense the rightness, or at any rate the inevitability, of that repression. It is to speak of forces in the mind whose operation and self-justification are all but unnoticeable—precisely because they render themselves something like the natural laws of a particular territory of thought.

Cavell's work contains very practical and methodical ways of studying the mechanisms and repressions by which philosophy excludes certain thoughts and procedures. The conviction that these mechanisms are worth studying constitutes an as yet unmeasured distance between Cavell's work and that of Richard Rorty. For Cavell, the drive to emptiness in our words is inseparable from the wish for transcendence. And he interprets the wish to speak outside of language-games as a version of the wish for transcendence—as if something about the very impulse to philosophy would itself forever block us from achieving the ambitions of philosophy. As if we have to learn from philosophy itself how to give up what we know of philosophy. As if that were the only way to put ourselves in a position to inherit philosophy.

What Rorty wants is evidently exactly *not* to inherit philosophy. Certainly, the last thing he wants is to internalize its desires and fantasies, as a means of undoing its mechanisms of defense. He is fond of the formulation that he takes from Iris Murdoch: "It is an attachment to what lies outside the fantasy mechanism, and not a scrutiny of the mechanism itself, which liberates."[5] Like John Stuart Mill's recommendation of "anti-self-consciousness," this recipe has its successes, and we should not begrudge them. But Rorty uses this sort of moment as a chance to make his getaway. From this point on, he wants to be done with the fantasies and mechanisms of philosophy.

Apparently, this wish has led him to think of the mechanisms by which philosophy invents and perpetuates its region of inquiry as merely a set of professional habits. Philosophy's triumphs of method and rigor are in principle indistinguishable from its professional deformations. And the self-defeating or self-impoverishing aura of the drive to philosophical purity is for Rorty indistinguishable from the self-definition and cultivation of the field itself. Rorty speaks of the definitions of philosophy as so many "polemical devices" intended to "exclude from the field of honor those whose pedigrees are unfamiliar."[6] He associates the idea of "philosophy as a kind of writing" with the idea of a literary genre. The genre is delimited not, so to speak, by its form or matter but by a tradition of writing about or addressing issues represented by certain figures. Here he only somewhat jokingly introduces the idea of the "family romance" of philosophy, speaking of "Father Parmenides, honest old Uncle Kant, and bad brother Derrida."[7]

It seems to me that Rorty eases himself into the idea of a family romance from his prior sketch of a more chivalric romance. In the chivalric version, what philosophers exclude as "not philosophy" Rorty characterizes as the "unfamiliar." But in most versions of the family romance what is excluded is not entirely unfamiliar. I have addressed this question before, in "Aftermaths of the Modern."[8] Here I extend those reflections to include the moment, later in the same book, where Rorty wants Cavell to give up the boring old round of questions and answers about the "external world." Rorty gives a kind of summary analysis of what he calls the "professional philosopher's skepticism," tracing it casually to the "theory of ideas." (This is the "theory," deriving from Descartes and Hume, that analyzes perception in terms of "ideas," regarded as the mind's basic contents, which can be immediately perceived and known without error.)[9]

Rorty's sketch is offhand enough to do little harm in itself. But with an oddly accurate perversity, he goes on to disconnect this sort of skepticism from what he calls "the Kantian-Romantic worry about whether the words we use have any relation to the way the world actually is in itself." At a stroke, Rorty cuts off the skeptical strand of the empiricist from the entire range of questions concerning the Romantic anxiety about using language to reach the thing itself. He also invites us to disconnect the "ritual interchanges between philosophy professors" concerning skepticism from the experience that Cavell discerns as fundamental to "classical epistemology (and, indeed, moral philosophy)." He cites a moment where Cavell is characterizing the skeptic's position as formed within "a sense of powerlessness to know the world, or to act upon it."[10] Rorty ridicules the idea that someone like Price could have had much to do with such an experience, and goes on to say virtually the same thing about Locke and Hume.

It is much less plausible to describe Hume as thinking of the skeptical consequences of the theory of ideas in the same way as the developers of a revolutionary scientific theory think of the "anomalies" in Kuhn's sense. Anomalies are puzzling but do not, of themselves, overthrow the paradigm within whose regime they occur. But the skeptical consequences were for Hume a kind of malady. More specifically, he thought of the malady as a form of melancholy, which he characterized—with a certain degree of clinical precision—in terms of its paralysis of human action.

> ... [A] Pyrrhonian cannot expect that his philosophy will have any constant influence on the mind; or if it had, that its influence would be beneficial to society. On the contrary, he must acknowledge, if he will acknowledge anything, that all human life must perish, were his principles universally and steadily to prevail. All discourse, all action would immediately cease; and

all men remain in a total lethargy, till the necessities of nature, unsatisfied, put an end to their miserable existence. It is true; so fatal an event is very little to be dreaded. Nature is always too strong for principle . . .[11]

It is true that Hume does not imagine that the mass of human beings will become permanently skeptical. It does not follow that the content of the skeptic's imagination is merely of academic interest to Hume. Nor, in particular, does it follow that the skeptic's anxiety about what would happen if others were to find themselves in his condition tells us nothing about the nature of skepticism. And it is not such a stretch as Rorty seems to imagine to think of Hume's skeptic as finding himself in a condition analogous to the one described by Cavell in *The Claim of Reason:* He is "outside" the realm of objects and action. Or perhaps he is better thought of as stuck in a fixed position, within the realm of objects, hence deprived from the outset of the possibility of acting on them. In either case, action and discourse tend to cease.

Perhaps we will find Hume's expression of anxiety about the skeptical paralysis to be uttered more for the rhetorical effect he wants it to have than as a genuine expression of anxiety. It seems to me generally true that philosophers in the Anglo-American tradition tend to downplay the means by which traditional philosophers have dramatized their positions. So, for instance, we are also likely to categorize as mere rhetoric or as stage-setting Descartes' concerns that he will be likened to a madman or Meno's comparison of Socrates to a stingray. The trouble is that we are also not very practiced in assessing even as "rhetoric" the kind of gestures that philosophers are inclined to make. Such gestures, it seems to me, often get made when philosophers find themselves pushed into some kind of skeptical corner. But they are not confined to such moments, and they are not readily analyzed into some well-known catalog of literary tropes and *topoi.* At any rate, to reach for a literary analysis as a way of confining or reducing these gestures brings us no closer to understanding the connection of the gestures to the philosophical movements of thought that produced them. Here the philosopher and the literary analyst of rhetoric are likely to agree in their willingness to keep the movements of thought and the gestures of rhetoric from touching one another.

If we did start to take such gestures seriously I think we would be drawn—as Cavell was drawn—toward the study of certain moments in Romanticism. Whatever Cavell's other reasons for writing about the Romantics, here at least he found writers and thinkers who anticipated his own obsessions and those of Wittgenstein. Whatever else they do, the Romantics took seriously the connection between a mind driven to contemplate its own limits and the various fates of language as it is submitted to those pressures. In the relation of Wordsworth and Coleridge to what they called Associationism (including certain ideas that derive from Hume) we might begin to assess the connection between the experience of the limits and conditions of knowledge and, on the other hand, the rhetoric in which that knowledge of limits is expressed.

To get some perspective on Hume, we might look, for instance, at Wordsworth's perception of the weight of custom:

> Full soon thy Soul shall have her earthly freight,
> And custom lie upon thee with a weight,
> Heavy as frost, and deep almost as life! [12]

For Hume, human nature cures the malady of skeptical consciousness by impelling us forward to meet our needs and rejoin the realm of custom and action. For Wordsworth, either the realm of custom is no cure, or else the cure hangs heavier on the spirit than the malady does. Something in our nature is able to help us survive the fate of growing up, because something in our nature survives the regime of the customary and "still remembers" the fugitive conditions of growing up.

Somewhat surprisingly, one of the conditions that our nature remembers is something like a kind of skepticism. Wordsworth himself called it a form of Idealism, but it presents itself like this:

> . . . those obstinate questionings
> Of sense and outward things,
> Fallings from us, vanishings;
> Blank misgivings of a Creature
> Moving about in worlds not realized . . . [*Ode*, 145–49.]

This is not a piece of full-fledged skepticism, if only because it does not emerge from a problematic of doubt. But it suggests that a certain condition of questioning is as natural to us as, for instance, our sense of limitless possibility. And it suggests that our grown-up nature still contains these possibilities of questioning and these questions of possibility.

In disconnecting the problem of Romanticism from the problem of skepticism, Rorty bars us from approaching a certain depth of language and feeling in the questions of skepticism. It is as if he shares with the "professors of philosophy" the sense that the philosophical problem of skepticism and self-consciousness must be insulated from the more human burdens of self-consciousness. And this insulation must occur even at the cost of restricting our ability to read the classical texts of philosophical skepticism with any serious attention to their literary or cultural context. Moreover, our skeptical and romantic perversities in words—driven by a need for reflection or perspective and finding ourselves in the posture of thought—are themselves capable of constituting at least some good analogies of ordinary human alienation and repressiveness. We will be missing more than Rorty seems to imagine, if we are barred from seeing analogies between these expressions of skeptical and romantic perplexity.

This need and this willingness to stay within earshot of the dominant forms of English-speaking philosophy and of Romantic poetry create problems for some of Cavell's readers. For long stretches of his work, you have to be able to activate enough philosophy in yourself to keep up with the pace and pressure of his prose. But if you know that much "real philosophy," you may also be wishing that he would hasten to his conclusions. Other readers, who are less impatient for the conclusion or less impatient with Cavell's interest in the routes the mind is taking on its way to its conclusion, might still find themselves wishing for a less active— or a less interactive—mode of writing. Even a quite sympathetic reader can sometimes wish that the pressure of his writing would ease up, allowing us time to dwell on one of his perceptions.

Taking up more explicitly the question of the audience for a book such as this one, I remark again that my very topic will be a kind of affront to several sorts of readers. As I noted at the beginning of this chapter, philosophical opponents and allies alike seem to have a stake in characterizing Cavell as possessing essentially no method at all. Cavell epitomizes for many readers the entrance of the personal element in philosophy. Whether they violently disapprove or violently approve of this entrance, they are likely to take Cavell as the kind of writer that would rather dispense with method altogether than be imprisoned by something thus impersonal. For many, Cavell fits the kind of Romantic stereotype of genius that Ray Monk's biography tries to make the key to understanding Wittgenstein. From such a perspective, Cavell's work seems to insist on the face of it that it is the product of spontaneity, founded on nothing more than the ultimately ineffable perceptions beyond the reach of our ordinary or academic philosophical measurements.

It would be difficult for such philosophers to imagine that Cavell possesses anything so regular and decorous as a philosophical method. It will seem even less plausible to argue, as I will be arguing, that Cavell employs two functioning philosophical methods, each of which can be followed and checked by an independent reader. I even go on to argue there is a perceptible and traceable development between these methods, and that Cavell's methodological evolution is itself instructive. To many Anglo-American philosophers, this would be about as sensible as arguing that there is some philosophical progress to be noted in Joyce's development from *Ulysses* to *Finnegans Wake,* or in the evolution of dogma from the Council of Nicea to the Diet of Worms. A more sophisticated objection might go on to connect this image of Cavell as related to a perception of his prose style as excessive and self-indulgent: What else could you expect from someone who has hitched the horses of his speech to the unappeasable demands of the unsayable? For a reader in the grip of this objection, to address the question of Cavell's philosophical method would be to beg the question of whether his writing should be regarded as philosophy at all.

This book does not take on itself the task of urging altered forms of reading and thinking on those particular observers of the philosophical scene. It is not that I think that there is nothing to say to such philosophers or that there is nothing abstract worth saying about the rationality of Cavell's procedures. But it seems more important to demonstrate my sense of the ways in which Cavell's methods can be rigorously *followed.* And perhaps the best way of demonstrating this is to produce some examples in my own writing of how his method is actually followed.

It is a corollary of one of the more general claims of this book that it is hard, if not impossible, to discuss the validity of a method at the same moment that you are trying to put it to work and to demonstrate its particular effectiveness. I have chosen, as a rule, to trace the workings of Cavell's methods and to show them at work in my own writing.[13] I hope this will not be taken as preaching to the choir, but I know it is better than standing outside the wedding feast and haranguing someone else's guests.

Beyond the settled camps of devotion and disdain, there is another sort of reader that I am interested in addressing. These are readers for whom Cavell's philosophical brilliance is undeniable, in everything from his early essays to individual lectures, to classes, to remarks made during the question periods following a talk. For these readers, what we can only call the "question of style" has become paramount. All too often, they experience a tension—and most often an unproductive tension—between the philosophical insight of Cavell's that they might like to dwell on and the forms in which that insight gets expressed. More generally, even readers who are at some level sympathetic to certain aspects of Cavell's work find themselves troubled and often irritated by the insistent gestures of his writing. Such a reader seems to have special difficulty with the tendency of the writing to fold back on itself—and to do so just at the moment when the argument might have led to a resolution.

I do not have a single set of responses to such readers, nor a single set of suggestions about how and why they might become more patient and more productive with Cavell's procedures and maneuvers as a writer. This book aims at opening up several paths on which the kind of answer I would like to give might start to make sense to such readers. This means that I am claiming that the question of Cavell's style is not a single question. I mean not only that the style is not monolithic but that the influence of Cavell's polyphony on our awareness of the content of his thought is also not reducible to a single region of difficulty. The impression that Cavell's writing has a single flaw (its self-consciousness or what is labeled its "self-indulgence") is just that: an impression. The fact that the writing makes just *this* impression on so many readers has to be understood, not merely dismissed or diagnosed away. I remain convinced that whenever the question of Cavell's style comes up, there is always something else going on in the reader. But the anxiety about Cavell's surface complications and about the demands his writing makes cannot be overcome by pointing to some other anxiety about the material that is surfacing in the reader's responses. (I say more about this below, in discussing Arnold Davidson's remarks on this issue.)

What I try to do in this book is to recast, as systematically as possible, the apparently immovable question about something called "Cavell's style" into a series of more tractable questions concerning the mutual impingements and creations of voice and method. For instance, I spend a lot of time in chapters 2 and 3 insisting that the immediacy of Cavell's authorial voice has to be heard in relation to the various voices of everyday life that his work is appealing to. My insistence on this point is connected to what I characterize as Cavell's *discovery* that Austin's and Wittgenstein's appeals to what we ordinarily say are to be treated as, among other things, appeals to the human voice.

My various treatments of the question of voice and method in Cavell will not settle, once and for all, the manifold issues of style and substance. But I think they will help us to see the questions about the manner of Cavell's writing as related to a series of significant issues about philosophical method and content. Perhaps those who hear his voice as nothing but a distraction from philosophical content might start at least to encounter the methodological issues of voice in writers such as Wittgenstein, Plato, and Augustine. (It may take somewhat longer, at least in Anglo-American circles, to get similar issues about voice and method raised in relation to, for instance, Descartes, Hume, Fichte, Kierkegaard, Mill, and Nietzsche.) And perhaps some of Cavell's students will find it easier to admit that his legendary manner of writing has its regions of potential mannerism, if the terms of the discussion include an appreciation of the necessities of that voice.

One of Cavell's increasingly explicit themes is the idea that the voice has its own risks, and that these are as dangerous, perhaps, as the risks of the voicelessness that he found at the heart of the skeptic's wish for knowledge. This sense of the risks in coming into your possession of your voice gets one kind of treatment in the third chapter of *A Pitch of Philosophy*, where Cavell turns to consider opera. A fuller account of these issues will require addressing the way the voice functions inside of academic philosophy (and indeed, inside academic criticism) and will exact of us some modes of listening and criticism that we are still not very practiced at.

To the extent that Cavell's writing incorporates within itself certain versions of his readers—hence certain versions of their anxiety—the problems of reception are re-created inside Cavell's own work. This in turn creates further problems for his readers, who are likely to be either further entranced or further appalled by Cavell's self-conscious enactment of the problems that his text is creating.

It is important to acknowledge that quite sympathetic readers of Cavell can experience the pressure of his writing as a source of discomfort. One of my main efforts in this book is to acknowledge this fact in some ways that might prove philosophically illuminating and useful. Moreover, I wish to specify some of the forms that a reader's discomfort may take. One might, for instance, experience a passage of Cavell's writing as refusing to let the reader alone and, more particularly, as refusing to let the reader dwell on a given thought or formulation. An unfriendly reader might take this refusal as related to Cavell's refusal to argue. A friendly reader might learn to think of it as the kind of restlessness that insists on exploring its own sources. Sometimes this restlessness is a refusal to remain content with the ways in which a thought first presents itself, and a refusal to let go of a formulation that the writer is not finished with. No doubt we ought to be thus prepared to refuse to accept conclusions arrived at for the sake of an argument, even if it is our own argument. But the refusal is still a source of restlessness and pressure, and not something a reader is likely to be grateful for.

One particular version of pressure on the reader dates from the composition of part 4 of *The Claim of Reason*. There are many transformations in that period of his writing. Most immediately, I link them to the crisis of the voice that I investigate in chapter 3. I also connect this moment of Cavell's development to his increasing explicitness in the fate of writing and the voice. Cavell clearly thought of this as a period in which he was discovering how to bring philosophical writing to a *close*. He associates this capacity for closure with a drive to the aphoristic and with a reconception of the idea of a philosophical *journal*. (Cf. *Claim*, foreword.)

What I am characterizing as the origin of a particular pressure on the part of Cavell's reader seems to be related to Cavell's discovery of a way of focusing and alleviating the pressure of philosophy on his own writing. My various explorations of a productive tension of voice and method can therefore be taken as pointing still further into regions that Cavell's writing has already begun to explore. In part 4 of *The Claim of Reason*, the tension of voice and method can be understood as the strain between the requirement of the aphoristic as a certain conclusive expenditure of the voice and the span of a day's thought, as it reaches words that you are willing to leave alone.

Exploring such tensions might help explore our sense that we often do not know what to expect from Cavell's writing: are we about to be stunned by a sentence that seems almost too good to be true? Or are we to be left alone with a perception that seems (once we have read it) so common that we ought to have been able to put it into words for ourselves? No doubt this latter sort of uncertainty will occur only to a reader who has managed to fathom a certain depth of connection between Cavell's prose and Cavell's thought. But such features of our response are just as much (or more) in need of exploration as the more superficial tensions in his writing. It may even turn out that the different levels of perplexity in our responses to Cavell's work have something to do with each other.

O ne good place to begin is by examining Cavell's own accounts of the question of method. Early in *Must We Mean What We Say?* Cavell is already working with the concept of method:

> So the different methods [of appealing to what "we would say if . . ."] are methods for acquiring self-knowledge; as—for different (but related) purposes and in response to different (but related) problems—are methods of "free" association, dream analysis, investigation of verbal and behavioral slips, noting and analyzing "transferred" feelings, and so forth. Perhaps more shocking, and certainly more important, than any of Freud's or Wittgenstein's particular conclusions is their discovery that knowing oneself is something for which there are methods—something therefore that can be taught (though not in obvious ways) and practiced. [66–67.]

"Method" is presented not quite as something impersonal, but certainly as something that exists beyond the possession of a particular person. It is something that can be—and in some sense *must* be—taught, or at any rate, communicated to another. That it can be *practiced* also implies that it can be *followed*. This is the conceptual spot where Cavell will come to locate the problem of inheriting a method, the place where one has to assume the burden of another thinker's knowledge. It is as if Cavell understands the burden of philosophical influence, at least in part, as the fact that a method is as much a burden as it is a gift. Method is here being thought of as consisting in steps that are always to be taken by oneself and for oneself. Yet a method is always to be reappropriated from its point of origin, at once within and beyond its particular human inventor.

In this essay, Cavell addresses what he characterizes as a kind of intellectual—even a spiritual—scandal about Freud and Wittgenstein: the existence of steps or routes to self-knowledge that are independent of particular persons and their spiritual accomplishments. It is not the presence of self or selfhood, as such, that concerns Cavell. It is necessary to remind ourselves repeatedly of this feature of Cavell's concern, because apparently something about reading Cavell repeatedly leads us to suppose otherwise.

I am not the first to have called attention to this aspect of Cavell.[14] But the absence of any sustained discussion of this tension between method and self-knowledge in Cavell's work suggests that he was more right than he knew. The scandal of philosophy is not the absence of the self—as some of his readers think. (A symptom is not necessarily a scandal.) What is expressly described as scandalous is the presence of impersonal methods of providing access to the self. In Cavell's vision, we have to relinquish the personal element in order, exactly, to know the self. ("I must disappear in order that the search for myself be successful" [*Claim*, 352].) The personal element of an author's writing is not what he struggles to assert or to achieve: the personal is what he is struggling *with*. And the reader is supposed to learn from this struggle by engaging in it on the author's behalf.

This will not seem like much of a struggle to those philosophers who take themselves to have already renounced the personal element. Perhaps they think of themselves as having renounced it, at least professionally, when they became professional philosophers. Or perhaps they think of themselves as renouncing mere personal concern and feeling each time they sit down to work. For some philosophical minds—and not necessarily the worst—"the personal" is simply another name for the self-centered or the self-indulgent. Only those who sense how pervasive the realm of the personal has become will have an intimation of the dimensions of the struggle with the personal that I am trying to characterize.

Those for whom a philosophical method is a set of rules and steps that can be picked up and put down at designated times will also not have to undergo this kind of perplexity about method. The struggle for the impersonality of philosophical method is a struggle of persons or selves *within* oneself, a struggle for a perspective *on* the self. It is only from a particular sort of angle that such a perspective will seem to be best characterized as a merely "personal" one. At the same time, the struggle over method occurs between selves, between those who bequeathed us the methods, and our need to be revising them and reinventing them. Ultimately, it is a struggle between our philosophical inheritance and our philosophical autonomy.

This vision seems intolerable both to academic philosophers and to the sentimentalism of some of Cavell's readers. The austere neighborhoods of philosophical argumentation are next door to the unruly suburbs of these methods of self-knowledge. And for more than one kind of philosopher this was, and is, too close for comfort. So the first scandal is succeeded by the next scandal: the methods exist, but we will not use them. No doubt there are often personal reasons for such a refusal—as there may well be personal reasons for listening to Cavell's voice but declining to pursue his methods.

The largest single claim I make on behalf of this book is that I have succeeded in tracking a specific development within Cavell's idea and practice of philosophical method. This claim implies another claim, equally large but harder to put into words. Not only do I take this effort to track Cavell's methodological development to be worth doing as an effort of explanation and interpretation; I take it to be philosophically instructive, beyond the instruction to be found within each particular stage of Cavell's writing.

I take this question of the development of method in relation to the characteristic themes and movements of Cavell's work to be largely missing from other accounts of that work. There have, however, been a number of substantial treatments of Cavell, stretching back to the still-indispensable essay "More on What We Say" by Stanley Bates and Ted Cohen (1972).[15] Their essay is, in my view, the treatment of Cavell's work that is most completely attentive to the issues of method contained in the appeals to what we ordinarily say. But for reasons having to do with the context of the debate about method, they do not directly raise questions about Cavell's style or voice, or about what we might call the philosophical location of those appeals to ordinary speech. (They make some useful remarks about the absence of language as a systematic theme in Kant, which are still worth following out.)

The most characteristic move of their essay is not to defend Cavell's work but to disarm its attackers. They demonstrate in staggering detail the heavy hand of polemical carelessness, resting on the shoulders of some of Cavell's first critics. In their arguments, in their efforts to use logical terminology, and in matters of textual interpretation, writers such as Fodor and Katz are found to be quite slack, almost casually so. Speaking in the name of the new science of Chomskian linguistics, they are not content with criticizing this or that result of Cavell's early essays. They need to explain that Cavell's version of the appeal to ordinary language, considered as an appeal to the "linguistic intuitions" of a "native speaker," constituted a repudiation of the spirit of empirical enquiry and therefore of anything that ought to be recognized as philosophy.

Bates and Cohen, writing some years after the height of the controversy—and with utmost patience and a leaven of sarcasm—exposed errors of logic and of analysis that might have occasioned some reconsideration of the terms of the debate. Perhaps it is of the nature of polemic that its participants soon forget the details of their passion, leaving only a residue of bad feeling about issues that no longer seem so important.

In the places where Bates and Cohen move past their explicit goal of criticizing Cavell's critics, it becomes clear that they are implicitly addressing the central methodological issues of ordinary language philosophy. They almost casually isolate the fact that Fodor and Katz (and elsewhere John Searle) have apparently confused "He joined the army voluntarily" with "He volunteered for the army." Noting that Fodor and Katz are forced to add "he wasn't conscripted" to make plain their meaning, they briefly suggest the continued relevance of Cavell's delineation of a "fishiness" attaching to the question, "Did you join the army voluntarily?" Here the contrast is between joining voluntarily and joining, for instance, under duress. Indeed, it would barely have been a paradox to ask, in those days, whether someone had enlisted voluntarily—or whether, for instance, he had enlisted only because he was about to be drafted.

Again and again, such apparently small points turn out to have a large yield. Bates and Cohen's ability to make such points count in a philosophically useful way gives precision and weight to their discussion of what we say. Above all, they advance the methodological discussion of how we know what "we" say and how we become *entitled* to make claims about what we say. Their discussion is technical because they are responding to opponents who have cloaked themselves in technicality, but it restores us exactly to the moment in Cavell's text that is frequently missing from later discussions. Cavell spends a significant amount of energy distinguishing between statements like S ("When we say that an action is voluntary we imply that the action is fishy") and statements like T ("'Is X voluntary?' implies that X is fishy"). Indeed, Bates and Cohen help to clarify some moments in Cavell's discussion, and they usefully suggest that S is not to be understood as purely or merely a statement, on a par with ordinary statements of current, empirical fact.

For Fodor and Katz the most outrageous idea in Cavell's philosophy of ordinary language is the idea that a native speaker needs no evidence for making statements like S. Bates and Cohen's discussion of this issue has prepared us to look again at Cavell's own words.

> Only a native speaker of English is entitled to the statement S, whereas a linguist describing English may, though he is not a native speaker, be entitled to T. What entitles him to T is his having gathered a certain amount and kind of evidence in its favor. But the person entitled to S is not entitled to *that* statement for the same reason. He *needs* no evidence for it. It would be misleading to say that he *has* evidence for S, for that would suggest that he has done the sort of investigation that the linguist has done, only less systematically, and this would make it seem that his claim to know S is very weakly based. And it would be equally misleading to say that he does *not* have evidence for S, because that would make it appear that there is something that he still needs, and suggests that he is not yet entitled to S. But there is nothing he needs, and there is no evidence (which it makes sense, in *general*, to say) he has: the question of evidence is irrelevant. [*Must We Mean What We Say?* 13–14.]

The region is difficult and perhaps Cavell would put some of these issues differently now. (So, of course, might Bates and Cohen.) But the issues Cavell raises continue to come up in his work, all the way down to the most recent issues about how Emerson imagines that we become entitled to voice the implications of what we say.

To some sensibilities, if a philosopher says that the issue of evidence is irrelevant to our ability to make a claim, he will be immediately understood as asserting that one *does*, after all, possess a peculiar kind of evidence. Perhaps the evidence is thought to be overwhelmingly superior to the mere outer evidence that painstaking scientific spirits are inclined to search for. This part of the conflict between Cavell and his critics verges on comedy: It is as if he had followed Austin in claiming, "It makes no sense to say that 'all the evidence of cheese is present,' when what is lying there on the table is, precisely, cheese." The empirically minded critic hears this remark and replies: "Oh, I see: by suggesting that the request for evidence is nonsensical or irrelevant or incompetent in these circumstances, you must be implying that you have a kind of internal intuition that gives you massive, irrefutable evidence of the presence of cheese, far superior to the external evidence that the rest of us require."

Perhaps the fact that these issues involve our possession of language rendered them especially fraught for those critics caught up in the apparently endless possibilities of the new linguistics. But nothing should have excused the critics from noting that when Cavell declared the question of evidence to be irrelevant, he did not suggest that our relation to our words was therefore incorrigible.

> The claim that in general we do not require evidence for statements in the first person plural does not rest upon a claim that we cannot be wrong about what we are doing or about what we say, but only that it would be extraordinary if we were (often). My point about such statements, then, is that they are sensibly questioned only where there is some special reason for supposing what I (we) say to be wrong; only here is the request for evidence competent. If I am wrong about what he does (they do) that may be no great surprise; but if I am wrong about what I (we) do, that is liable, where it is not comic, to be tragic. [Ibid., 14.]

Bates and Cohen's discussion of how the individual can be the source of data for what we say remains one of the best routes of access to this topic in Cavell. But even they (and, I think, even Cavell) might be a bit surprised at the sudden gesture toward tragedy at the end of these remarks.

Even among Cavell's best readers, this particular set of issues about our possession of language has been somewhat neglected—perhaps with increasing exceptions. It puzzles me that the Bates and Cohen essay has been so little referred to by later commentators. But I have the impression that it nevertheless continues to be read enthusiastically by successive generations of readers and students. Discovering the continuing resonance of old perceptions (of Austin as well as of Cavell) has been part of my sense of discovering a community of readers. If the interplay between voice and method is as central as I take it to be, my account may prove useful to others in charting still further options in reading Cavell.

Accounts of Cavell's work differ in how single and monolithic a presence they take the edifice of his work to be, and they differ, accordingly, as to what kind of access they take themselves to be providing to that edifice. There is a tendency to look for a single perspective that might provide a way to unify the proliferation and variety of Cavell's recent work. I have tried to overcome that tendency in myself by keeping in mind the idea of a kind of path through Cavell's work—a path on which various unities and pluralities could emerge in their own time, and take their various places.

The accounts also differ as to how much of the surface of the writing they are willing to take responsibility for, and how much, on the other hand, they would like to disown, or at least apologize for. This implies, also, the question of their sense of the connection between the manner of the writing and the method of the thought. No one (not at least since the article by Bates and Cohen) can avoid for very long the question of such connections.

Michael Fischer's elegant and thought-provoking *Stanley Cavell and Literary Skepticism* has demonstrated the greatest capacity to take the ins and outs of Cavell's writing in stride.[16] Fischer sets out to explore Cavell's relation to what Fischer calls "literary skepticism," and his book displays the considerable virtues and also some of the risks of so controlled a focus. His argument is clear and lucid, and he has something useful to tell us on every page—about Cavell, about criticism, about Romanticism, and about the aspirations of literary theory. But his central claim about the subject of "literary criticism" is hard to keep within the focus that he sets for it. On the one hand, Fischer lays out in detail the way in which the "deconstructive probing of texts *parallels* external world skepticism as represented by Cavell" (10, my emphasis). On the other hand, he sometimes seems to be suggesting that deconstruction is a *species* of skepticism.

The latter suggestion is more appropriate when responding to something like Walter Benn Michaels's treatment of *Walden*, or the various enterprises of Stanley Fish.[17] Such an idea tends to make deconstruction seem more mystified about its own philosophical origins and tendencies than is plausible in the case of a writer like Derrida. Of course, it *is* plausible that deconstruction is the kind of term that can embrace a range of tendencies, from the lucid to the self-mystifying. But Fischer's book also does not quite challenge itself on a very particular and very fundamental question: Why doesn't Cavell himself explore the access that his skeptical problematic provides us into the literary phenomena known collectively as deconstruction?

Fischer wrote his pioneering study just at the moment when Cavell was beginning to get beyond his first tentative forays in the direction of Derrida and de Man, and certainly long before Cavell's more sustained encounters with Derrida and Lacan. Fischer was certainly aware of this, but the point is not merely a matter of the timing of his study. For the question about whether deconstruction is an analogue to skepticism, or is somehow contained within it, is also a question about the nature and location of reading. Cavell's reticence about engaging with deconstruction is the other side of his being drawn further and further into the problematics of his own reading and his own models of reading. In chapters 2 and 4, I suggest that the pressures of deconstruction are far more specific in the texts of that period than the pressures of skepticism. Indeed, these pressures are explicitly part of what draws Cavell into the twin problematics of reading and the voice.

If one looks at the appeals to the ordinary as appeals to the place from which skepticism must begin and to which it must return, then the activity of reading might be conceived of either as on the side of the ordinary or as on the side of the appeals. Reading might be presented as the activity that skepticism undermines, as if reading were analogous to seeing. Or it might be presented as the activity that allows us to track our doubts and our less mentionable anxieties, as if it were analogous to the activities of philosophical reflection. Fischer seems to want the act of reading to have the security of ordinary perception—no doubt not an unshakable security—while retaining the power and intricacy of good criticism. There are good reasons for wanting this. But granting this double set of features to reading as a kind of empirical status will tend to undermine any parallel between the act of reading on the one hand, and the lucidity of the appeal to ordinary speech on the other.

In fact, at this stage of Cavell's work, the intimacies of reading and the everyday world are part of his sense of what he calls the "underwriting of the ordinary." But, as I am suggesting, a focus on this underwriting and these intimacies tends to undermine the independent lucidity of the appeals to the everyday: if the appeals need to be underwritten, then perhaps their legibility is less secure than we had imagined.

Far from converging in a more human acceptance of human finitude, the model of reading reveals the world of the everyday as unsecured and unprotected. Given Cavell's willingness to provide a hearing for Emerson's thought of the "infinitude of the private man," one should not be too happy with the idea that Cavell is praising or recommending an acceptance of our finitude. No doubt he would oppose the idea that we should merely, as it were, *deny* our finitude. But for all the recent talk about philosophers who deny such features of our common humanity, what do we actually imagine that such denials and affirmations amount to? For Cavell, it is in the "transfigurations" (a word he borrows from Emerson) that philosophers are able to assess their yearning either for transcendence or for the presumably finite everyday. And it is in the methods of a philosopher's address to an audience as well as by his wording of an insight or a principle that we glimpse what the philosopher will, practically speaking, accept as the limits of a philosophical aspiration.

The moment-by-moment success of our appeals to the ordinary does not provide a haven for interpretation, whether of our literature or of our symptoms. These appeals now show the ground of our exposure. What is at issue is not our exposure to uncertainty—Fischer is surely right here—but our exposure to the false certainties and false closures that underlie our theories as well as our skepticism. Fischer is also surely right that part of what deconstruction wants us to see about language is part of what skepticism knows (or takes itself to know) about language. But whereas Fischer usefully focuses on the claim to polysemy, the arbitrariness of the signifier, and the instability of the interpretive enterprise, the deadness of the separate sign comes in for a less sustained treatment.

Fischer has a great many useful things to say about what happens when the "sign" is taken in isolation and detached from the movement of the work, and also about how inevitably criticism ends up picturing a text in images of objects or structures. But here again, we must look to the grammar of a thinker's proposed cure in order to understand the thinker's picture of the problem. In Fischer's treatment, there is a tendency to conflate the returning of the word to the life contained in our ordinary forms of life with the returning of the word and the world to the mutual life sustained in a work of literature. (As we will see, Stephen Mulhall takes this tendency even further.)

In thinking of Emerson and Thoreau as "underwriting" the appeal to the ordinary, Cavell does not mean us to confuse the state of mind in which I am inclined to try to mean the words "I can know of another's pain only indirectly" with the state of mind in which I proclaim my joy in a "nasal twang," as Thoreau puts it. No doubt these states of mind are related. In both, one might say that the voice is constrained. But the constraints on our expressions of joy are not immediately treatable as if they were constraints on our knowledge of coffee cups and lumps of wax. In our self-restricted expressions, the life of our words is threatened, and our voice is perhaps damaged. In his constraining of our concepts of knowledge and directness, the skeptic displays his wish to forgo the voice altogether.

It is not easy to determine which damage is the greater damage to the human voice or spirit. The important thing is not to swamp the different paths of analysis and diagnosis by assimilating them too quickly. After all, when the skeptic sequesters the human voice, it may well be that he intends its safe return on some other occasion. (Perhaps he imagines a kind of holiday from the demands of thinking.)

A starting point for any encounter with Cavell's writing is contained in Arnold Davidson's review of *Themes Out of School*.[18] Although this is a relatively short piece, Davidson is one of the few commentators to have developed a central insight into the positive structure of Cavell's writing. Many of my own themes can be traced in relation to Davidson's remarks.

> Cavell writes not primarily to produce new theses or conclusions, nor to produce new arguments to old conclusions, but, as Kierkegaard and the later Wittgenstein did, to excavate and transform the reader's sensibility, to undo his self-mystifications and redirect his interest. This is a distinctive mode of philosophizing with its own special rigor, in which the accuracy of description bears an enormous weight. In aiming to transform a sensibility, one must capture it precisely, and if one's descriptions are too coarse, too rough or too smooth, they will hold no direct interest, seeming to have missed the mark completely. Cavell's writing places extraordinary pressure on itself to describe, undistractedly and specifically, the forces of the mind. [234.]

Davidson is giving an account of one of the pervasive features of Cavell's writing, for those who are willing to follow his lead. In such moments of reading, Cavell's descriptions of the positions and movements of other philosophers and artists possess the kind of accuracy and interest that reward the reader's attentiveness, and produce the kind of illumination that is hard to capture in a paraphrase.

But Davidson is also preparing the way for a description of how Cavell's writing can fail its readers, or at least appear to fail them. Though the general region of this account seems accurate enough, there is a slight slippage in Davidson's account, which bears some notice. When Davidson remarks that if Cavell's descriptions are too rough or too smooth, they may seem to "have missed the mark altogether," he passes over what seems to me a crucial step. Before a reader is inclined to take the accuracy or lack of accuracy of Cavell's descriptions as grounds for acceptance or dismissal (as hitting or missing the mark), the reader must already have accepted something fairly substantial about this "distinctive mode of philosophizing."

A way of writing that aims to transform a reader's sensibility must seek out readers who are at least partly willing and ready to have their sensibilities transformed. Only a reader who is somehow or somewhere prepared to have his self-mystifications undone or his philosophical interests reoriented is likely to find that this sort of transformation happens in response to a *description* of the condition to be transformed. Only such a reader is likely to think that the accuracy or inaccuracy of the description is at issue. And only such a reader will find that when Cavell's descriptions do miss the mark, this alone is the reason why the writing sounds inflated or self-absorbed. Davidson reminds us that those who are philosophers by professional training are both "best-placed and worst-placed" to understand Cavell's work. But in the regions of academic philosophy where Davidson and I got our training, it is more than just bad manners to diagnose the opposing view instead of arguing against it. Such diagnosis— even in the form of description—is likely to be regarded as hostile to the very spirit of philosophy. (For instance, it may be taken as a species of the so-called ad hominem fallacy, or even as a sort of apotheosis of it.)

Davidson is surely aware of all of this, and he leaves room to describe what it is, on a first reading of Cavell, that gives his philosophical readers enough material to keep them coming back for more. This "something more" is the feature that gives the text a chance with the reader, and gives it the time required to do its work of diagnosis and demystification. I take up some of these issues in chapter 3, where I cite Cavell's own sense of this "something more" as an explicit problem, not only for his writing but for his shifting sense of methodology. In the same context, I am suggesting that what constitutes the attractive surface of his text gradually changes in the course of the 1970s and early 1980s. These changes reflect the changes in his philosophical methods, and perhaps in turn are reflected by them.

Davidson's account is not meant to be an account of the whole impact of Cavell's writing regarded as a medium of his philosophizing. He is perhaps inclined to pass over a description of the early phases of this impact, in order to get out a couple of other features of Cavell's style. He remarks on Cavell's sometimes nearly uncanny ability "to get 'inside' a position and uncover its motivations, as if he were a diagnostician of the spirit in which things are said . . . " (232). A bit later, Davidson amplifies his description of Cavell as wishing to transform sensibilities and to redirect his readers' interests, suggesting that Cavell's ultimate ambition is to overcome certain kinds of resistance.

This introduction of psychoanalytic terminology has some of its roots in Cavell's reading of Wittgenstein. (Cavell is not alone, if sometimes rather lonely, in his sense of the importance of the vocabulary of resistance and therapy in Wittgenstein's work.) The pervasiveness of this language is a mark of the later phases of Cavell's work, the phases I characterize as marked by the model of reading. It is, however, important to note here that the two kinds of diagnosis that Davidson singles out in Cavell are facing in different directions. One kind points in the direction of the text Cavell is providing a "reading" of. The other kind faces the current reader, and offers—or threatens—to turn that reader into a text for his or her own perusal and edification.

Both directions are indeed present in Cavell, and both involve the idea of reading and the idea of the self as a text, or collection of texts. And Davidson is quite right to suggest that at certain moments the one direction collapses into the other. Or rather, the lines along which Cavell engages his reader suddenly and strikingly coincide with the lines along which he has been engaging the text that he is reading. For some, these moments of coincidence and merger are the most exhilarating moments of Cavell's work. For others, they are among the most infuriating and pretentious. Some readers, of course, never get far enough with Cavell's writing to discover the power of such moments of coincidence and self-reflection at all. But surely we will not be able to see what makes these moments so satisfying if we produce them too quickly. Initially and normally, the two modes of address and diagnosis face—and *must* face— in different directions. And these directions will also tell us something about how Cavell's own text provides interest and sustains attention long enough to do its further work.

When we diagnose the movement of at least one kind of text important to Cavell's enterprises, we enlist the reader on our side, and suspend conviction in the self-evidence or self-subsistence of the problem that the text purports to address. That suspension is already one kind of offense to philosophers, and the fact that Cavell shares this mode of offense with Austin and Wittgenstein is not likely to improve the situation. Normally, the writer must be able to describe, as it were objectively, enough of the features and enough of the issues of the text that the reader becomes willing at least to listen to the diagnosis. In Cavell's case, this implies (as he puts it in "More of *The World Viewed*") a further willingness to wait for the words of the contending positions—the contending fragments of the mind—to express themselves in their due course.

This willingness to wait, to suspend the urgency of arriving at a solution, is indeed present in Cavell, and not merely when he is discussing explicitly philosophical texts. This impulse is part of the source for an aspect of Cavell's writing that Davidson does not mention: Some readers have responded, with varying degrees of impatience and irritation, to what they think of as Cavell's refusal to come to a resolution. It is easy for them to connect this to another aspect of his text, namely, a sense of

its increasing refinement, its urge to make minute distinctions and to record them in what seem like merely fussy variations of wording.

To readers like Davidson and me this may seem more like a matter
of Cavell's efforts to suggest the right word for the right theme, perhaps
by exploring the theme's capacity for significant variation. But to other
readers, the same enterprise can evidently seem as if he is merely circling around the theme, refusing to let the obvious notes emerge. Such
readers sometimes respond as if, having bought a ticket to hear Rosemary
Clooney, they had been forced to listen to Thelonious Monk. But they
cannot be so easily dismissed. To such readers Cavell is not just refusing
(like Wittgenstein) to advance theses or arguments: he is refusing to allow his work to have any cadence or resolution at all.

D avidson is interested in those moments where Cavell turns to the
reader and invites the consciousness that the reader is a kind of text.
One may argue that such moments are implicit already in the model of
the appeal to what we ordinarily say. There the reader (as I suggest in
chapter 2) is first of all a source of philosophical data and conviction. The
reader is a source that must be invited to offer words of her own, allowing
herself to be prompted by the text's formulation of examples and assertions. But in these circumstances the reader *must* be, at least potentially,
a *competing* source of such data. Otherwise, the resultant agreements and
harmonies are without philosophical weight. If the eliciting of attunement is the goal of such appeals to what we ordinarily say, then the
opportunity for disagreement is the price for any worthwhile philosophical achievement of this kind. It follows that the option of diagnosing the
reader's lack of accord must not be exercised too quickly.

In fact, it is relatively rare for Cavell to turn to the reader directly and
suggest that she is *currently* caught up in a specific piece of resistance.
Davidson can certainly maintain that Cavell's work tends to get increasingly involved in such forms of diagnosis. But in the passage we now turn
to, what is being called upon is not so much the kind of diagnosis latent
in Cavell's work as Davidson's own capacity for diagnosis. This is not surprising, given that Davidson's treatment of this issue is bound up with his
response to the incessantly repeated charge that Cavell's writing is self-
indulgent.

In this passage, Davidson begins with a somewhat polemical reversal,
converting this habitual charge of self-indulgence into something that
itself requires diagnosis. As Davidson develops his diagnosis, his own posture as a reader merges quietly with Cavell's. I take this gradual merger

as a kind of confirmation of my formulation of the reversals of reading: Davidson takes over the position of what I call the "philosopher-reader."

> What does [Cavell's prose] indulge itself in, and what picture of philosophical writing must one have to view this writing as indulging in something? Suppose one were to understand the self-indulgent as the uninhibited. Then that might mean that one was opposing this kind of writing with inhibition, call it repression. And repressed writing might look like rigorous writing, where rigorous ended up associated . . . with stiffness. From this view-point, Cavell's writing might look like a form of acting-out, which generally has an impulsive character and may be aggressively directed either at oneself or at others. . . . However, one must not forget that Freud contrasted acting-out with remembering: acting-out is a kind of resistance that refuses to recognize one's unconscious wishes and fantasies. Cavell's ambition is precisely to overcome this resistance to allow one to recall or remember wishes, fantasies, temptations, illusions, urges, desires, and hopes. This explains why Cavell understands reading and writing as redemptive and therapeutic, and why he says that any credible model of such reading and writing will have to be psychoanalytic in character. [239–40.]

Davidson is surely right to suggest that at least one source of the sense that Cavell's prose is constantly referring to itself is an unwillingness on the part of the reader to investigate the sources of his own image of a problem or a text. The professional philosopher does not wish to know where the words are coming from in which our response to the problem or the text gets formulated. That is to say, there seems to be something right about the suggestion that a characteristic criticism of Cavell's writing is produced by a mechanism akin to projection.

But dangers abound: the image of Cavell's writing as involved in a therapy-as-diagnosis seems appropriate enough, especially given the explicit idea of a therapeutic reading in Cavell's later work. Sooner or later, however, the suggestion should remind us that when Cavell propounds the model of a therapeutic text, it is not typically the text that he is engaged in writing that is thus characterized. Ordinarily it is the text that he is *reading*—or that he depicts himself as reading—that Cavell goes on to characterize as therapeutic.

> It ought to help to see that from the point of view of psychoanalytic therapy the situation of reading has typically been turned around, that it is not first of all the text that is subject to interpretation but we in the gaze or hearing of the text. [*Themes*, 52.]

On my understanding, it is not merely rhetorical reticence or deference to the earlier writer that leads Cavell to characterize the prior text as the therapeutic text. His implicit invitation for us to join him in the "gaze or hearing" of Thoreau's text is not a ploy to distract us from the therapeutic work of his own text. It is part of Cavell's invitation to read Cavell that we should find him in the posture of reading—and being read by—Thoreau. It is precisely such reversals that my model of reading is designed to take account of. I specifically intend the idea of "reversal" to capture what Cavell has in mind when he says that "the situation of reading has typically been turned around" (ibid).

Furthermore, Cavell characterizes the text in question as maintaining a kind of silence or stillness. This is something I take up in chapter 3 and at length in chapter 5.

> Of all the problems that beckon and seem to me worth following from the sketch [of such a therapeutic text], the one that is perhaps paramount in terms of my work on skepticism . . . is . . . one I only mention here, namely, why or how the same silence, or rather the stillness of the text, the achievement of which perhaps constitutes textuality, or a text's self-containedness, should be interpretable politically as rebuke and confrontation and be interpretable epistemologically as the withholding of assertion, on which I have found the defeat of skepticism, and of whatever metaphysics is designed to overcome skepticism, to depend—as if the withholding of assertion, the containing of the voice, amounts to the forgoing of domination. ["Politics," 199.]

It is this silence or stillness that is the heart of the model of reading as therapy, and the heart of the analogy between psychoanalytic therapy and the situation of reading. The intensity of Cavell's verbal presence is no bar to this form of stillness or self-containedness. What *would* work against Cavell taking over from Thoreau the withholding of the voice and of assertion is the reader's sense that Cavell needs the reader as a subject of his diagnosis.

Thus Cavell's depiction of himself as reading an earlier text is designed, in part, precisely to get the reader *off* the spot, and to provide room and time for the work of therapy and liberation: "But what is a text that it has this power of overcoming the person of its author?" Cavell is well aware of the seductive power of the teacher or the text that pretends not to need us. In the foreword to *Must We Mean What We Say?* he writes: "The great teacher invariably claims not to want followers, i.e. imitators. His problem is that he is never more seductive than at those moments of rejection" (xxv). If there is a moment when the teacher is more seductive than at such moments of rejecting the student's wish to imitate, it might well be when the teacher is calmly and tactfully *discussing* the need for such rejection.

There is in Cavell's writing a wish to engage in such discussion to ease the student and the reader through such transitions from imitation to independence. (I discuss a version of this in chapter 3, in relation to some remarks of his about Austin.) Such a wish may have something to do with wanting to avoid certain kinds of confrontation with a reader, as well as with certain kinds of assertiveness and assertion. It may also have to do with an unwillingness to relinquish the presence of the student or the reader, since it is, after all, their presence that constitutes Cavell's authorial voice as teacher and as writer.

Whose problem is it, in the end, if the teacher is never more seductive than at these moments of rejection? It is as if the teacher is unable, on his own, to stop being a teacher, to stop being seductive. This topic leads naturally to the topic of how writing is brought to an end, a topic that increasingly occupies Cavell's attention throughout the 1980s. But this does not exhaust the question of how the teacher stops being a teacher. Put otherwise, it may well be that the teacher in the text—or the teacherliness of the text—is not as easily appeased as the text's writer.

If this characterization of Cavell's wish to ease the reader's transitions to independence is accurate, then it becomes more obvious how this wish is appropriate to Cavell's sense of how writing works. It might help us understand how his work can be seductive and useful to some readers, and irritating to others. Remarks designed to help me through a transition that I have no intention of making are not going to register as helpful. And since these remarks may well refer to Cavell's presence, or the presence of the prior text in his words, the reader will have the impression that Cavell is referring to himself. This impression will be partially correct. That is, Cavell is indeed discussing and enacting the connection of a reader to a text that Cavell is already involved in (as its reader and hence as the one who is being read by the prior text). And if the current, empirical reader of Cavell's text has not found himself among its acts of reading, then Cavell's references to his own enactment of reading will be read as references solely to Cavell himself. The other party to the transition has left early, or has not shown up at all.

Such moments of transition are part of a larger issue in relating Cavell's own text to a model of therapy. In eliding the role of the prior text, Davidson creates an obstacle to taking the work of reading Cavell as like the work of therapy. Normally, my resistances to therapy are not elicited merely by having my therapist describe them to me. There must be a situation in which my resistance is revealed as having already been elicited by someone or something (relatively) neutral. (Otherwise, characterizing my resistance in detail is likely to be inappropriate and counter-productive.) Cavell's own text is not initially to be found in this posture of neutrality and silence, and I imagine that it is never seen in such a light without a certain preparation. His writing works both to achieve this neutrality and independence within his text and to prepare his readers for this condition. But he presents himself in the first place as the one who is always to be found in the posture of reading. Cavell is the one who has already been seduced and is already beginning to work through his entrancements and his other passivities in the gaze of the text.

We take over the situation of reading in the middle of things. This is necessary since, like any critic, Cavell is to some extent debarred by the nature of the situation from giving us a view of his prior seduction (e.g., by film, by Shakespeare, by Emerson, or by Freud). Writing such as Cavell's cannot assume a neutral position from which to describe the moment at which his neutrality as a reader came to an end. Such writing must do some work, in order to give us even a provisional view of the moment of seduction. Cavell's writing, in particular, presents itself as working back to the moment of encounter that dispatched him to his writing, and dispatched his writing on its various paths. The reader discovers Cavell's seduction by making some sense of his various quests and errands, as well as by making a pattern of his various insights into the text.

It is for such reasons that I characterize Cavell's exemplification of the transitions and the exchanges of position as composed of what I call the reversals of reading. And while Davidson is surely right to describe the liberation of the reader as the ultimate aim of writing such as Cavell's, one must not be too quick to characterize the liberation in exclusively psychoanalytic terms. In fact, I think it is important to *deny* that Cavell's model of philosophical method—or for that matter his model of reading—is *based on* psychoanalysis. Cavell's model borrows features of psychoanalytic therapy in order to further develop a model of philosophy as a kind of reading. The results may open up our sense of what philosophy is and what reading is, in psychoanalytic terms. But until we have a clearer account of reading and therapy it will be difficult simply to illuminate the situation of reading by appealing to some well-known mechanisms of therapy. Even if there are such mechanisms, it is notoriously difficult to apply them beyond the limits of the therapeutic encounter itself.

Conversely, however, Cavell's specific borrowing of analytic terms to elucidate the situation of reading might also suggest that we reexamine certain crucial elements of therapy and psychoanalysis. First of all, I think one would want to examine the possibility of accounting for the situation of therapy as itself already containing elements of reading. A starting point here would be the fact that the patient tries to *read* the therapist's silences, and that silence may be perceived as a text, and moreover as a text of withdrawal and withholding. Here would be a place to reinsert the problematic of the other (and perhaps indeed the animation of the other) that Cavell finds Freud a bit too willing to avoid. (Cf."The Uncanniness of the Ordinary," in *In Quest of the Ordinary*.)

Davidson does not quite make the claim that Cavell's text is meant to be therapeutic in the same way that therapy is meant to be therapeutic. But he clearly relates the mode of remembering released by psychoanalytic therapy to the mode of remembering (as opposed to acting out) that is, on his account, released by Cavell's writing. This is very much worth pursuing. But it is also worth bearing in mind that when my therapist's silence helps me to unlock a piece of resistance, the resulting restoration of memory and of the circulation of thought has no further reference to his mind, or to my fantasies about the sources of his silence.

By contrast, when I work through the silences and withdrawals of *Walden*—or for that matter of *The Senses of Walden*—I have learned something not only about what is frozen in my personal season of winter, nor merely about my private thawing out. There remains something very like a book for me to know about, something at any rate that others may also know about and care about in ways that may prove to be essentially similar to mine. Of course, there are also things that I will never know about *Walden*. The sort of memory and acknowledgment of loss released in Thoreau's writing or in Cavell's writing must always contend with the reader's prior stake in the text that is under discussion. So, too, there will still be a text in the room, when I have learned how to leave it alone. Naturally, this point may suggest further analogies to the situation of therapy. But they remain to be worked out.

Of the books that have appeared on Cavell, the one with the greatest scope is Stephen Mulhall's *Stanley Cavell: Philosophy's Recounting of the Ordinary*.[19] Like Fischer, he harbors a double image of Cavell's reading—as an activity that is at once extraordinary and somehow representative. But he goes further than Fischer in attributing the extraordinary, redemptive aspect of reading to Cavell's own particular powers of animation, or reanimation. At the same time he goes further than Davidson in taking Cavell as "transposing the psychoanalytic model to the domain of reading" (210).

Mulhall provides any number of useful insights about the results of such a transposition, including the idea that the text will contain an "image (or fantasy) of its readers." But he has not, to my mind, sufficiently clarified what there is about the situation of reading that invites this transposition. In particular, he leaves fairly inert what ought to have been the fairly volatile idea that we are "read by" the prior text, and that we are to enact Cavell's enactment of this reading.

He seems to take the presence of the reader to the text that he reads (and is read by) as essentially a matter of recognizing similarities—a species of identification, one might say:

> Cavell's Thoreau has therapeutic designs on his readers; just as he conceives of his own readings (of nature, of words) as a matter of allowing himself to be read, so his text is intended to subject its readers to interpretation; his writing contains a particular image of them and their needs (they are lost, lacking interest in their own lives), and it involves presenting himself in such a way as to elicit his reader's transferences and to encourage them to interpret those transferences (e.g. "He is isolated, but then so am I"); from which activity his readers are supposed to learn how they might recover themselves, whilst maintaining their freedom from the person of the author. [*Cavell*, 254.]

It is not exactly clear from this last sentence *which* activity we, as Thoreau's readers, are supposed to be learning from. I suppose the activity that I am to learn from is my interpreting of my own transferences, rather than, for instance, Thoreau's "presenting himself in such a way as to elicit his reader's transferences."

Either way, Mulhall's picture flattens and constricts the model of reading that he places at the center of Cavell's later work. If I am to learn freedom and self-recovery by interpreting my transferences to that text, then my imagination of that text's activities as well as its silences seems crucial. But if the point my "transference" attaches to is my recognition that the author ("Thoreau") is also alone ("He is isolated"), then my interpretive activity seems to give out fairly quickly (" . . . but so am I").

Mulhall strives to show the connection between this depiction of our transference to a text and issues of mourning and the realization of loss. He characterizes the goal of such reading as that of releasing what he calls "frozen or distorted investments of desire" (256). And he characterizes Thoreau as interpreting "his reader's recovery from skeptical despair as a matter of a recovery of the self—or more precisely, as a progress towards a new state of the self" (256). But it seems hard to get from any of the things that Mulhall depicts Thoreau as doing to the transferential relationships that the reader is supposed to interpret and learn from.

It is hard to see, for instance, how the fact of being isolated, or the ability to depict oneself as isolated, would take a reader very far. It takes us a bit further if we notice that Thoreau's writing possesses strategies for enforcing a sense of his "withdrawal" and "his text's disinterest," and that these are designed to deliver an "impersonal rebuke to his reader, one which specifies her autonomy as lost but recoverable." We can see why a withdrawal of the author's interest from the words on the page might rebuke us for bringing the wrong kind of interest to that page. But how do that withdrawal and that interest teach us "to take an interest in our lives"? Mulhall does little to connect what Cavell isolates as Thoreau's strategies of writing to the powerful, transferential effects that are supposed to result. If the point of working through the transferences is ultimately liberation from the person of the author (as Mulhall notes at several junctures), then there doesn't seem to be much of an author present for us to be liberated from.

What Mulhall leaves out is precisely what Cavell insists on: Thoreau's achievement of a voice in words. One of the most powerful voices in American literature, it is all the more impressive for emerging within earshot of Emerson's voice. And it is precisely this voice of Thoreau's that Cavell characterizes Thoreau as having withdrawn. For instance, it is the withdrawal of Thoreau's voice that links his "impersonal rebuke" to the reader with his refusal of his voice to a society complicit in slavery.

Mulhall seems convinced that he can explain Cavell's philosophical progress almost wholly without recourse to the idea and fact of his voice. The word *voice* does not appear in Mulhall's index, and there are only a few occasions on which he comes close to presenting the issues of the voice in alternate terms. Until the present book, I have also tended, for various reasons, to avoid formulations that relied too heavily on the voice. But in writing about Thoreau one pays dearly for such abstinence. Mulhall's discussion of the social contract contains one of his few references to the "voice." But Mulhall seems to isolate this discussion of the social contract from the problem of criteria. He places the discussion of giving or refusing one's voice to the social realm in what he calls a "parallel" field of investigation, thus ensuring that the political notion of "voice" will remain segregated from the appeal to the voice in the methods of ordinary language (63–65).[20]

One reason why Mulhall may not have felt the constriction of his reading of Thoreau may have to do with his general sense of Cavell as a reader:

> In his writing on these particular texts, Cavell is acknowledging the absolute specificity of his particular experience of reading them; and— since reading is the most fundamental activity of his life, since it is that to which he has most deeply committed himself—he is thereby attempting to declare and to enact the specific texture of that life, the particular con-

> stellation of thoughts, feelings and experiences that go to make him up as
> a person. He is, in short, not only furthering a philosophical argument and
> engaging in a mode of cultural analysis: he is also attempting to enact his
> own existence as an individual by bringing his personal world of experience
> to our common words, and by acknowledging us, his readers, by asking us
> to acknowledge his words, and so himself, through reading them in the
> spirit to which their writing aspires. [194–95.])

(I discuss the passage again in chapter 5.) As in the case of *Walden*, Mulhall does not ask why Cavell's enactment of his experiences of reading
should prompt us to acknowledge him or the spirit in which he is writing.
What is so particular about Cavell's words, or the spirit in which he writes
them, that we should be invited to some sort of acknowledgment? Why
should acknowledgment take the form of our working through the transferences to his text?

Following out Mulhall's own sense of the transference from Cavell's
text to us, we might ask what image of ourselves we encounter as har-
bored by that text. Perhaps it is an image of us as unable to declare the
specific texture of our experience, and unable to take responsibility for
the specific words at our disposal for recording and enacting that experience. Then what bars us from taking up this responsibility? And what is
it about Cavell's text that helps me get beyond the impediment to my
specific existence, and that helps me to shoulder my responsibilities in
this regard? Surely it is not merely the autobiographical element of Cavell's prose, nor his success at forging a personal style and exhibiting the
"particular constellation" of his person. I could get something similar from
Rousseau's *Confessions* or, for that matter, from Mill's *Autobiography* or
Newman's *Apologia Pro Vita Sua*. It is surely not enough to look for eloquence and precision in someone's personal narrative. Even if most philosophy contains an element of autobiography, perhaps hidden or unacknowledged, it is still not the case that all autobiography is philosophy.

Perhaps what we are seeking is to be found in the more general characterization that Mulhall gives just prior to this passage. He means to be
providing grounds for linking the earlier and the later work:

> [Cavell's] investigation of modern skepticism leads him to think of his
> Wittgensteinian practice of recounting criteria as a mode of thinking whose
> prosecution constitutes a reanimation of words, self, and world—a way of
> declaring and enacting one's own existence and that of others through the
> full acknowledgement of the life in (that is, our life with) words. [193.]

This notion of a writer's power to acknowledge our life with words is
promising, as are the companion notions of animation and reanimation.

Here is certainly an image that Cavell's text could harbor of us, an image of me as taking my words in isolation from my existence: They are as dead to me as I am to my existence.

But how is Cavell's exemplary text supposed to bring me back to my words, and my words back to life? The account of reading attributes a nearly magical power to Cavell's ability to animate the words of what he reads. Having slighted the realm of the ordinary as the place where our words are already alive if we but restore them to circulation, Mulhall is now impelled to overestimate the life that Cavell brings to the page. The life of our words that a writer must live off cannot be entirely the work of the writer.

If I follow Cavell's words too closely, then I am precisely not finding my own. Or I am following the wrong thing about his words, failing to listen to what his words might have in common with anyone's words, and hearing only the specialness of his voice. Or is the danger rather that if I do not follow his words precisely, then I will not learn from his text how to follow the precise syllables I am now contending with?

This would be a good moment to invoke the idea of the reader's prior seduction by the author (in this case someone we can call "Cavell"), and our need to work through and liberate ourselves from the mechanisms of this seduction. But what specifically are we to liberate ourselves from? The author here is an enactment of the text, and I imagine that the primary phenomenon that this text harbors is the voice of its author and the impression that voice makes. (I take this thought further in chapter 5.) More specifically, Mulhall is surely right to think of something like the animation and the acknowledgment of specific words. But, again, Mulhall tends to conflate two different sorts of animation, and two streams of life to which our words might be restored.

Wittgenstein already suggests that the sign by itself is dead, and evidently within our forms of life it is restored to its own kind of life. Many philosophers have felt a qualm about Wittgenstein, as if words were alive only when they were at home, and as if our words had to be kept indoors, permanently grounded. Some Wittgensteinians accepted this as a small price to pay for avoiding philosophical nonsense. Cavell's revision of this understanding does not replace the dimension of the life and death of our words with the phenomena of voice. But his problematic of voice begins the process of characterizing the deadness of the sign as a kind of voicelessness, a condition more drastic than the inertness of an unused sign. And this in turn begins a further effort to locate this region of voicelessness—of being outside language-games—with the kind of damage to the voice explored by Thoreau and Emerson.

The latter life of our words is something a writer might undertake to supply, perhaps by teaching us to listen more closely to the sources of our own words, to let ourselves be overcome by the specific syllables to which we are partial. When I restore, for instance, the word "indirectly" (as in "I can know of another's pain only indirectly") to the language-games that are its home, I am unlikely to discover very much about how I bring my "personal world of experience to our common words." At least I hope not to discover that the philosophical problem of other minds stems primarily from, for instance, my inner distraction in the face of other people's pain, along with perhaps my willingness to concoct philosophical cover stories for my distraction and incapacity.

My conviction that this is a problem worth taking seriously, studying, and writing about may, of course, also stem from personal problems. But you can read, for instance, the whole of *The Claim of Reason* and not discover very much about any personal difficulties Stanley Cavell might happen to have in responding to the pain of others. What presents itself as "personal" in these texts has more to do with Cavell's response to a specific philosophical problem or text, along with his drive to keep on articulating the form of the problem and his various responses to it. But his responses to the problem or text in question are (almost always) intended as *representative* responses, not responses belonging to him alone. Of course, one may fail to recognize one's response in Cavell's various reconstructions of responsiveness. Then this mode of writing is likely to fail. But one might also come to recognize that Cavell has found words for a response that one had not yet managed to find for oneself. Then how do we know that he hasn't been putting words in our mouths, rather than locating a common region of response?

If we are to locate such writing as Wittgenstein's and Cavell's on a philosophical map, such issues will have to be worked out. These are also matters of what I am characterizing as the tensions between voice and method: between the need to find the words that will let you articulate the depth of your position and the need to find words that will let others acknowledge your position as one that they can share. However sympathetic a voice such as Cavell's may come to seem, it must be something we can work with.

This doubleness of Cavell's voice—its eloquence along with its workaday proposals for steps to be taken—seems to be quite hard to get hold of. Sympathizers and detractors alike sometimes seem to have a stake in making it harder than it is. If there is a lesson about the contribution of our inner disorders to the problem of the other, then that is a discovery of Wittgenstein's and Cavell's (and perhaps also of the much-neglected

John Wisdom's). Following out the ways our words get away from us, words like *indirectly* and *directly,* and restoring them to the stream of life within our forms of life, is not a substitute for psychotherapy. (Such philosophical therapy might of course work in some hitherto unexplored conjunction with psychotherapy.)

In this book, the changing relation between the voice and the life of our words will be explored as a transition between the model of the appeal to ordinary speech and the model of philosophy as a series of reversals in our reading. In the first case, the voice that the author recovers and enacts is played off against the voices that are invoked by the appeal to the ordinary. The life of our words that we obtain by restoring them to their ordinary places in our speech is either a life we can share or it is no life at all.

In the latter case, there is as yet no common life in our words. But there is something already there, when we arrive, something we can still call a text. The voice of the author emerges as the voice of a prior text. In Cavell's later writing, his voice emerges most commonly as the voice of one who depicts himself as *listening.* And what he is listening to are the voices of a prior text, voices that have been sequestered or shunned, voices that need to be recovered. The idea and practice of recovering the voice is a substantial piece of continuity between the model of ordinary language philosophy and the model of philosophy that is founded on elements of reading. But in recent years, Cavell finds himself reading texts in which a voice is known by the voices it shuns. (His writings on Derrida and on operas such as *La Traviata* and *Pelléas et Mélisande* are good examples of this.)

In the philosophical writing that proceeds from ordinary language, Cavell's work often gives the impression that the words are returning from a kind of lifelessness. But it is a lifelessness for which no one in particular is responsible. For the skeptical impulse to speak outside of language-games and to deprive one's words of the voice in which they are uttered is not exactly the responsibility of any one person or any one text. (No doubt that is part of the problem with the impulse to skepticism.) But to recover the voice that the skeptical impulse has banished is consequently not to recover the voice of some particular author or text.

To engage in the philosophy of ordinary language you have to be willing to let the words in question be as common as gravel. And if Cavell's voice is nonetheless distinctive in his practice of these methods, that voice is also intended to exhibit its responsiveness to the most ordinary reaches of language. The willingness to say that somebody's expression of joy is nasal or constricted, that somebody else's words are mean and sneaking, is as important as Emerson's wider perception that "every word they say chagrins us." The life that the great Romantic writers and their successors bring back to our words is not quite the same as the life that skepticism takes out of our words. If the latter can be characterized as the suppression or repression of the voice, the former life must come from sources beyond the ordinary language-games we all must live on. Of course, it may be that to pursue the voice that knows how to appeal to the ordinary will already take us beyond the voices we have heard. To relinquish that voice, even perhaps to shun it, may be the precondition for hearing it afresh. And that relinquishment is something that we can learn from Romantic texts as far back as *Walden* or the *Prelude* and as recently as portions of the *Philosophical Investigations*.

If someone were to give voice to the life in our words and show us the life in our most ordinary acts of speech, we might well need ears behind ears before we were ready to hear it. But then where would we find the words to acknowledge the possibility of such a voice, or find the methods to pursue it?

2

VOICES

THE APPEAL TO ORDINARY SPEECH AND
THE VOICES OF THE EVERYDAY

It is not hard to make out that the idea of voice is central to the philosophical and critical work of Stanley Cavell. Long before the publication of *A Pitch of Philosophy*, with its triptych of voices, Cavell had been harping on the human voice and its affiliations with philosophy. Of course, it was not just a question of the voices that philosophy wishes by turns to deride and to inflate but also of the voices within the various arts. In an age where American criticism has been dominated by Foucault, Lacan, and Derrida, it is hard to find a philosopher who keeps insisting that the genuine artist is the one who learns how to speak, and the genuine critic is the one who best shows us how to listen.

The recovery of the voice that skepticism banishes is essential to Cavell's methods of undermining skepticism, and essential to any adequate characterization of this project. The skeptic's suppression of the voice represents the suppression of the myriad connections and criteria by which the mind is ordinarily located in the world of objects and others. Hence, the voice is essential to Cavell's inheritance and revision of Austin and Wittgenstein. Suitably sketched in, the idea of voice forms part of Cavell's analogy between the skeptic's precipitous fall into world-annihilating doubt and the drive of the tragic hero to know and not to know.

Still further changes on the voice are rung in Cavell's treatments of

Romantic poetry and prose, of Emerson and Thoreau, of the melodrama of the unknown women, of what he calls the "conversation of justice" lodged within Rawls's *Theory of Justice*, and, only somewhat less surprisingly, in his chapter "Opera and the Lease of Voice" in the recent *A Pitch of Philosophy*. Some but not all of the increasing sway of the idea of voice has to do with Cavell's increasingly explicit delineation of what he calls moral perfectionism. An important suburb of this delineation has to do with his refusal either to disengage from or to give in to Derrida's treatment of the "voice" in opposition to the idea and practices of writing.

The possibility of perfectionism can be represented as a voice—usually released in writing but sometimes in film. The voice is meant to provoke us to recover possibilities that we had either dismissed outright or kept at a distance. Emerson tells us that the voice occurs to us often, as if its very existence were a warning, or rather an "admonition." We hear such voices so vividly precisely as a kind of compensation for our failure to attend to our thoughts. This casts the efforts and methods of listening and reading as moments of necessary self-estrangement. Our alienation allows the voice of the writer to emerge with uncanny clarity as a sort of amplified version of the return of the repressed.

Often the prior possibility has occurred to us as a voice that we had previously dismissed. We may not have listened to it because it was faint, or perhaps because it was familiar. The voice may have been saying something that we did not want to hear, or drowning out some silence we did not wish to fathom. What we have repressed (whether as a voice or as some other phantasm) is no longer exactly ours, but it is also not entirely foreign to us. The voice we are now attending to, coming from what seems like someplace beyond us and external to us, is also likely to sound neither wholly foreign nor wholly familiar.

The various resonances of the idea of voice thus ramify throughout the work of a writer whose branchings are already hard to keep track of. Moreover, throughout the proliferation of these methods of attending to various voices or various aspects of the voice, Cavell maintains a strong centripetal undertow toward a kind of unity in his conception of the function of voice in philosophy. As perhaps with notions like "criterion" or "acknowledgment," Cavell would deny that he is using the term in any technical sense. He wishes to invoke whatever aspect of the voice is appropriate to the issue he is pursuing. But if the idea of a technical sense of the word is not of much use in understanding Cavell, we are surely right to apprehend in his writing a sort of heightened or intensified significance of the voice.

If it is hard to know where to begin with these issues of the voice, we

are not without some signposts. As Cavell's work takes on a certain tra-
jectory in the years following the publication of *The Claim of Reason*, he
comes to use the idea of voice in the perspectives developed by that later
work. Indeed, as I have already suggested, the idea of the voice is crucial
to those emerging perspectives. But the emerging ideas of voice also afford some perspective on Cavell's earlier work. We need to guard against
the dangers of rereading the earlier work solely in the terms provided by
the later work. Nevertheless, we can find in the later work an important
clue to the structure of the earlier work, and we can discern the elements
of an instructive series of exchanges among the different stages of Cavell's
development.

The later work offers a retrospective sense of the significance of voice
in his own work, reaching back to its earliest recognizable beginnings. In
one of his most recent pieces of work (*A Pitch of Philosophy*, 64–67), he
argues that the "metaphysical voice" in Husserl is criticized as much by
Wittgenstein and Austin as it is more famously by Derrida. In each case,
what is being targeted is a version of the impulse to think of metaphysical
and incorrigible knowledge as present to the mind in a way that is independent of the uncertainties of actual language. He asks us to consider
whether Husserl's question about the function of voice in establishing the
unity of sense and presence might be framed analogously to the older,
Lockean question about how we acquire the meaning of general terms
from the collection of particular things. He invites us to consider the relation between the fantasy of the particularity of words that is embodied
in the picture of language as a collection of names and the fantasy of the
(mere) externality of words. The latter gives rise to the fantasy of language as a collection of inanimate signs. Giving voice to these latter fantasies, Cavell continues: "Since language is only external, how does it
come into the origin of self-presence . . . ?"

(*Self-presence* is a crucial term in Derrida's critique of Heidegger and
Husserl; he uses it to suggest the persistence of metaphysical categories
in the critique of those very categories. Here, the mind's capacity for self-
presence, for example, in something like a *cogito* is found to be something
on which both sense and knowledge depend.)

Circling back to his earliest public reflections on Wittgenstein and
language, he speculates about the paths he took and the paths he might
have taken. Within this speculation, the theme of voice acquires one of its
richest and most complicated sets of variations:

> Though I did not, I might just possibly then, as now, have captured in
> my experience, and theorized, a fantasy of a voice that precedes language,

that as it were gives itself language. This is not quite the fantasy of acquiring language by stealing it, since that carries the implication of coming late
to language, not preceding it,—so that there always remains a problem
whether language is mine, something that giving myself a language should
precisely settle. . . . In practice, however, the moment I felt that something
about ordinary language philosophy was giving me a voice in philosophy,
I knew that the something was the idea of a return of a voice to philosophy,
that asking myself what I say when, letting that matter present itself as a
defiance of philosophy's interest in language, as if what philosophy meant
by logic demanded, in the name of rationality, the repression of voice
(hence of confession, hence of autobiography). Thus when in my second
paper in philosophy, the first in response to reading Wittgenstein . . . I
identified the *Investigations* as a form and work of confession, I set words
out that I am following to this moment. [*A Pitch of Philosophy*, 69; cf. 67.]

I count at a minimum three distinguishable ideas of voice at work in
this passage: (1) a version of the metaphysical voice, i.e., a voice "before"
language, a version of a pure consciousness or pure understanding that
assigns meanings to the words that it knows itself to require as means to
express its essentially extralinguistic thoughts; (2) the human voice that
philosophy is characterized as banishing; and (3) Cavell's "voice in philosophy," the thing he began to acquire as a writer when he began to
listen for the voice that philosophy has banished.

It can seem to be nothing more than an accident of words that allows
Cavell to speak of finding his voice in philosophy by finding the track of
the voice that philosophy strives to suppress. This idea of the voice that
philosophy has banished or repressed is meant to remind us, for instance,
of the recognition that the *point* of uttering some words and the circumstances in which they get uttered are as much a part of the significance of
those words as what philosophers are inclined to call their "meaning" and
"reference." This is the region of Cavell's first prolonged encounters with
Austin and Wittgenstein. In summarizing the lessons of these encounters, he will say things like this: What the philosopher loses when he is
driven outside language-games is not what the words mean, but what he
meant in saying them. It is such losses that Cavell will eventually characterize as a loss of voice, and ultimately as philosophy's repression of
the voice.

The third idea of voice is contained in Cavell's depiction of himself
as finding his voice in philosophy. He characterizes this arrival at the
voice as the primary effect of his encounters with Austin's version of ordinary language philosophy. But this idea of a personal voice seems to
point us in a very different direction from the voice that is suppressed by

philosophy. Finding your voice in a field of work, like having your say in a discussion, is a way of characterizing your contribution to a chosen field. On the face of it, this idea seems to pull us in quite different directions: The idea of the voice as repressed points toward some general elements of human utterance and expression that have been driven beyond our serious consideration by the present constitution of philosophy. The idea of finding one's voice points toward something like Cavell's own access to the subject of philosophy.

As I argued in the first chapter, some readers have found it far too easy to focus on the supposedly personal aspect of Cavell's work. In some cases, this is true not only of those who dislike such intrusions of the personal but of those who admire them. Passages in which different regions of the voice abut each other in the space of a paragraph can facilitate these particular misreadings of Cavell. For instance, in the passage we have been examining, it becomes too easy to think of Cavell's effort to find his voice in the field of work called philosophy as an effort to make his presence felt by other practitioners in that field. This effort may in turn be thought of as essentially one of locating certain means of self-expression, or of making himself comprehensible to a particular audience. Here the idea of Cavell's finding a voice in philosophy becomes dangerously close to the idea of his arrival at that distinctive style—a style so easy to allude to and so difficult to characterize in any useful fashion.

In such moments, Cavell is not at pains to prevent the directions of misreading that I am trying to isolate. Nevertheless, it seems quite clear that Cavell's depictions of arriving at his voice are always also pictures of his arrival at his work. In this instance, the arrival at his work in the field of philosophy is depicted as his arrival at a voice that works to undo the suppression of voices. Cavell obviously wants this doubling and even tripling of voices. It is clear enough, even from this passage alone, that Cavell is interpreting Austin's methods of ordinary language as offering him his voice. At the same moment, he recognizes that the feature of Austin's practice that most immediately offers him voice is the feature of that practice which can be characterized as "a return of the voice to philosophy" (ibid.).

I am arguing that Cavell's recognition of this double emergence of the voice is something that developed in the course of his work. The terms of voice in which he describes the encounter with Austin's work were not available to him in forms accessible to his writing until sometime after the publication of *The Claim of Reason*. Even if these terms of voice had been thus available, it would still be an error to characterize Cavell's arrival at his voice as essentially the same event as the voice returning to philosophy.

The achievement of the authorial voice may happily be seen to echo, or even to coincide with, a certain moment of the voice being recovered for philosophy. But to ignore the difference between these voices is precisely to pass over the intellectual and the human conditions that permit the emerging voices to call for one another. This would prevent us from seeing why Cavell's authorial voice is suited to activate and revise Austin's appeals to ordinary language. It would prevent us from seeing the stroke of originality that allows Cavell to characterize these appeals as, precisely, appeals to the voice. And it prevents us from understanding what it was about just this writer Cavell and his various aspirations that allowed him to find a way through certain reaches of philosophy and back to his own sense of his words and his voice.

If we free ourselves from the idea that Cavell's arrival at his voice is essentially the same event as his beginning to speak in that distinctive style, other and more interesting questions become discernible. One might ask, for instance, how Cavell's voice was *able* to emerge in the field of philosophy. This is worth asking, since Cavell evidently remains convinced that it was exactly there that he found his voice, even though he seems equally convinced that his contribution to the field has been passed over or even repressed. Academic philosophers sometimes mention the latter idea, as if to suggest that Cavell complains too much and to confirm that his irrelevance is self-imposed. But if Cavell is not suggesting that the emergence of his voice in the field of philosophy simply coincides with the rise and fall of his fortunes among professional philosophers, then we might interpret these issues as a further instance of the problematic relation of voice to audience.

In any event, the question of who is listening to an authorial voice in philosophy is an especially poignant one to ask about a voice like Cavell's, which began its career with the discovery that philosophy has traditionally banished the voice. How will such a voice encourage the emergence of other voices? Granting for the moment that finding his own voice had something to do with his ability to find the voices that philosophy has repressed, we need to ask with still more precision, What does the one voice have to do with the other voice or voices? This question leads to another: What does the picture of the voice as embodying the contribution of an author have to do with the picture of the voice as embodying an aspect of the expressive endowment of all human users of language?

(I leave aside, for now, the third idea of voice, the idea of a metaphysical voice. This requires further exploration of the idea of a metaphysical power of reasoning, which locates and consolidates its sense of significance in the image of a voice existing prior to all empirical human utterances.)

I offer a couple of preliminary remarks, which will lead in turn to some further questions. Not every sense of being able to contribute to the field of philosophy will represent itself as finding one's voice. Not every achievement of voice in philosophy and not every sense of Wittgensteinian liberation in philosophy will take itself to be engaged in lifting philosophy's repressions of the voice. What is so special about these voices that Cavell evidently thinks he is able to hear and to set down in writing? Such a question cannot usefully be answered unless it is raised in tandem with another question: What is so ordinary about these voices? What is the ordinariness that Cavell keeps insisting upon? And how can these voices be characterized as ordinary when it takes so much extraordinary talent and effort to arrive at them and so much insistence to keep them in view?

These are the questions this chapter is trying to answer. We should not imagine that it will be easy to sort these issues out, nor perhaps that a voice in philosophy can be acknowledged by any means short of some analogous expression or achievement of voice. This much seems fair to say: If Cavell's happy coincidence of voices is in some sense a fortunate accident, it is not something that can be reduced to a play of words.

The signposts Cavell sets up within the territory of his development seem clear enough. But they soon turn out to lead us into some thickets of interpretive and philosophical difficulty. The paths they point back to have become somewhat overgrown, or perhaps it is rather that we never quite got used to taking *those* original paths. It was never very easy, at least outside of Oxford in the 1950s, to become accustomed to the practices of appealing to what we would ordinarily say in a given case. And for many readers, the perplexity grows with Cavell's very efforts to illuminate his own development. If it is difficult to understand Cavell's reading of Austin, it is not going to get easier when Cavell's rereadings of Austin, Wittgenstein, and his own earlier work tend to bind together regions of concern that were initially, perhaps, not obviously so tightly linked.

Moreover, it can seem as if every time Cavell revisits the methods and scenarios of his philosophical youth, he emends or annotates the script. Too much illumination or too much interest in one's philosophical origins can leave even a sympathetic reader more than a bit lost. And those whose training tells them that the origins of a method or a problem are irrelevant to the practice of the method or the solution of the problem are very unlikely to get interested in retrospective accounts of someone's philosophical itinerary.

I am suggesting that the procedures of Cavell's reconstruction of his own itinerary contain useful clues about the development of his philosophical methods. What Cavell produces when he looks back at the paths he has taken cannot, however, be safely used as a straightforward guidebook to the development of his views. His references to past work are not pristine declarations of information about the author's progress, presented to us from the privileged vantagepoint of authorship. But neither are they merely a product of the kind of self-referential consciousness that congratulates itself on its intellectual progress. Cavell's references to past work are not static reminders of what has already been accomplished. They are intended to mobilize philosophical insight and energy for work that is still to be done. Demonstrating that the intellectual path in question has already been taken is in part a way of demonstrating that the path is still open. Indeed, to go down such a path only once is not to know what it is to be on it. Such paths are always to be taken over again. We find out what they are when we find out what was blocking them and what finally permits us to go further along them.

There are certainly occasions on which Cavell seems willing to give the impression of having been everywhere and done everything. More to the point, he sometimes betrays the frustration of having had to discover that something that he managed to say a long time ago is still not getting heard. Such moods are not, however, the primary source of Cavell's references to his past writing. When he does arrive (for instance, in *The Senses of Walden*) at an explicit sense that everything has already been said, this sense is not uttered in weariness.

If there is intermittently a kind of weariness in Cavell's writing, it is not the world-weariness of the misunderstood but self-satisfied insider. Cavell is less likely to depict himself as having heard everything than as straining, at this very moment, to *listen to everything*. A certain philosophical fantasy that everything significant and intelligible is somewhere, somehow, present to us, all at once—if only we are alert enough—merges with the idea of the voice as the origin and bearer of human sense. The fantasy of philosophical alertness is no doubt more active at some times than others. It emerges in Cavell's work periodically in the early 1970s, most strikingly as the sense that not only has everything been said but everything *is now being said*—at this moment and pretty much all at once.

In *The World Viewed* and especially in *The Senses of Walden*, what reaches expression is Cavell's sense that the cacophony of public and private voices is approaching the pitch of madness. This fate of public madness is an aspect of what he sometimes calls "amentia." At least once, he relates this perception of our amentia to his depiction of Thoreau as engaged in withdrawing his voice from the writing of *Walden*. Cavell characterizes Thoreau as withdrawing the voice in order to *protect* the voice—to protect it from further damage and to teach our society something about what Cavell calls its dysphasia (*Senses*, expanded edition, xv).

I take Cavell's little sketch of a concept of dysphasia to be making room for cultural vicissitudes more desperate even than a tendency to muteness or voicelessness. These outcomes might rather be characterized as cultural forms of *a*-phasia. Cavell is discerning a wish or impulse to *damage* the voice. To imagine oneself the sole or even the primary victim of the culture's attack on its own voices would not be altogether safe. Nor is it methodologically wise to imagine that one is free of the impulse to damage our voices, however much one has learned to cherish them in the abstract.

Misprisions of Style: Conflating Voice and Method

It is not surprising that sympathetic readers should become a little bewildered by Cavell's deployment of these ideas and practices of voice. Perhaps the most ubiquitous of these confusions is hardly ever made explicit: It is a confusion between the singularity of Cavell's *style* and the distinctness and the pertinence of his voice. And this in turn confuses the question of Cavell's self-expression with the question of his contribution to philosophy, a contribution that he takes himself to have been on the track of since his encounter with Austin's work (cf. *Pitch*, 8). No doubt the finding of his voice in philosophy and the development of that singular, seductive sound to his prose were achieved together and are difficult to separate in practice. But it is one of the burdens of this book to suggest that, nevertheless, a great deal depends on disentangling them.

If the presence of Cavell's voice in his writing is taken as equivalent to the effectiveness of his distinctive style, this suggests a very particular idea of the power of writing and its effects on an audience. At least according to one common legend, a voice such as Cavell's either irritates and repels you or it engages and seduces you. At the same time, this idea of the singularity of Cavell's voice points to a particular way of marking words and phrases as his own, of enlisting them in the service of a sound uniquely his. It is as if Cavell's accomplishment as a writer were thought to lie in the creation of a sort of dialect or accent, which could then be recognized essentially in every syllable he utters.

I am not denying that his writing can have this effect. If Emerson's prose can be seen as a golden mist, Cavell's can evidently give the impression of Chopin, or perhaps Debussy.[1] Even some detractors can admit that the style is melodious and intricate, though they may regard its success as merely aesthetic and hence not pertinent to philosophy. But what Cavell means by "finding his voice in philosophy" cannot comprehensibly be seen to lie in the direction that such impressions suggest.

To begin with, the sheer singularity of Cavell's authorial voice grants no clue as to how, within the impressive range of this voice, we are to recover the representativeness of the everyday voices it invokes. Short of undertaking that work of recovery, the singularity of Cavell's voice and his impressive contributions to literary and film criticism will not have a great deal to say to philosophers. If we do not seek the representativeness that Cavell's voice aspires to, then we are not hearing how that voice seeks to locate its contribution to philosophy. Failing an appreciation of that effort, Cavell's sense that his arrival at his voice was, in fact, his way of having his say in the field of philosophy would turn out to be unsecured and ungrounded.

Evidently we need to hear this singular voice of Cavell's as seeking to elicit a voice that is almost anonymous in the appeal to "what we say." The use of the word *we* does not invoke some existing group of people (e.g., "living speakers of standard English") but invites the recognition that some other speakers might recognize an aspect of themselves, of what they say and do with their words, in what I say and do with mine. In appealing to what we say, I am inviting you to recognize that you are (if you are) implicated in what I say.

We need to know more about how the impressiveness of Cavell's writing contributes to the provocation of this mutual recognition. It may not miss the entire point of his writing, if we use the impression of his words to recognize our own potential impressiveness as readers or as writers. But we are likely to have missed the chance to seek the philosophical work that Cavell's writing is engaged in. And this in turn might allow me to evade the necessity for doing the kinds of philosophical work that we are, in turn, called upon to do.

To imagine that you can take in the sound of his authorial voice as the source of his philosophical authority is exactly to suppress the aspiration to representativeness that forms itself within that voice. Furthermore, it is to suppress the practices and methods that took shape along with that voice and gave it a series of local habitations. Suppressing this dimension of the idea of a philosophical voice suppresses the need Cavell articulates to let oneself be expressed within the common conditions and confines of the most common media of our intelligibility. To take his style as the substance of his achievement of voice is to take his voice as working in isolation from the resources available to everyone—the flawed syllables and the stubborn sounds of language, along with our knowledge of what we would say in a given circumstance. It is to suppress, therefore, the slim resources of methodology that can still prompt a genuine line of philosophical questioning in those who find themselves impeded by their professional training.

It would be useful if we could learn to hear the singularity of Cavell's voice as a writer and the representativeness of the voices that he discovers for philosophy as made for each other. But this achievement would still not explain how these voices are made *by* each other or how they call for each other. A first approximation would be to say that they make each other *audible*. The singularity of Cavell's style can be used as a kind of listening post or as a medium of amplification. His voice is supposed to be precisely *not* all-encompassing. Rather, it is supposed to help us detect the voices that animate our ordinary utterances.

One way in which this works is when we can hear Cavell's prose as written, so to speak, above or below the common pitch of speech. The idea would be to make the commonness of an expression *evident*, not as a way of showing its meanness but as a way of showing its appropriateness in a given context. But this would not yet explain how it is possible for some readers to attend to Cavell's voices and his methods at a distance from one another, and as functioning independently. Or rather, since it seems relatively rare to be attuned to Cavell's claims of representativeness *apart from* his claim to singularity, what we need to explain is how someone can hear the singularity of that voice without attending to the representativeness of ordinary language that this singularity is meant to invoke.

At one extreme, the admiration of his style becomes the counterpart of its detraction. As his dectractors take his style to have become an end in itself or a means to serve the end of self-display, this particular sort of admirer takes Cavell's words as so many deeds of self-expression. The claims that Cavell is making are evidently made good merely by his success at self-expression. This can come very close to a fantasy that the mere utterance of the words intended for his self-expression can make them into successful acts of self-expression and hence successful acts of speech.[2]

Such fantasies are analogous to certain literary fantasies of "performativity" or to some Heideggerian program of preserving the authentic word, without regard to audience or to the substance of the investigation at hand. These seem to me to be perverse variations on Cavell's theme that Emerson's words don't need us, and even that they rebuke us for needing them. In these fantasies Cavell's words need us, but only as the audience for these vehicles of intimate and privileged insights. Typically, in this mode of reception, his words are quoted but not really *used*. (This is at least some improvement on the words being used but not quoted.)

I would not be preaching against these dangers had I not been exposed to them. I do not pretend to be immune to all the dark corners of these fantasies, only to have explored my share of them. I know enough about these fantasies and images of reception to know that the line of thinking they harbor is ultimately unfriendly to Cavell's ambition to stay within earshot of philosophy.

To spell it out more explicitly: Attending to the sheer singularity of Cavell's voice, and to whatever compacts you may find that voice to promise, is so far a betrayal of what that writing proposes. I do not claim that no good work can be done in the grip of such a picture of his voice. Moreover, I am aware that no one is likely to recognize his own responses to Cavell's work under these descriptions. So I will not insist that so melodramatic an irony is one of the principal fates of Cavell's reception. It would not be the first time that the uniqueness and glamour of a writer's powers of expression — or perhaps something like sheer stage presence — became the medium by which that writer's achievement is circumvented or denied.

In Cavell's case, the peculiar irony of being denied precisely by those who are devouring his words would have to be measured against two other sorts of reception: those who know, almost without reading the work, that nothing written like this *could* ever make a contribution to philosophy; and those whose own work bears the marks of an exposure to Cavell's writing and who claim to be beyond the effects of his language, even as they relentlessly paraphrase his "results." This partial immunization produces some surprising effects.

In the meantime, I want to begin the process of reversing the relative values of Cavell's voices and focus some attention on his arrival at what he calls his voice in philosophy. This will require that we look more closely at some of the philosophical methods and practices that he characterizes as eliciting the human voice restoring philosophical effectiveness. In the first place, this means the practice of Austin and Wittgenstein in asking for *what we should say when,* or for the home of a concept or assertion in our ordinary ways of talking.

THE PERVASIVENESS AND THE OBSCURITY OF THE APPEAL TO THE VOICE IN CAVELL'S EARLY WORK

It is the beginning of some kind of wisdom in reading Cavell to appreciate how pervasively he means this invocation of the voice. Once he finds it, he finds it almost everywhere: Recovering the voice becomes the primary goal of philosophy, and appealing to the voice (by appealing to what we ordinarily say) becomes the primary means by which philosophy accomplishes the goal. But it has become equally important to appreciate how *unobvious* it is to describe Cavell's early philosophical work as explicitly depending on such appeals to the voice. Or rather, we might say that in Cavell's earlier understanding of the philosophical appeal to the ordinary, the appeal to the voice is latent but obscured. To hear the voice in these appeals will require a shift of perspective or a refocusing of attention. A few general comments will help to orient the readings that follow.

The pervasiveness of voice: The voice figures both as the source and medium of our utterances and as the life of our criteria. It also figures in the expression of our interests. This means at least two things. The cost of voicing something becomes an essential measure of whether it was worth saying. But you can also—sometimes—actually *hear* how interested a person is in what he or she is saying. Excitement gets into the voice, as do curiosity, anticipation, wonder, sympathy, neediness, despair, and desire. You can sometimes also hear how *uninterested* some people are in what they are saying. And, of course, there are those who have a stake in *seeming* uninterested.

These questions of the interest and the worth of *saying* what we say point to a region of study that Cavell calls "the economics of speech" (*Claim,* 93–96). At that stage of his work, he does not explicitly draw a connection between the interest in what we are saying and our (no doubt closely related) interest in saying it. I take both these forms of interest to be part of what Cavell goes on to characterize as the aesthetics of speech. Both aspects of our interest—or lack of interest—in our words point toward a new wrinkle to an old question about how the "sense" of saying something is affected by the occasion on which you say it.

Cavell will pick up these themes in the 1980s when he returns to take a fresh look at Austin's work. One trail he explores goes like this: The wish to speak "outside of language-games" was the primary scene of the crime of philosophy against the voice. It was the first suppression of the voice to be identified and tracked down. Cavell built the indictment and the analysis of these transgressions in *The Claim of Reason*. But this monumentally detailed story about the suppression of the voice is not the only story that Cavell tells, and this suppression or repression is not the only damage that philosophy has done. We are far from finished with exploring the effects on our voices of straining to say what we really have no interest in saying. The damage is surely akin to the damage we do to our minds by pursuing intellectual problems whose connection to our real interests has been severed from the outset.

For the moment, I remark only that Cavell follows Wittgenstein in taking our concepts to be *expressions* of our interests, to shape our interests, and to guide our investigations. It would not be claiming too much to say that in Cavell's work voice and concept contest each other for the field of human expression and ultimately of human value. The voice cannot dispense with concepts, on pain of turning back into the metaphysical idea of a voice "before" language—the voice that aspires to do without the necessity of being voiced. And concepts cannot do without the life of the voice, on pain of becoming suddenly reduced to that static order of concepts which philosophical analysis has often taken as a sufficient end for philosophy.

P. F. Strawson writes of what he calls "the stage of conceptual self-consciousness" as essentially equivalent to "philosophical reflection" (*The Bounds of Sense,* 44). Investigations guided by such ideas have certainly yielded significant philosophical results, and they do indeed reflect a certain sort of human self-consciousness in which we retain just enough self-reflection to be aware that we *possess* certain concepts, but not enough to become aware that these concepts express our interest in the world and that our use of them will exhibit the nature and degree of our interest.

Such austere philosophical reflection seems to presuppose our interest in our concepts, or at least some connection that goes beyond the merely contemplative. But it is not particularly successful at explaining the interest we continue to take in our own concepts and words, and it seems powerless to sustain that interest. No doubt such philosophers do not think it is their business to explain or sustain our interest in our concepts or our words. Nor, perhaps, do they feel obliged to give an account of the interests that lie underneath our concepts, the ones that our concepts are meant to capture and to express. (To argue explicitly for the connection between these different forms of interest in our words would take us back to the argument of the *Philosophical Investigations*.)[3]

We can say at least this much: It is in our *use* of these concepts that they have their life, and the interest they express is surely one source of the interest we continue to take in them. Any philosophical reflection that tries to ascertain the logic of our concepts, as detached from the intelligibility of our interest in them, is likely to detach us even further from the conditions in which we use our words and concepts. And this is likely to contribute to the withdrawal of our interest in them, and hence in the withdrawal of these words from the life that they ordinarily possess. This loss of interest in our concepts tends to get expressed as the loss of interest in saying anything in particular. A philosopher may learn to cover this loss of interest by acquiring the conviction that he can analyze the meaningfulness of any utterance, no matter what the occasion of its being uttered, no matter who is making the utterance, and no matter what potential interest there is in making it. The image of those denatured utterances as the proper subject matter of philosophy is one of the consequences of what Austin called "the descriptive fallacy." And it is another way of characterizing the condition Cavell refers to as philosophy's suppression of the voice.

In suppressing the need for voicing our words and criteria as itself an expression of interest, philosophers have repressed not only a primary access to human value but also one of the primary *sources* of value. At any rate, we would be suppressing those capacities for evaluation which seem essential to a particular form of value. In Cavell's conception of philosophical method, the recovery of voice and the perspicuous presentation of our criteria are both to be taken as sources of representativeness. (The link between the value of saying something and the representativeness of what we say is an early expression of the ethical dimension of Cavell's investigations of language and the voice—the dimension that will blossom later into what he calls moral perfectionism.)

These activities of recovery and presentation must one day go together naturally—but they are not likely to fit together very easily, or of their own accord. And it is important to see that in Cavell's own work, the ideas of voice and of the other kinds of exemplariness do not emerge evenly or without disruption. The ideas of voice and the ideas of method emerge as if born from each other, but they do not emerge full grown.

The obscurity of the voice: This characterization of Cavell's work as teaching philosophy to recover the voice that philosophy had itself repressed, however inevitable it may now seem, is quite *unobvious* as a description of his first contributions to philosophy. From the standpoint of those first contributions—collected as *Must We Mean What We Say?*—the ideas and practices of voice remain obscured, fragmentary, inexplicit,

and out of alignment with the issues of representative expression that
they will ultimately go so far to formulate and indeed to resolve. Where
the practices (primarily but not exclusively those of Austin and Wittgenstein) are most in evidence, the word *voice* stays in the background.
Where the word comes to the fore, it is for the most part to be found
slightly askew in relation to Cavell's philosophical practices.

Here is an example of a use of voice that seems to be different from its
appearance in Cavell's later philosophical concerns. It occurs in his reading
of *King Lear,* "The Avoidance of Love," in a passage about the relation of
teaching to critical method in the New Criticism. Cavell is interested in
understanding something about the tendency of such critics to focus their
attention on longer poems and away from the lyric. He tries to characterize a certain difficulty in the teaching of lyric poetry:

> . . . [I]t is not clear what would count as training someone to read a lyric.
> You will have to demonstrate how it rests in the voice, or hauls at it, and
> you will perhaps not be able to do that without undergoing the spiritual
> instant or passage for which it discovers release (that is, unable to say
> what it means without meaning it then and there); and you may or may
> not be able to do that during a given morning's class, and either eventu-
> ality is likely to be inopportune in that place. [*Must We Mean What We
> Say?* 269.]

What seems striking here is Cavell's emphasis on the nearly physical relation between the words of the poem and the voice that is enacted in
those words. Cavell describes a kind of uneasy struggle between the lyric
("it") and the way it "rests in the voice, or hauls at it." The slight per-
sonification in the tension between the poem and the voice suggests the
existence of a more mundane struggle between the voice and the words
in which the voice resides.

This is not a matter of two different struggles but of different ways of
trying to get out the movement of the words and the voice. It is as if
Cavell saw the most immediate point of the words of the poem not as a
medium for the expression of the voice but as a medium for resisting it.
Naturally, without such resistance the lyric voice would have no place to
live—and hence no way of "expressing" its moment of feeling or being.
To adopt a figure from Wittgenstein, the words must create the rough
ground on which the voice can begin to move.

The passage is also among the first occurrences of Cavell's lifelong ob-
session with what is and is not teachable in a given enterprise. The ability
to give voice to something might turn out to be exactly the element that

isn't teachable. We might even use the achievement or the release of the voice as a way of characterizing the unteachable moment within the otherwise teachable steps. This is the point at which the teacher must call on powers of exemplification that may not be available on a given day, and may not ever be appropriate in a classroom.

The question about the academic success of the New Criticism, like Cavell's later analogous questions about deconstruction in American universities, has everything to do with Cavell's more general concern about the appropriateness of philosophy as a discipline within the university. And these concerns about the possibility of teaching philosophy have almost everything to do with the tensions between method and voice, or more generally, between the steps that you can tell someone how to take and the steps that you must show yourself as taking.

The other quite radical suggestion in this passage is located within the parentheses: The idea is that you cannot mean certain things, certain forms of words, without meaning them then and there, at a quite particular moment in a quite particular setting. Cavell suggests that this sort of meaningfulness will exist only when the speaker of the poem undergoes a certain spiritual passage or movement from one "state" of mind to another. Such a movement cannot be reduced to a single expression of "emotion." The passage is already a kind of movement or transition, and we do not yet know how to calculate the relation between this inward movement of "passage" and the presumably outward movement of expression. Moreover, since we have just been told that the lyric resides in some engagement or struggle between word and voice, there is more than a slight suggestion that there is, at certain moments of using words, an irreducible connection between meaning something and voicing it.

If I am right about these signs of impending developments, then there are some good reasons for Cavell to have quarantined or even repressed certain connections of voice to questions of meaning. For the view that meaning a stretch of words depends on an achievement that is, in a certain sense, private—along with, no doubt, a certain willingness to let go of privacy—is not exactly Wittgensteinian. Or if it is not quite antithetical to the lessons of the *Philosophical Investigations*, it is still difficult territory for a serious reader of Wittgenstein to enter happily. Such an emphasis could, for instance, have swamped the necessarily delicate emphasis on criteria and a shared capacity for meaning things. By the time he completed *The Claim of Reason*, Cavell was prepared to claim that Wittgenstein was emphasizing the individual's responsibility in the "shared edifice" of language. He even speaks of the fragility and privacy of the moments in which we take on that responsibility (*Claim*, 36). But that was later. Sometimes an initial piece of philosophical self-repression is necessary to get a line of thought going.

Some readers will find the idea of repression to be unnecessary at this stage. It is not implausible to imagine that a concept such as "self-restraint" might be adequate to cover the features of Cavell's development that I have been pointing to. We might use the idea to cover both the uneven emergence of the voice and the relative slowness with which Cavell drew connections between the different regions of his thought. Even those who grant the relevance of concepts like repression and resistance to philosophy in general may balk at the idea of applying the notions to a description of a primarily positive development. Nevertheless, it seems to me that we can study this gradual emergence of the idea of voice in Cavell's writing as an image or enactment of the lifting of at one least one sort of repression. I have in mind the type of repression that Freud characterizes as separating the "idea" or representation from the "associated" feeling or affect. More generally, we might speak of a repression that separates and quarantines our interest in a word or other means of expression from the sense of our need for (further) expression.

I am taking the lifting of such a repression as at least analogized in Cavell's alignment and synchronization of the various aspects and ideas of voice with the various methods of his philosophizing. Even if this idea of the lifting of a repression seems too extreme, it suggests the independent possibility of tracing out the various sources of the idea of voice in those early essays, and, moreover, it suggests that this tracing will have something to teach us about the present status of the concept of voice. The idea of voice as a description of the earlier work can be taken as the emergence from obscurity of a new perspective on that work (hence on Austin, and Wittgenstein; hence on the contemporaneous state of philosophy) from within the later periods of Cavell's work.

This understanding of Cavell insists on the fact that a new perspective on the past is itself some kind of new step—an arrival at a particular ledge—within the progress of that later work. This is perhaps a way of saying that even inside the career of a single writer, there is no such thing as metaphilosophy, as Cavell used to put it. There is no place from which to get outside your work and assess its progress and its obstacles—no place, that is to say, that is not already implicated in philosophical entanglements and methods. To put it in terms that relate these thoughts to the concept of therapy, every interesting philosophical obscurity will turn out to have been in some fashion self-imposed. The only aspects that can dawn on me are the ones to which I have been blind.

One might very well credit this inseparability of methodical progress from the process of self-illumination (conceived here in the form of self-revision) without resorting to the idea of the lifting of a past philosophical repression. What has to be made out here is the way in which the ideas of repression and resistance help to make clear the *kind* of illumination that philosophy produces, the kind of work that philosophy does. I take it as a sort of practical definition of the subject that there are specific types of obscurity that philosophy is meant to dispel, obscurities that in turn specifically resist the work of philosophy. Apart from such a sense of philosophical work, which is certainly connected to what I am calling philosophical method, the idea of therapy in philosophy is little more than an empty reassurance that somewhere and somehow the possibility of philosophical health still exists.

WITTGENSTEIN'S VOICES OF CONFESSION AND THE WORDS OF PHILOSOPHY

I am claiming that either the first appearances of the idea of voice in Cavell's work remain inexplicit and unthematized, or else they are not clearly synchronized with the philosophical practices that the idea of voice will later be meant to capture. I am at the same time claiming that these unthematized appearances are of fundamental significance to the issues of *Must We Mean What We Say?* and hence to Cavell's origins as a philosopher.

Here is the first emergence of this aspect of the voice at a site that Cavell has already singled out for attention. In that late passage quoted above from *A Pitch of Philosophy*, Cavell recalls his early identification of both the form and the work of Wittgenstein's *Investigations* as *confessional*. This remains a valuable insight into one of the principal modes of composition of the *Investigations*. But Cavell then goes on to *interpret* his own discovery of the forms and tasks of confession in Wittgenstein's philosophizing as releasing the further task of returning the voice to philosophy (*Pitch*, 69).

Let us look more closely at this passage, which is drawn from "The Availability of the Later Wittgenstein" (*Must We Mean What We Say?* 44–72). Cavell there characterizes Wittgenstein's writing as "choosing" the mode of confession and "recasting" the form of the dialogue.

> It contains what serious confessions must: the full acknowledgement of temptation ("I want to say . . ."; "I feel like saying . . ."; "Here the urge is strong . . .") and a willingness to correct them and give them up ("In the everyday use . . ."; "I impose a requirement which does not meet my real

need"). (The voice of temptation and the voice of correctness are the antagonists in Wittgenstein's dialogues.) In confessing you do not explain or justify [or theorize], but describe how it is with you. And confession, unlike dogma, is not to be believed but tested, and accepted or rejected. Nor is it the occasion for accusation, except of yourself, and by implication those who find themselves in you. [*Must We Mean What We Say?* 71.]

What seems to me worth dwelling on in this passage is, first of all, this slight lack of alignment between the explicit use of the word *voice* and the philosophical claim that carries the primary burden of the idea of the voice. Twenty-five years later Cavell points to the discovery of Wittgenstein's mode of confession as the moment that releases the idea of the returning of the voice to philosophy. But the explicit—and, as it happens, parenthetical—mention of voice introduces the contrast between what Cavell calls the voices of temptation and the voices of correctness.

The emphasis falls not exactly on the sheer fact of their existence as voices (e.g., on their capacity to express or indicate a human presence) or on their condition as a mode of saying something (e.g., as giving voice to it). Rather, it seems to fall on the fact of their being *different* voices, hence serving different needs and emanating from different regions of the mind. Cavell has in view not primarily the voice as, so to speak, the second-best picture of the human soul, nor as a token of a human presence or of the self's integrity. The voice is here the sign of the division in a particular self: a very particular self, though not one that can be reduced to being the possession of a particular empirical person. The distinctness of these voices in Wittgenstein is a function of the claims they make, claims on us and claims on each other as well as claims about the problem at hand. From this distinctness derives the capacity of Wittgenstein's voices to enact the intimate antagonism—in part, the sound of a family quarrel—that goes a long way toward constituting the sound of a Wittgensteinian dialogue.

Obviously, the voices of this dialogue have everything to do with the voicing of the confession that Cavell is discerning in Wittgenstein's words. It is not just that Cavell is entitled to his retroactive emphasis on the voice disclosed in the act of confession. Beyond this, my point is rather that his later interpretation is making explicit something that was originally left inexplicit. (Making something explicit in such a fashion is, of course, a function that interpretations often serve.) Moreover, the later interpretation contains an insight that is sufficiently powerful to make us underestimate the complexity of the very texts that Cavell means to be interpreting.

It should not be surprising that the emergence of the idea of the voice in philosophy is not always explicitly tied to words like *voice* and *voicing*. There is no wide range of canonical treatments of voice and language for us to choose from. Without a sense of the alternatives, it is difficult to know much about how such ideas of voice take shape, either in relation to Wittgenstein's practices or in relation to the Western philosophical tradition. Of course, with the assistance of Cavell's later interpretation we can see that the reinsertion of a mode of confession into philosophy is a good vehicle for the discovery of the voice: A confession must after all (grammatically? logically? theologically?) be *voiced*—that is, somehow expressed or uttered. An unexpressed confession (which is not the same as a tacit, or unspoken, confession) is not a confession. The act of *making* a confession is indispensable to the existence of the confession. (This is, naturally, not meant to deny that you can inadvertently confess something, or at any rate inadvertently *admit* to something, e.g., to knowing someone's secret. But this possibility should serve to remind us how special such circumstances are.)

This aspect of confession—that it must be *performed* in order to exist—is surely part of what was drawing Cavell to this characterization of Wittgenstein. So is the fact that a confession is something that you must do for yourself, though as Cavell points out, it is a crucial feature of Wittgensteinian confessions that they may implicate others. We can see the movement toward this idea of confession if we look back a paragraph at Cavell's efforts to connect the difficulties of Wittgenstein's writing and the difficulties of philosophizing. Cavell is suggesting that Wittgenstein's difficulty is related not only to the difficulty of his own thought, but to a new sense of the difficulty of philosophizing altogether. Wittgenstein discerned new difficulties—along with new possibilities—in philosophy conceived of as a medium of human reflection.

It is worth reminding ourselves of some of the texture of this passage.

> His literary style has achieved both high praise and widespread alarm. Why does he write that way? Why doesn't he just say what he means, and draw instead of insinuate conclusions? . . .
>
> The first thing to be said in accounting for his style is that he *writes:* he does not report, he does not write up results. Nobody would forge a style so personal who had not wanted and needed to find the right expression for his thought. The German dissertation and the British essay—our most common modern options for writing philosophy—would not work; his is not a system and he is not a spectator. My suggestion is that the problem of style is set for him by the two aspects of his work which I have primarily emphasized: the lack of existing terms of criticism, and the method of self-knowledge. [Ibid., 70.]

This last sentence refers to Cavell's practice of isolating the "terms of criticism" in a philosopher's work. The effort to exhibit such terms is one of the earliest explicit pieces of method in Cavell's own practice as a philosophical reader. By this practice, he intends to focus attention on the means by which a philosophical text will characteristically locate itself in relation to other texts, whose work it hopes to criticize or to reject. In the next chapter, I will say something about the connection of this search for the terms of criticism to the idea of "self-knowledge" as a goal of the Wittgensteinian philosopher. Already in this early passage, both ideas are functioning as counterweights to the ideas of voice and confession.

What Cavell calls the "problem of style" in Wittgenstein is not here—and not, I think, ever—essentially a question of self-expression. The issue is not one of expressing the *self* of Wittgenstein—if that means expressing something "inward" such as his immediate pains or desires or the things he is ashamed of. Cavell characterizes the problem as one of finding an adequate expression for Wittgenstein's "thought." And this problem is not dictated by a need for the "personal" element in his style. The element of the personal must serve to advance the forms of thinking and to discover new materials for thought. Cavell is quite explicit that the problem of style—hence the problem of its element of personality—is set by the need to supply a lack in our capacity for philosophical criticism and the need to arrive at and to enact a new regime of philosophical method.

Furthermore, it is quite clear that "method" is here construed as something "impersonal" in its outcome. That is, a method is something essentially independent of the individual psychologies of those who practice it, something that can be followed by someone other than its inventor. Provisionally, we might say this: If no one else could follow the steps that you have laid down (laid down, it may be, in taking the steps), then whatever else you have done, you have not constructed a method. In practice, this requirement perhaps amounts to the effort to imagine what keeps another from taking the steps that you take. Not everything is permitted to count as such an explanation. One way to allow for such an explanation is to discover connections between what kept the insight obscure to you and what might be keeping the insight obscure to your reader.

At the same time, for Wittgenstein and for Cavell, the possibility of method insists that you must take the step, do the thing required, for yourself. Methods in philosophy must be undertaken individually, one by one: It is you who must acknowledge that you are the one at this juncture of the exposition who craves generality or who requires the subliming of logic or who insists on a picture of understanding as a kind of inner mechanism. In this mode of philosophizing (and surely not in this one alone), you cannot sit back and watch the argument unfold, waiting to see if all the steps are valid. Unless you respond to the voices by which the position is being unfolded and exhibited, there will be no position worth criticizing. This is a good reason why so many philosophers writing about Wittgenstein have gone astray: they have tried to reconstruct his argument without first going through the necessity of responding to the voices within the various phases of his exposition. In this quite particular sense, there is after all a personal element in Wittgenstein's methods of presenting his thought, and also in our ability to understand and follow those methods.

Voicing the Experience of Film and Speaking in a Philosophical Voice

The issue of method is always also an issue of the representativeness of a thought or of a line of thinking. I want to say a little more about the relation of methodology and representativeness, and I will use some of William Rothman's work to articulate my point. My sense of the depth of my disagreement with some aspects of Rothman's account of Cavell's philosophizing is matched by my sense of the success of Rothman's own methods as a philosophical critic of film. His work strikes me as that of a powerful critic, making good use of a powerful philosophical sensibility and converting insights gained from Cavell's work into insights of his own. But if Rothman's momentum as a writer is impressive, it sometimes takes him into troubled waters.

In his books and articles, Rothman articulates his own way of reading a Hitchcock film by articulating his sense of its intimate differences from Cavell's way of proceeding:

> Cavell . . . aspires to put into his own words what these [melodramas and remarriage comedies] say to their audiences. Speaking in his own philosophical voice and out of his own experience of these films, he declares himself to be, despite everything, a representative member of that audience. The films' Emersonian aspiration of creating a more perfect human community, shared by their audience, is his as well. I find myself continually called on to make discoveries, to see things that viewers don't ordinarily see, or to see familiar things in an unfamiliar light, discovering unsuspected connections. The *Vertigo* that emerges, at least in fragments, in this essay is not the film as viewers ordinarily view it (although my reading is meant to account for the ordinary experience, which it interprets as

the experience that fails to acknowledge Hitchcock and hence misses his meaning).[4]

Rothman evidently takes Cavell's method to be one of putting common experiences—experiences that Cavell shares with an ordinary audience—into Cavell's own words. He then takes this "putting into his own words" to be equivalent to speaking in his "own philosophical voice," which is evidently taken to be the method by which Cavell manages to evince his own uniqueness and to declare his "representative" membership in a film's audience.

In another essay, Rothman consolidates his sense of Cavell's voice as creating itself by expressing Cavell's unique existence.

> This is what it means for a philosopher like Stanley Cavell to perform his own *cogito ergo sum*. To claim his birthright, all he has to do is give voice to his experience, and claim this voice as his own. To play the role his philosophical fathers created before him, the role his mother gave birth for him to play, all he has to do is create himself.[5]

This uniqueness of the individual voice is taken to constitute the uniqueness of Cavell's contribution to philosophy. It seems at best an accident that Cavell—or Cavell's philosophizing—could ever speak for anyone else.

Given that Rothman takes Cavell to declare the "representativeness" of his experience *in spite of* the uniqueness of his voice, it is clear that Rothman takes the representative to be something like the average, the typical, or the commonplace. The averageness of a typical member of Hitchcock's audience implies that he or she is for the most part missing its "meaning." What is representative in our experience of *Vertigo* is not what we see but what we fail to see. Generally speaking, Rothman understands us as failing to see any connection that wasn't previously suspected: We do not appreciate the unsuspected connections, and we see the familiar things only in the light of their familiarity.

What is most disturbing here is Rothman's implicit suggestion that a critic's ability to see things in new ways tends to render that critic "unrepresentative" of the audience. If a critic claims to see what others have not seen, or manages to say what others have not been able to say, he forfeits his claim to representativeness. Indeed, Rothman's account contains the strong implication that we can be representative of one another only if we have the same experiences of a work of art, or if the work "says" the same thing to us.

When Rothman accounts for the experience of the audience of a Hitchcock film, he is not accounting for an error or an obscurity that he might himself have shared. He is accounting for a state of blindness toward Hitchcock's worth that he himself has been delivered from. It is a state of sight and mind that cannot be alleviated by any ordinary act of viewing, nor by anything that Rothman would be willing to call "representative." The viewing of the ordinary American moviegoer is blinded by the most intimate workings of American culture. It is blind from birth—doomed in advance, like one of Hitchcock's "wrong men." In Rothman's critical vision, we either give in to the commonplace viewing of a film, or we rise above what is (merely) representative in our viewing and achieve a state in which we are capable of acknowledging Hitchcock's authorship.

This view of representativeness is far from impossible to maintain. Although Rothman intends to be leaving plenty of room for Cavell's philosophical voice, his views make it difficult to see what room he is leaving for Cavell as a critic. Moreover, what is left of philosophy, in Rothman's account, is only the voice and the vision of the philosopher, not the steps by which we are to acquire the vision and respond to the voice. It is not nothing to recommend the courage it takes to live in a world without transcendence or actual community. But it is hard to see in Rothman's account of Cavell that there is anything left of the quest for method. And it is still harder to see why Cavell would spend so much methodological energy on precisely the search for representativeness.

What is left of the voice for Rothman is the sense of Cavell's individual expressiveness. It is Cavell's ability to locate what Rothman calls "his own words" that infuses even the commonest of Cavell's experiences with the stamp of his uniqueness. Given such a view, it is difficult to see Rothman as searching for obscurities in himself that are representative of obscurities that anyone might come to have. Nor is he likely to search for methods by which our shared obscurities are to be overcome.

Rothman's theorizing of the practice of criticism—if not his critical practice—drives a wedge between the existence of the philosophical voice and the methods by which we might respond to that voice. Conversely, his acknowledgments of Hitchcock's meaningfulness and unknownness are presented as exclusively the effects of Rothman's critical insight and, indeed, as exclusively Rothman's. They are not acknowledgments that might allow others to hearken to the same voice, or follow the same path of self-illumination, but are acts of private devotion to a greatness that is at once public and hidden. Rothman takes himself, perhaps rightly, to be going public with such acknowledgments at the risk of sharing Hitchcock's destiny of unknownness.

Rothman has produced critical work on Hitchcock of unparalleled skill and detail. Perhaps the frame of mind that I have been sketching was indispensable to the production of this body of work, which strives to remain in touch with certain underlying insights in Cavell (and in Emerson and Wittgenstein). What remains unclear is the relation of such criticism to philosophical method, and to the very idea of voice, conceived of as part of the method and part of the goal of philosophy.

The Personality and Impersonality of the Self

If it is not for the sake of some sort of self-expression, what then is the point, within the field of philosophy, of "forging an intensely personal style"? It should be clear enough that the point is not merely to put a kind of personal stamp on one's voicing of the most common experience. The point is not, for instance, to ensure that one's authorship or ownership of the words will prove to be unmistakable, despite the commonness, or the widespread nature, of the experiences. That is no doubt a goal of certain writers. Perhaps it is not entirely alien to Cavell's way of doing things. But it is alien to the spirit of philosophy. Consequently, whatever other ambitions Cavell's writing exhibits, his enactments of style and voice must also exhibit a kind of *struggle* against a certain image of self-expression.

Hence, if the struggle against false ideas of self-expression is to be made visible, Cavell must also make visible the possibility of various outcomes to that struggle—including the possibility of failure. This is not just a matter of the author's providing a sense of his own humility in the face of his task. It is rather that a revised sense of what philosophical writing might achieve must also offer a revised sense of how to criticize this achievement. We learn to see what philosophical progress consists in by learning to see how the writer goes astray or bogs down. (In chapter 4, I pursue the more detailed interpretive work necessary to fill in the significance of new forms of philosophical failure for Cavell's inheritance of Wittgenstein.) It is difficult to connect the specific power of Wittgenstein's expressiveness with the specific genres of writing—in particular, his invention of a kind of *fragment*. In later work, Cavell has a lot more to say about Wittgenstein's construction of fragments and his less noticed power to make paragraphs succeed one another. Already in this early essay, Cavell is reading Wittgenstein as finding ways to voice the circumstances in which a philosophical problem emerges. Wittgenstein does not deliberately propound the need for fragmentariness. He is looking to characterize not only the problem but the form of a philosophical problem as such. It is the form that reaches words, for instance, in the sentence "I don't know my way about" (*Philosophical Investigations*, #123).

Wittgenstein's fragments and dialogues result, at least in part, from the wish to give voice to the circumstances of the origin of the problem, along with the particular sense of lostness and obscurity that gives a kind of form to the problem. Even without the lengthier consideration that this issue deserves, we can see that Wittgenstein's sense of the fragmentary is not to be conflated with Schlegel's or with that of certain other Romantic writers. In the Romantics, the fragment can be regarded as a way of improvising and dramatizing a responsiveness to the contingency of the human condition. Sometimes the fragment tracks the rise and fall of inspiration or vision. In Wittgenstein, what the form of the fragment responds to is almost invariably some particular irruption of the temptation to philosophy or "metaphysics."

Neither Wittgenstein's breaking up the flow of the writing into strings of remarks nor the fervor of certain passages within those remarks is best understood as the spontaneous outbursts of a Romantic genius, unwilling to systematize his thoughts. This is a theme and even an organizing principle of Ray Monk's biography of Wittgenstein. (I have been arguing that similar perceptions have affected the reception of Cavell's work.) Wittgenstein's forms of writing embody, among other things, the fact that the impulse to philosophy is neither predictable nor manageable. Philosophizing has its outbreaks and irruptions, and the only thing we can be fairly sure of is that it will keep starting over again. Indeed, Wittgenstein's willingness to pursue the form of the fragment and the dialogue suggests that philosophy *must* always begin over again. Our responses to situations that call for philosophy are unpredictable. We do not know when philosophy will start to happen, or how long it will last, or to what degree of complexity we will become entangled in our words, our concepts, and our criteria.

What we do know—or what Wittgenstein's way of writing keeps attempting to teach us—is that without the entanglement there is no philosophy. In opposition to the English essay, Wittgenstein's writing proposes not the "personal" element of a particular personality but the intimacy of a human desire for speech. It is a desire that might have remained unspoken and does in fact remain to some extent anonymous. Wittgenstein must somehow motivate the voices of his writing in ways that not only demonstrate their intimate struggle with each other and with the question at hand but at the same time invite the reader to a corresponding intimacy.

In claiming that the point of the personal element in the writing of Wittgenstein and Cavell is not primarily self-expression, I do not need to deny that there is *some* kind of self-expression going on. In both writers, the work bears the stamp of individuality. You could also say that such writings created their authors, created the *persona* that the writing gives voice to. Or you could say that the writing created the very individualities that those authors were learning how to become—in part by learning how to write like that. So you could, I suppose, go on to say that writing such as Wittgenstein's and Cavell's expresses some kind of selfhood.

Saying such things would do no harm, if we could figure out a way to remind ourselves that there is a region of the self that is impersonal. The trouble is that this is hard to remember—or hard to let yourself remember. Remembering the impersonality of the self is remembering a region in which we have to forget, at least temporarily, what we know of particular persons and what we incline toward in the personality of persons. One important aspect of Cavell's fate as a philosopher is to be taken as at his most personal when he is most at pains to remind us of the impersonality of the self. His audience is inclined to interpret his fervor as the fervor of self-expression, which is also how they are inclined to interpret Wittgenstein. Like most audiences caught up in the aftermath of Romanticism, they know little of the fervor of method, of the struggle to take things intimately without taking them personally. But that is exactly how Cavell defines the seduction of philosophy. (Cf. *The World Viewed*, 100–101.)

Cavell insisted on the importance of the confessional mode in Wittgenstein in order to capture Wittgenstein's personal address to the impersonal. This is a mode of address that I have elsewhere characterized as a public offer of philosophical intimacy.[6] It is common but not inevitable to respond to writers such as Wittgenstein and Cavell with a kind of private wish for intimacy, expressed as a form of discipleship. Intimacy often seems to be construed in such discipleship as a wish to perpetuate the moment where the singular voice was first heard. The voices of such teachers are heard as breaking down barriers and breaking through to a region of thought that the student had taken to be private and perhaps inexpressible. But it would be a poor expression of gratitude for such moments where the writer's voice breaks through, if the reader's reception remained on the level of a need for some further expression of intimacies. The real acknowledgment of such moments of reading and discipleship requires the achievement of utterance, some new version of public response that breaches the circle of private exchanges, however gratifying. Only the renewed commitment to a philosophical practice, the willingness to take a step in public, can enable our response to the method of such writing.

These reflections on the personal element in such philosophizing give us the chance to take a closer look at Wittgenstein's voices of temptation and the voices of correctness. Cavell's depiction of these voices can help rectify a misapprehension about the kinds of expression that Wittgenstein's style is giving to his thought. For these voices in his dialogues are not exactly personal voices of Wittgenstein's. That is to say, first of all, they are not his property and do not, sentence by individual sentence, express his individual thoughts. This is part of what it means to have created, or re-created—Cavell says "recast"—a dialogue form: The sound of a passage of Wittgenstein is often the sound of an exchange that typifies its participants. Sometimes it is the sound of someone recoiling from an exchange or a series of exchanges, a voice of one who is trying to step back from a struggle that is going nowhere. These voices accomplish their philosophical work to the extent that they capture agreement among various voices and attunements in judgment. Or else they work to the extent that they evoke precisely the terms of our disagreement, encouraging a reexamination of our lack of attunement in a given case.

The voices in question are accordingly not, on the whole, imitations of previously known or previously existing voices.[7] And they are not obviously the same as the voice that Cavell will later suggest has been repressed by philosophy. What Cavell describes is an exchange between voices, or an *interplay* of voices. And the voices help to bring each other into existence by defining each other's tone and subject matter.

These voices cannot be characterized as dictated by personal need in any normal sense of the word. Here again, it is a certain pull or drive to philosophy that is in question, a drive that is accessible only to those who submit themselves to the problem at hand. These written voices are discoveries or enactments of human voices, but they are elicited precisely by a situation *within* philosophy, or by a situation in which philosophy is getting under way. They are voices elicited at moments of lostness or self-entanglement; by philosophical perplexity, or bewilderment that is self-induced, but not obviously self-imposed. Such a state is not obviously curable by an act of will or resolution. Hence the philosophical relevance of the wish to bring philosophy to an end and to give it peace. (Achieving the condition Wittgenstein calls "peace" will not seem like much of an accomplishment if philosophy is the sort of thing that you are able to put aside at will.)

It can seem that it is, after all, the voice of temptation which carries the largest freight in this idea of confession. For without the temptation to speak in certain ways, the corresponding pull to "correctness," to what Cavell will later call a return to the ordinary, either would not exist or would turn out to be merely the assertion of the right and proper way to speak. Claiming to be able to speak with this voice of correctness is one of the more common ways of proceeding among students of Wittgenstein and also, it seems to me, among certain readers of Cavell.

This emergence of the idea of voice from the interplay of confession and dialogue is itself food for thought. It suggests that the voice is never discovered in something like a pure state of expression. The voice is discovered, or recovered, in the *act* of confession, or in the passivity of being repressed. In this passage of Cavell's from *Must We Mean What We Say?* (70), the idea of these voices forms part of an account of how Wittgenstein's practices are comprehensible as forms of confession. Just as significantly, the passage gives some clue as to how we can take such forms of confession to be part of the work of philosophy.

At this moment, Cavell begins his persistent interrogation of our impoverished understanding of what a confession is.[8] He takes implicit aim at the idea that a confession is some sort of elaborate apology or excuse. Such an idea of confession often goes with an idea of autobiography as giving vent to your formerly unexpressed feelings, perhaps by narrating a satisfying version out of the many possible versions of your life. On the other hand, some sympathetic readers of Cavell have perhaps paid insufficient attention to the differences between the functions of confession and the functions of autobiography.

Give or take an Augustine or a Rousseau, the function of a confession is not to tell the story of your life but to reveal something quite specific to someone quite specific. Autobiographies are sometimes said to create the lives that they are supposed to be narrating, and hence, perhaps, to create the audience capable of appreciating that story. If it were, in general, true of confessions that they create the piece of oneself that one is struggling to reveal and also the audience for that revelation, the practice of confession would be a lot easier than it is. Or perhaps there would be no such thing as a confession. Only in quite special cases, as perhaps with Rousseau or in certain forms of philosophical writing, can one think of a confession as creating the audience that is capable of appreciating it. Only in special cases can we think of confession and autobiography as coinciding. Cavell's characterization of Wittgenstein's writing as a mode of confession ought, therefore, to raise as many questions as it answers.

What is it about the world or about human thinking that elicits this voice of temptation—or, as Cavell will later put it, this temptation to voice a kind of emptiness, a modern version of madness? These questions will become increasingly thematic in Cavell's work. But initially what seems to elicit this voice is a situation that calls for, in terms drawn from Wittgenstein, completeness or generality (of a certain kind) or explanation (of a certain kind) or a certain sublime order "behind" or "within" our language or our bodies. The voices that philosophy banishes from our use of language (for instance, from our expressions of pain) keep turning up as efforts to make words as regular as the order of things is supposed to be.

Long before Cavell depicted us as haunting our own lives, he had noticed that Wittgenstein portrayed us as haunted by voices containing our wishes for knowledge. As philosophers we make ourselves into the spokesmen of our project to know the world. We become the ventriloquists of a knowledge that we have yet to achieve. The philosophical project can accordingly be characterized like this: first you suppress the ordinary connections of mind to things, and of the voice to things and to other voices. Then you try to recapture them in an ideal structure, with an ideal ordering of precise expressions.

This remains a pretty good picture of what many moments of philosophy are like. But these descriptions of Wittgenstein's writing and of his characterization of philosophy tend to raise the issue of philosophy's claims on its audience. More particularly, they point to questions about the claims of Cavell's writing to intervene in the formation of its own audience. Wittgenstein's writing "confesses" to temptations, and it acknowledges pieces of grammar that are, apparently, there for all to see. Is the implication that he is confessing for all of us? If so, on what occasion and to what end would such an implication be appropriate? Does the acknowledgment of grammar and the "acceptance" of our forms of life as "given" make sense to those who have not yet acknowledged their flight from their ordinary? Must the knowledge of that flight be inflicted on a reader before the return flight can find its point of departure? How does one inflict such knowledge, and who authorized Wittgenstein or Cavell to inflict it on us?

Kant's "Universal Voice" and the Partiality of What We Say

In the next essay of *Must We Mean What We Say?*, written a year after "The Availability of the Later Wittgenstein," Cavell makes explicit a crucial aspect of the philosophical voice. This moment is, I think, unique in the early work, and in retrospect it is not surprising that Cavell should have been borrowing a term from Kant. This appearance of the voice is potentially so surprising in Kant that it can seem to authorize Cavell's appropriation of this difficult thought: "Kant's 'universal voice' is, with a slight shift of accent, what we hear recorded in the philosopher's claims about 'what we say': such claims are at least as close to what Kant calls aesthetical judgments as they are to ordinary empirical hypothesis . . . " (94). The "voice" is something we hear recorded in writing, and it requires a certain attentiveness to hear it. It requires a further attentiveness to hear it in relation to the aesthetic claim.

Examples are not hard to come by but are difficult to attend to. Where do we end up if we number the likenesses and differences between claiming that "the *Hammerklavier* sonata is a perverse work" and claiming that "When we ask 'Do you dress like that voluntarily?' we must be implying that there is something odd or untoward about the way you are dressed"? Cavell notes that no one would even be tempted to collect *data* as to whether the *Hammerklavier* was indeed perverse, whereas, at least in the 1950s and 1960s, there were voices raised in favor of taking a poll or a survey to determine what "we" would in fact be meaning or implying in asking whether you dress like that voluntarily.

A difference that Cavell does not dwell on is this: It is fairly easy to imagine the circumstances in which someone might be claiming something about the musical perversity of a Beethoven piano sonata. You might imagine an audience that is in agreement with the speaker, or uncomprehending, or respectfully astonished, or struck by disbelief, or perhaps vehemently scornful. It is harder to imagine the circumstances in which someone has to remind us of the implication of oddness in asking whether you dress like that voluntarily. There might be circumstances of inadvertent rudeness: for instance, I am trying to confirm my hunch that you have taken religious vows, or that you are pledging a fraternity. The circumstances are more likely to be those in which we have been drawn into philosophizing. But what circumstances are those? Even if one accepts the Wittgensteinian characterization of philosophy as getting away from the ordinary and, moreover, accepts the usefulness of Austin's procedures, it remains difficult to see how these insights are supposed to work together. We need to ask whether Cavell takes it that Austin's procedures can help respond to, for instance, a Wittgensteinian confession of a temptation. Or else we need to know more about the posture of mind that we respond to by reminding ourselves of what we imply when we ask whether you dress like that *voluntarily*. (Or for that matter, what we imply when we ask this of someone who walks on a treadmill three hours a day for a year, or drinks cod-liver oil, or invests in the mayor's nephew's new business.)

While no one would be likely to characterize J. L. Austin as proceeding in a confessional mode—at least not on a regular basis—it is characteristic of Cavell's own procedures to press the issue of the "spirit" in which the appeal to ordinary language is made. Of oneself—of one's representative self as a speaker—Cavell wrote this:

> I am not saying that evidence about how (other) people speak can never make an ordinary language philosopher withdraw his typical claims, but I find it important that the most characteristic pressure against him is applied by producing or deepening an example which shows him that *he* would not say what he says "we" say. [95.]

Such words, uttered in the teeth of an ascendant Chomskian linguistics, were more liable to inflame disdain or anger than to provoke methodological reflection.

> The philosopher appealing to ordinary language turns to the reader not to convince him without proof but to get him to prove something, test something, against himself. He is saying: Look and find out whether you can see what I see, wish to say what I wish to say. [95–96.]

The activation of the etymology of the word *proof* as a kind of test is somewhat more typical of a later strand of Cavell's writing. This "turning" to the reader imports something of a modification, even a little moderation, of Wittgenstein's implied assault—or assault by implication—on his reader.

Even short of Wittgenstein's writing, the stakes and the risks in the appeal to "what we say when" remain, for Cavell, quite high—higher, I continue to imagine, than Austin would have been willing to play for—at least explicitly. Playing for these stakes will lead us back to the fact that what we say in a given case is something we have to learn how to voice in a given set of circumstances.

From the side more specifically of Wittgenstein's writing, the appeal to what we say is mounted in such a way as to invite the reader to undergo a sense of assault, a demand not only for self-examination but for "inner change." It is this oscillating sense of invitation and assault—of a certain kind of seduction or of a certain parody of seduction—that is one of the features of reading Wittgenstein and, to some extent, of reading Cavell's version of ordinary language philosophy. The reader is invited to find herself implicated in what is said—and then hauled up short by the sense that someone else has had to remind her of it.

It seems to me, furthermore, that this feature of such writing is something that Cavell comes to bank on. For the fact that this sort of philosophizing can be thought of as assembling a series of reminders does not get us around the fact that someone had to step in and perform this act of remembering on my behalf. It is, after all, something I could have done, and said, for myself. If what is remembered is not thus held in common, the remembering of it will not be a *philosophical* reminder. And if the remembrance is not only of something held in common but of something commonly *available* to both of us, there will be no point to the act of remembering—much less in recording this act in writing.

I explore these issues further in chapter 3. For now, I will say this: I think Cavell surmised that the kind of writing that breaks in and voices an act of recollection that we could have performed for ourselves is exactly suited to be the kind of writing that it takes to break the control of the past. In part for this reason, it is in terms of this specific effect of their writing that Cavell first links the names of Wittgenstein and Freud. Or perhaps it would be better to say that this connection between the aims of their writing is the first one that Cavell goes public with:

> Because the breaking of such control is a constant purpose of the later Wittgenstein, his writing is deeply practical and negative, the way Freud's is. And like Freud's therapy, it wishes to prevent understanding which is unaccompanied by inner change. Both of them are intent upon unmasking the defeat of our real need in the face of self-impositions which we have not assessed (#108), or fantasies ("pictures") which we cannot escape (#115). In both, such misfortune is betrayed in the incongruence between what is said and what is meant or expressed; for both, the self is concealed in assertion and action and revealed in temptation and wish. ["Availability," 72.]

By now, we should be ready for the idea that the realm of "incongruence" between what is expressly said and what is implied in the saying of it is the realm of the voice. Even without this reading, we can readily see that the "control" that is meant to be broken by such writing is the control of past voices. Cavell is thinking of prohibitions that are all the more effective for being almost inaudible, and dictates of the mind that are all the more pervasive in that they seem to be part of the most familiar structures of the world.

There is a kind of confirmation for this interpretation in the suggestion that Cavell goes on to make: the corollary of liberation from the past is something like discipleship in the present:

> Such writing has its risks: not merely the familiar ones of inconsistency, unclarity, empirical falsehood, unwarranted generalization, but also of personal confusion, with its attendant dishonesties, and of the tyranny that subjects the world to one's personal problems. The assessment of such failures will exact criticism at which we are unpracticed.
>
> In asking for more than belief it invites discipleship, which runs its own risks of dishonesty and hostility. But I do not see that the faults of explicit

discipleship are more dangerous than the faults that come from subjection to modes of thought and sensibility whose origins are unseen or unremembered and that therefore create a different blindness inaccessible in other ways to cure. Between control by the living and control by the dead there is nothing to choose. [Ibid.]

What Cavell does not quite say explicitly is something like this: We have to pass through the phases of being controlled by the living in order to get out from under the control of the dead. And since the medium through which the dead control us is principally the deposited and fantasied voices and residues of voices among the unseen and unremembered modes of thought and sensibility, it will take a therapy of the voice to recover. We are to use the present possibilities of giving voice to these modes of thought and feeling to dissipate the dictation of the all but inaudible voices of our education (philosophical and otherwise). This idea of therapy common to Wittgenstein and Freud is perhaps most visible in the thought I just cited that relates Freud's idea of fantasy to Wittgenstein's idea that a picture held us captive. In both cases, something unspoken has to be put into words, in order to free us from its inaccessible power.

We will take a longer look at these questions in chapter 4. For now I want to just signal my interest in the following features of this passage: Cavell seems to be conflating the issue of bringing a certain source of influence to *consciousness*—perhaps lifting the repression of this influence—with allowing ourselves to be influenced by the living rather than the dead. This doesn't quite say that the repression of influence is designed to assassinate the one who influences (though an earlier footnote suggests such a connection). And then it becomes unclear whether we are dealing directly in the idea of repression or whether we are dealing with Cavell's fantasies about the power and motives of his own repressions. Fantasies about the power of repression may occur at various times and may be perhaps the product of repression or of the partial lifting of a repression, for instance, in the course of analytic therapy. In chapters 3 and 4, we will have occasion to look at the fantasy and at a certain mythological level of the reality in the idea of words having the power of life and death—that is, once they are brought back from their death at the hands of a philosophical repression. As early as Cavell's first book, these considerations occupy the territory that he will later explicitly populate with voices and the idea of voices. On the other hand, these are the kinds of considerations that are already drawing him deeper into the distances of the voice.

3

CRITERIA AND CRISIS

America's best writers have offered one another the shock of recogni-
tion but not the faith of friendship, not daily belief. Perhaps this is
why, or it is because, their voices seem to destroy one another. So they
destroy one another for us. How is a tradition to come out of that?
—Stanley Cavell, *The Senses of Walden*

Voices are so often disappointing.
—Willa Cather, *The Song of the Lark*

ENACTMENTS OF VOICE OF *THE CLAIM OF REASON*

Cavell's next steps within the problematic and the practices of the voice were taken between 1970 and 1972. This is the period in which he was writing *The World Viewed* and *The Senses of Walden*, and in which he produced the most central revisions of his account of criteria in Wittgenstein's later work. These were the revisions that began the transformation of his dissertation *The Claim to Rationality* into the work that was published as the *The Claim of Reason*. Something that he discovered in this period evidently made possible the publication of these investigations in the form of a book. No doubt this discovery was partly personal, but some of it was a discovery of the voice.[1]

I have been arguing that a major aspect of this discovery is to be thought of as impersonal. Throughout *The Claim of Reason* we can observe Cavell in the process of discovering that the methods of appealing to what we ordinarily say are, at the same time, methods of recovering the voice. This discovery is "personal" in the sense that Cavell is the one who made it. And making such a discovery philosophically accessible depends on a certain literary achievement, which might also be characterized as an achievement of voice. But this double discovery of the voice must not be confused with Cavell's achievement of a distinctive style.

Some connections of voice and style are, of course, unavoidable. A voice that is produced in written words can be discovered only through certain experiments of style. And for some writers—Cavell is one of them—the achievement of a voice seems to dominate all other accomplishments. Perhaps by now, Cavell's voice is inextricable from his writing, hence inextricable from what most readers think of as literary style. Nevertheless, something crucial about the voice of the writer and the voices that he recovers for philosophy remains to be worked through. And when we move beyond the personal elements of style—conceived of as something idiosyncratic and unshareable—we will begin to uncover the idea of the voice as something that needs to be communicated and, in that sense, shared.

One of the main points of my project has been to investigate the relationship of these different voices. But now the story gets more tangled and more fraught. As we shall see, the perception of the voice within the appeals to ordinary language unleashed further insights in Cavell's work. It is as if, having recovered the voice for the use of philosophy, Cavell was able to find his voice in a variety of fields. But this emergence of the voice, and the developments in his writing that were part of that emergence, also led to a kind of philosophical crisis. In the first part of this chapter, I bring into view more of the emergence of the voice in *The Claim of Reason.* In the second part, I try to show some of the consequences of this crisis.

Some of the steps Cavell took in this period had already been prepared for in his early engagements with Austin's procedures. But here again, though his progress in *The Claim of Reason* toward the idea and practices of voice is unmistakable and decisive, his full and explicit insistence on the role of the voice in the characterization and undoing of skepticism comes later, looking back. For instance, at the edge of his critique of Kripke's account of Wittgenstein's "skeptical solution," Cavell gives us this insight into *The Claim of Reason:*

> The idea of my voice in my history, in my acceptance of criteria, in assessing my agreement or attunement in language, is a principal theme of *The Claim of Reason,* which proceeds by way of taking Wittgenstein's idea of a criterion (in conjunction with grammar) to account both for the acceptance of attunement in the appeals to my voice in ordinary language procedure, and at the same time to account for the rejection of this attunement, hence of my voice, in skepticism; to show the character of our agreement

in our words—that our consent or agreement in words cannot be contrac-tual—as well as to show our falling, and our wish to fall, out of attune-ment. Since criteria and skepticism are one another's possibility, criteria cannot be meant to refute skepticism; on the contrary they show skepti-cism's power, even something one might call its truth. I sometimes think of this theme as our disappointment with our criteria. [*Conditions Hand-some and Unhandsome*, 64.]

This is a decisive interpretation of *The Claim of Reason*, a step that de-mands the kind of close rereading that the book deserves. This inter-pretation has shaped the ways in which we now read *The Claim of Rea-son*, and it deserves to have done so. But because of its power and, no doubt, in part because of the authority of its origins, there is a danger that we will accept this interpretation prematurely and as possessing perhaps the wrong kind of authority.

I am not interested in making an argument that Cavell's having written *The Claim of Reason* is a poor reason for accepting his interpretation of it as authoritative. Of course, as with any putative advance in our under-standing of a difficult text, we need to test its point-by-point contact with the work it claims to be interpreting. But beyond such issues of authori-tativeness, my idea of a premature acceptance of an interpretation is in-tended to suggest a further danger. If I am right at least about the *kinds* of steps by which Cavell brings the idea of voice into the open, there is a series of philosophical risks and perhaps also some private dangers in ac-cepting this idea of voice without taking at least some of the steps for oneself. The idea of voice is not merely a useful interpretive stroke but a continuation of the book's own work of lifting an obscurity or repression. What I think we need to recognize is that Cavell's ability to continue the work of *The Claim of Reason* was achieved by an interpretive step that was actually *discontinuous* with the self-characterizations of *The Claim of Reason*. Jumping too quickly to Cavell's later depictions of his appeals to the ordinary as appeals to the voice, we will tend to miss precisely how Cavell's rereading of himself evolved into those later expressions and for-mulations of voice.

There is, in fact, a tendency in reading Cavell to reinterpret the earlier appeals to ordinary language in the light of his later work on the "under-writing" of the ordinary in Emerson and Thoreau. Sometimes this ten-dency has the effect of leaving to one side the parts of his earlier work that are harder to assimilate to the later model. This tendency helps to produce a sort of rift, separating his work with ordinary language from his work on, for instance, Shakespeare, Freud, and film.[2]

Such a rift is not necessarily a bad thing, and there are good reasons for trying to understand the various forms it takes. Cavell himself has consistently tried to avoid eliminating or papering over some related rifts in his own cultural topography. He insists, for instance, that we should not pretend to have overcome the divisions between "analytic" and "Continental" philosophy; between philosophy and psychoanalysis; between philosophy and literature; and (what is not the same division) between philosophy and criticism. However painful these divisions are for a given thinker, they are not mere accidents of our cultural history, and they may still prove instructive. Cavell's aim has often been explicitly to work within the pains and tensions of these rifts and divisions, perhaps even to get some energy from keeping the tensions live and out in the open. Whether or not the case of the rift in his own work is exactly parallel to the other cases, there is little to be gained by leaving one side of the rift out of the picture. Nor is it very useful to encapsulate his attention to ordinary language as something like a phase he went through as an "ordinary language philosopher." It is not so easy to demonstrate which parts of his work are in touch with the philosophy of ordinary language and which may be taken as standing more independently.

I have been suggesting how far we will have to go in order to hear the shift between the original sense of the appeals to ordinary language and the later sense of those appeals as appeals to the voice. I have not fathomed all the intricacies of this shift. Nevertheless, I am claiming (1) that Cavell takes some critical steps in *The Claim of Reason* toward this new understanding of the appeal to ordinary language; and (2) *The Claim of Reason* does not make it explicit that these steps are steps toward the recovery of the voice. Certainly, Cavell does not characterize the steps he takes in *The Claim of Reason* with anything like the same explicitness and methodological compression displayed in the passage I just cited. And the same comparison holds between the relative explicitness of the methodological self-conception in *The Claim of Reason* and that in the passage from *A Pitch of Philosophy* that I quoted at the beginning of chapter 2. There Cavell speaks of "the return of a voice to philosophy," and in *Themes Out of School* he speaks of the suppression of the voice by metaphysics and analysis and of its recovery ("as from an illness") in the methods of ordinary language. Such explicitness about the voice does not occur in *The Claim of Reason*.

In fact, there is no single place in *The Claim of Reason* where Cavell *explicitly formulates* the connection between his various treatments of skepticism and his conception of Austin's and Wittgenstein's procedures as appeals to the voice. The revisionary conception of the appeals will go hand in hand with a new characterization of skepticism. And this is precisely the one that is now so current in his work, the conception of skepticism as containing a rejection or repression of the voice. What we *do* possess in *The Claim of Reason* is something like the *enactment* of the steps by which Cavell arrived at these new conceptions of the role of the voice as suppressed by skepticism and as recovered by way of the appeals to ordinary language. Cavell shows us these conceptions and their interconnections before he ever names them. We have the taking of the steps toward the fuller realization of the voice, but not the full characterization of those steps. In some important sense, we have the methods of recovering the voice before we have the voice as such.

Does this matter? Is it perhaps merely an accident of his personal intellectual history? Or is it merely a matter of Cavell's penchant for indirection? In chapters 1 and 2, I have already suggested some reasons why this inexplicitness or reticence about the voice ought to matter to a reading of Cavell. Without an appreciation of this reticence, we would tend to overlook, for instance, the interplay between the voice of the philosopher and the voices of ordinary speech that he is invoking. And because the methodological appeal to ordinary speech is not yet explicitly characterized as an appeal to the voice, there is a tendency to elide the methodological preoccupation, in favor of a kind of unbalanced attention to Cavell's literary achievement of a distinctive voice.

Furthermore, I began to suggest that Cavell's enactment of the emergence of the voice in his own work presents *us* with a kind of working model of the lifting of a repression. In this chapter, I work through this suggestion most specifically in relation to *The Claim of Reason*, and I continue to elaborate my suggestion that there are even more specific and more positive advances to be made from a study of these developments in Cavell's work. Within my larger story about the emergence of voice, I have a second and more cautionary tale to tell. In the absence of a more explicit account of the different tasks performed by the idea of the voice at different stages of Cavell's work, and of the specific practices that are devoted to the undermining of skepticism, the possibilities for misreading Cavell's most central ideas are far greater than they need to be.

One such tendency in interpreting Cavell has become fairly widespread. This is the idea that when he speaks of "living your skepticism," he is in some way recommending this as a more mature, more human, response to skepticism.[3] More generally, readers have taken away from these regions of Cavell's work—again, most notably from part 4 of *The Claim of Reason*—the idea that Cavell wants us to have a greater appreciation of human limitation and a greater acknowledgment of our finitude. This misreading derives from a number of sources, but a confusion about the phases of Cavell's diagnosis of skepticism makes it easier to maintain. Later in this chapter I offer a partial response to this interpretation.

There is yet a further motivation for tracing out the emergence of the voice in *The Claim of Reason*. This book tells in various ways of its own construction and of the various temporal and conceptual strata that compose it. Cavell's own various rereadings of *The Claim of Reason* provide us with clues and traces of the paths of its understanding. But the new paths inevitably tend to cover up the older paths. It is worth uncovering some of the steps he took along those paths in order to see how they looked before they were subjected to rereading.

To trace out each of the themes of voice in *The Claim of Reason* would be close to a full-scale reading of the book. It would certainly go a long way toward situating this book as not only at the center of his originality but at the heart of his development as a writer and a philosopher. Failing that, I want to at least present a series of different strands of Cavell's use of the idea of voice. For starters, this should enable us to appreciate the feat of self-reading that goes into a passage like the one quoted above from *Conditions Handsome and Unhandsome*.

I single out six themes in *The Claim of Reason* either explicitly involving the voice or pointing to its eventual emergence in Cavell's later work:

(1) Wittgenstein's writing as a mode of attentiveness to the human voice (p. 5).

(2) The voice as an emblem and means of consent to a social existence (traditionally understood as a "compact" or contract) in which we are complicit but of whose origin we are unaware (pp. 22–28).

(3) The sketching of an analogy of the existence of criteria with such a social or communal existence, in which we are complicit but of whose origin we are as yet unaware (pp. 28–32).

(4) The methods of recovering and representing Wittgensteinian criteria and Austinian "samples" of what we say.

(5) The sense of the voice as emerging from a privacy yet deeper and more inward than the privacy constructed by skepticism. (This phase of Cavell's investigations forms an important piece of continuity between parts 1 and 4 of *The Claim of Reason*. And this characterization of the voice is directly tied to Cavell's developing sense that the intellectual doubts of the skeptic are designed to cover over a still scarier region of knowledge. And here we might add that one kind of knowledge that skepticism covers up is precisely our knowledge of the voice.)

(6) The voice as the means by which I "have a voice in my own history," the emblem and medium of my having a say in my own existence.

This list is not exhaustive. But I take it to suggest how far we are from an exhaustive study of this issue and how crucial such a study might prove to any full-scale understanding of Cavell's philosophical accomplishment. I have already said something about how we are to appreciate Wittgenstein's writing as enactments of voice and dialogue. I cite here an early passage from *The Claim of Reason*, where Cavell is fleshing out his view of himself as contributing to philosophy as a set of texts rather than, in his phrase, to "a set of *given* problems" (3–4). Cavell adds the following comment, not quite in passing, to a remark about oral and written traditions:

> I may say that while Wittgenstein's philosophizing is more completely attentive to the human voice than any other I think of, it strikes me that its teaching is essentially something written, that some things essential to its teaching cannot be spoken. This may mean that some things he says have lost, or have yet to find, the human circle in which they can be usefully said. [5.]

While this passage nicely undercuts any easy way of identifying voice with speech—hence of *opposing* voice to writing—it also undercuts the idea that Wittgenstein's attention to voice constitutes an imitation of some previously existing voice. Such an imitation might well be at home in the same human circle in which that voice first existed, that is, the circle in which it first made its actual utterances.[4]

There is more to say about the second and third themes on this list, and more to say about the links between them. It is striking how often Cavell returns to the issue of the voice in its political and social registers: key passages occur on these matters in *The Senses of Walden*, in *Pursuits of Happiness*, in *Conditions Handsome and Unhandsome*, and in the introduction to *Disowning Knowledge*. From a certain perspective, he is also quite close to this question of the social and political dimensions of criteria when he takes up what he calls the "biological" reading of the idea of a "form of life." He contrasts such an understanding (which might emphasize the difference between a human's call for help and a bird's cry of warning) to the "social" treatment of criteria (which might tend rather to emphasize the grammar of different calls and responses within the forms of life of a given tribe or tribe-like group).

Despite this substantial anthology of passages where Cavell discusses the social and political aspects of criteria, the discussion of the social contract in *The Claim of Reason* is often apparently treated as if it were a

self-contained discussion of political theory—as if Cavell had just casually dropped some remarks about Rousseau and Hume into the middle
of a discussion of Wittgenstein.[5] Other readers have wanted to absorb
this abrupt entrance of the theme of one's voice in the social contract
into a larger, more unified vision of the general nature of the human
community. We are unlikely to get very far with Cavell's work on criteria if we remain in the grip either of the view that Cavell is merely
offering some sort of loose analogy between the political and the linguistic sources of community, or of the view that Cavell is offering us a
chance to merge them into a yet deeper, more humanistic, sense of
community.

Characterizing the search for criteria as a search for community, Cavell
wonders "how I could have been party to the establishing of criteria if I
do not know what they are." He suggests that the best answer will go
something like this. We are to

> . . . [m]ake out that there are (what Wittgenstein calls) criteria (i.e. pro-
> duce some), and to admit that nobody could have established them alone,
> and that of course whoever is party to them does know what they are
> (though he or she may not know how to elicit and state them, and not
> recognize his or her complicity under that description); and to emphasize
> that the claim is not that one can tell a priori who is implicated by me,
> because one point of the particular kind of investigation Wittgenstein calls
> grammatical is exactly to discover who. [*Claim*, 22.]

Admitting that this is probably not the answer the reader had been hoping for, Cavell explicitly sets the stage for the actual production of some
criteria. But he is also, it seems to me, setting the stage for a certain disappointment with that very production of those very criteria. There is at
this moment a kind of admission that we are already disappointed in criteria even before we actually start looking for them.

Cavell's excursus into the region of the social contract breaks into his
exposition of criteria at this critical moment. The motivation for this excursus seems rather casual: "The question it answers [about how I can
have been party to the establishment of criteria] sounds like a familiar
moment in the history of modern philosophy, the moment of Hume's
attack upon the idea of a social contract." The casualness of the association to Hume's attack does not quite disguise Cavell's radical break from
the traditional lines of discussion about the *Investigations*. Where commentators have pursued the social aspect of forms of life they have almost
invariably done so in a quasi-anthropological spirit. They have spoken
either of tribes or else of groups that are conceived as having the same

coherence and relative insularity that tribes are thought to possess. Such enquiries have rarely, if ever, pursued a quasi-political understanding of the nature of community in the era of nation-states. Cavell mentions both the sense in many philosophers that Hume had succeeded in rendering the idea of a social contract "disreputable" and the somewhat opposite feeling—however "unestablished"—that "the mutual meaningfulness of words must rest upon some kind of compact or connection among the users of a language" (22). He pursues this grouping of ideas, he remarks, in order to show what he calls a "natural outcropping of concepts which will later come more thematically into play" (ibid.).

What comes into play does not have much to do immediately with the meaningfulness of words or with the linking of criteria to the implication or complicity of others in what I say. The far-reaching questions of what Cavell characterizes as part of the epistemology of the social realm do not get tied directly to the question of words and criteria but to the question of who speaks for whom. It is precisely this issue of who speaks for whom that provided Cavell with the first overtly philosophical impetus to speak of the voice in *The Claim of Reason:*

> To speak for oneself politically is to speak for the others with whom you consent to association, and it is to consent to be spoken for by them—not as a parent speaks for you, i.e., instead of you, but as someone in mutuality speaks for you, i.e., speaks your mind. Who these others are, for whom you speak and by whom you are spoken for, is not known a priori, though it is generally treated as a given. [27.]

The discussion proposes an analogy between speaking for yourself and for others in the realm of politics and, on the other hand, speaking for yourself and for others in the (philosophical) voicing of our criteria. In each realm, we risk rebuff from those we are implicitly claiming to speak for. But in each realm, the mutual implication of the speakers is not something that is up to our personal decision. (The discovery of such moments of mutual implication may appear to be private. But here again we face the issue of the private discovery of a condition that must be conceived of as shareable.)

> To speak for yourself then means risking the rebuff—on some occasions perhaps once for all—of those whom you claimed to be speaking for; and it means risking having to rebuff—on some occasions perhaps once for all—those who claimed to be speaking for you. There are directions other than the political in which you will have to find your own voice—in religion, in friendship, in parenthood, in love, in art—and to find your own work; and the political is likely to be heartbreaking or dangerous. So are

the others. But in the political, the impotence of your voice shows up quick-est; it is of importance to others to stifle it; and it is easiest to hope there, since others are in any case included in it, that it will not be missed if it is stifled, i.e., that you will not miss it. [27.]

Whatever else this discussion accomplishes, it pushes Cavell further into the open on these particular issues of voice. Almost without breaking stride, he goes on to raise the stakes:

The alternative to speaking for yourself politically is not: speaking for yourself privately. (Because "privately" here can only either be repeating the "for myself," it means roughly, "I'm doing the talking," or else it im-plies that you do not *know* that you speak for others, which does not deny the condition of speaking for others.) The alternative is having nothing (political) to say. [27–28.]

"Having nothing (political) to say" points us toward the still more radical fate of voicelessness. Only those creatures who breathe (politically) can be stifled by political power. "Voicelessness" speaks of a more radical, if perhaps less politically violent, condition. Shortly, Cavell will be suggest-ing that it is the prevalence of a tendency to voicelessness that allows the prevailing absence of serious political speech to go unheeded.

If I am to have a native tongue, I have to accept what "my elders" say and do as consequential [as Augustine depicts himself doing in the passage quoted at the beginning of the *Investigations*]; and they have to accept, even have to applaud, what I say and do as what they say and do. We do not know in advance what the content of our mutual acceptance is, how far we may be in agreement. I do not know in advance how deep my agreement with myself is, how far responsibility for the language may run. But if I am to have my own voice in it, I must be speaking for others and allow others to speak for me. The alternative to speaking for myself representatively (for *someone* else's consent) is not: speaking for myself privately. The alterna-tive is having nothing to say, being voiceless, not even mute. [28.])

That the philosophical and the political should interpret one another is no more out of the ordinary than that the individual and the political should interpret one another—as they do, for instance, in the *Republic*. In re-turning his discussion to the question of "my voice in my language," Cavell raises for the first time the issues that I began this essay by exam-ining: the various relations between (a) my voice in my language, (b) the voice that philosophy suppresses, and (c) the voice that is to be returned to my language and hence to philosophy. He is getting ready to suggest that the most basic appeal in the methods of ordinary language is from, so to speak, my words to the voice that I have withheld from my words.

Although these issues are, from this point on, at least partially out in the open, they are still not connected explicitly. I now turn to the questions of voice as they appear in (4) and (5) on my list, more explicitly in relation to the point of Wittgensteinian criteria and to the uncovering of further reaches of privacy, not accessible to philosophical skepticism.

Here is a passage where Cavell is actually discussing the suppression of the human in philosophy, an aspect of the human that we are meant to recover by means of Wittgensteinian appeals to ordinary language-games. But Cavell does not here name the voice as the aspect of the human that philosophy suppresses:

> "The meaning is the use" [a slogan frequently used to summarize Wittgenstein's teaching] calls attention to the fact that what an expression means is a function of what it is used to mean or to say on specific occasions by human beings. That such an obvious fact should assume the importance it does is itself surprising. And to trace the intellectual history of philosophy's concentration on the meaning of words and sentences, in isolation from a systematic attention to their concrete uses, would be a worthwhile undertaking. It is a concentration one of whose consequences is the traditional search for the meaning of a word in various realms of objects, another of which is the idea of a perfect understanding as being achievable only through the construction of a perfect language. A fitting title for this history would be Philosophy and the Rejection of the Human. [206–7.][6]

Cavell goes on to identify being driven "outside language-games" with losing the point of what you are saying. Soon after concluding the work of The Claim of Reason, he will come to say that what is lost outside of language-games is the voice. This will prove to be decisive for his later work. It suggests that we can use his detailed investigations of the fate of our words and expressions under the pressure of skepticism as studying the myriad and sometimes surprising ways in which our voice can get lost in our words. But in this passage, the attention is still focused not expressly on the voice but on the links between language-games (and hence the criteria that have their home in those games) and what human beings are thereby enabled to mean and to say. This passage is from a stratum that the book identifies as having been written before the passage in chapter 1 that I was just discussing. It should not be surprising or alarming, on my reading, if the different strata of composition contain different degrees of explicitness and illumination about the voice.

Cavell singles out the ways in which a familiar and easily misunderstood slogan of Wittgenstein's calls attention to the fact that human beings use their expressions or voice their utterances, meaning them differently in different circumstances. (This is not the same as saying that

meaning is "context-dependent," if only because we can sometimes determine the relevant context only when we know what someone is trying
to say, or mean. This question of context requires a much longer story.)

Cavell's thought about the difficulty of attending to the sheer *fact* of
the human use of words to mean something suggests that philosophy has
more than one difficulty in attending to the human sources and engines
and media of meaning. Very soon, Cavell will begin to use the idea of
voice to capture precisely this fact of utterance and, more widely, to capture the unrelentingly interesting distances and intimacies between what
the words we are using mean and what *we* mean to say in using these
words, in voicing them.

The word *attentive* (in the passage about Wittgenstein's attending to
the human voice in writing) suggests some difficulty in attending to the
voice. The voice requires more—or more continuous—attention than
it has been getting. Wittgenstein's "calling attention" to the sources of
meaning in the act of uttering or voicing our words suggests that philosophy's rejection of the human can be understood as a mode of inatten-
tion. Philosophy does not just set out to repress the human, as if one's
humanness were *merely* a source of anxiety or shame. Philosophy, for
reasons and motives still to be unearthed, finds it easy enough to look
away from the ordinary and attend to something else as a source of order
and meaning.

These seem to me exactly the kinds of considerations that will lead
Cavell to the idea of philosophy as repressing the voice. They lead him, I
suggest, to think of the voice as the primary *instance* of what philosophy
represses when it rejects the human element from the human capacity to
make meaningful utterances. But the idea of such a repression of voice
points more exactly to how the mechanisms of repression are, in general,
supposed to work in philosophy. Indeed, already in *The Claim of Reason*,
we could say that the voice is not only the principal mode of human being
that philosophy represses, but also a principal feature of the therapy by
which the human is to be recovered. Like childhood sexuality, the voice
is not some accidental content that happens to get repressed. The voice
is part of the form and part of the representative content of everything
about the human being that philosophy would like to be rid of. Something like this thought is enacted in the exposition of *The Claim of
Reason*.

Evidence for this reading will have to emerge in the course of my exposition of each of the topics of the voice. Nevertheless, a small preliminary piece of evidence is suggested by Cavell's use of the quotation from
Feuerbach as the epigraph to part 1: "This philosophy . . . speaks the

language of men, not an empty, unknown tongue." Here, however, the association of the emptiness of language with a certain kind of unknownness does not reach all the way to Cavell's thought. For Cavell, it is the ease and apparent familiarity in the ways by which we fall into philosophy that constitutes a rejection of the ordinary.

I am building a case for the significance of the fact that the very book in which the links between the suppression of voice and the distortion of criteria are most thoroughly and demandingly laid out does not quite name the voice as the point where the philosophical skeptic applies the pressure required for this repression. If I am right that *The Claim of Reason* is enacting the lifting of philosophy's repression of voice, and if "repression" is more than an analogy, it is not surprising that the returning of the voice is not always named, or not named to the same degree of methodicalness by which it is enacted.

It is not merely that it was rightfully the first order of Cavell's business to trace in detail the ways in which the skeptic's progress drives him "outside" of the language-games, forcing him to distort the criteria of our ordinary expressions and at the same time the ordinary circumstances of pain. Or we are driven outside the circumstances in which it makes sense to say that we are seeing the "whole object," or that we know of someone's feelings "from their behavior." Until this methodical labor of tracing the skeptic's progress was accomplished, there was not only no point in relating that progress to the repression of voice, there was nothing present—in writing—for Cavell to pin that formulation on. There were as yet no systematic examples of the distortion of our criteria and the circumstances of their employment to be interpreted as a repression of voice.

In the absence of such samples of distortion and suppression in the skeptic's words, the characterization of skepticism as a repression of the voicing of these words (his own words and, by implication, our words) would have been empty. The emptiness would not have been neutral, because it would have suggested false solutions and a false sense of progress. (This seems analogous to the consequences of offering premature interpretations in other forms of therapy.) In fact, I think that a failure to connect the details of the work on the distortion of our criteria to the idea of the repression of voice has been responsible for some of the more prevalent and often harmful interpretations of Cavell on skepticism and the voice.

I want to take my intuition about this gradual and unsynchronized emergence of the voice in *The Claim of Reason* a little further: each step

Cavell takes toward releasing the voice exposes some impediment or in-hibition of the voice. Often the obstacle is a false sense of privacy or a false picture of inwardness, and exposing these obstacles exposes whoever wishes to follow Cavell to further risks of inwardness and falsity. If each such step potentially releases a further reach of the voice, each step also creates the possibility of a false reliance on the tokens and the assurances of the voice. There are thus ample grounds for being reticent or guarded about the voice, precisely in a piece of work that is trying to demon-strate the centrality of the voice and to exhibit its recovered existence for philosophy.

I am suggesting that the idea and practices of voice are liberated for Cavell, in proportion to his ability to realize and demonstrate that Witt-gensteinian criteria are not intended, and not bound, to refute skepticism. This realization, which explicitly organizes and governs the entire project of the book, leads Cavell into some practical shifts in his writing and in his reflections on that writing. The recapture and perspicuous represen-tation of criteria becomes not only a means to, for instance, philosophical recollection. This effort at perspicuous representation keeps turning into the issue about how criteria are to be written about, expressed to an au-dience: in a word, how criteria are to be voiced. As *The Claim of Reason* constructs its progress, the issue of finding ways to voice criteria in a philosophically useful fashion becomes the issue of how to represent cri-teria in ways that show their mutual implication and dependence on the voice. This is meant to teach us that the voicing of criteria is, at the same time, a demonstration that the appeals to criteria enable the reemergence and recovery of the voice.

It is always difficult to get back to the realization that criteria are not meant to refute the skeptic but rather to show how the skeptic's progress is possible. What I have been saying should suggest that the difficulty of this realization has a great deal to do with the difficulty of appreciating the emergence of the voice. If we do not know what we are appealing to criteria for—what they are supposed to *do*—we are unlikely to under-stand what the voice that utters the criteria is for.

The realization that criteria are not meant to defeat skepticism is ex-plicitly announced in chapter 2 of *The Claim of Reason*. The realization leads to Cavell's development of the companion ideas of the "truth of skepticism," of our "openness to the threat of skepticism." Just as cru-cially, it leads him to explore what he calls our disappointment over the limits of knowledge, which is most specifically exhibited in our disap-pointment with criteria. In the English-speaking philosophical world, it is hard to take in the thought that a philosophical position may have "its truth" without therefore being true—holding true propositions and maintaining true theses.

Cavell's phrase "the truth of skepticism" does not refer to something like the portion or grain of truth in somebody's views. The skeptic emerges not as saying something true but as harboring a truth. The truth in question is more like the "truth" of a situation. The situation is a reality whose mode of appearance could be said to disguise or falsify the truth it embodies. The skeptic will not see his own hand in the collapse of the criteria that bind us to the world, even as his striving produces that collapse.

The skeptic is alienated from the very truth that he has nurtured: So he will not learn from it, or listen to it. That is why Cavell speaks of defeating the skeptic's "interpretation" of his discovery. This is the form in which the skeptic's human condition presents itself to him. But without that form of interpretation, there is nothing like a *discovery* of some calamitous limitation of human knowledge. There is only the condition in which the skeptic began, the one we all share. Consequently, there is no "fact" about the limitation of our knowledge to be discovered by his procedures. So there is also no fact for him to be making a true statement about.

When Cavell speaks of the truth of skepticism, it is not as one might speak of chiropractors or self-help manuals or astrologers as having, appearances to the contrary, amassed a certain number of facts or truths. To speak of the "truth of skepticism" is more like saying "the truth of marriage is the struggle for mutual recognition" or "the truth of capitalism is the alienated development of the social character of human labor."

The skeptic (the skeptic in us) has got hold of something crucial in the human situation, but that something is not accurately represented as a kind of fact. It is more like a kind of relationship or relatedness, something about the way in which the world is present to us, and we to the world. But the skeptic interprets this aspect of the situation—that the presentness of the world to us does not reside in our knowledge of the world—as the discovery of a disastrous fact. The idea is not so much that skepticism has true things to say about our situation, but that the skeptic is *in* a situation. He voices that situation as best he can—given the way he got into it. But he interprets it as a kind of catastrophic progress. His interpretation of his chastened sense of human knowledge presents us not with truths that we should learn to deal with but with developments that we can learn to read.

These ideas have caused a great deal of perplexity, perhaps especially when they are hooked up to the thought (first broached in part 4 of *The Claim of Reason*) of "living one's skepticism." Before I try to untangle those knots and show their connection to a failure to appreciate the idea of voice, I want to reconnect the idea to some earlier themes and discoveries. In particular, I think it has not been appreciated how much the idea that criteria do not refute skepticism is related to Cavell's slowly dawning recognition that Wittgenstein's notion of a criterion is at least significantly and structurally dependent on the ordinary notion of a criterion.

After some years of writing and teaching about the *Investigations*, Cavell arrived at the sense that "criterion" was to be construed neither as a quasi-technical term, nor as simply identical with our ordinary notions of criteria (such as the criteria for admission to a certain college, or the criteria to qualify for a loan, or the criteria for the ranking of a race car or a college football team). On the one hand, this means that Wittgenstein can legitimately rely on a *certain* level of familiarity with this crucial notion, and that he need not, for instance, make special preparations for the introduction and use of this notion or for the companion notion of "grammar." On the other hand, the use of the term is not *more* than analogous with the ordinary use. And this is part of what leads Cavell to his fateful recognition about criteria: The notion and the facts of criteria cannot supply a more forceful or rather a more *direct* response to skepticism than is provided by the existence of language itself. (This question of the existence of language "itself" and how it does and does not constitute a response to skepticism is taken a step or two further in "Declining Decline.") The notion of the "directness" of a response constitutes one starting point for interpreting what a "refutation" of skepticism would mean.

Most of this has been said before—first of all, by Cavell himself (*Claim*, 6–13, 15). Other philosophers have taken some kind of reliance on the public existence of language (of conventions, shareable rules, language-games, forms of life) as crucial to Wittgenstein's response to skepticism. Such philosophers take Wittgenstein's treatment of "private language" to point essentially away from false pictures of the private and toward a truer picture of the shared and public quality of language and "mental" predicates: A number of philosophers have responded sympathetically to such thoughts as, for instance, "An 'inward process' stands in need of outward criteria." Cavell shares with other philosophers influenced by Wittgenstein some sense of the task of insisting on an account of the "outward" criteria, that is, on insisting that what we call "inward" and what we call "outward" help to define each other. To lose touch with what may seem like the outer circumstances that we *call* his having a toothache (his clutching his cheek, calling his dentist, stoically staring at the television set, and pointedly ignoring our offers of sympathy) is to lose touch with whatever inward state we take to be expressed in those circumstances.

Cavell, however, *was* pretty much alone in imagining that when Wittgenstein combats false philosophical pictures of the "inner," one of his primary goals is to arrive at a deeper and more dangerous sense of inwardness.

> The *Investigations* takes many ways of approaching ideas which construe the inner life as composed of objects (and if objects then for sure *private* ones). To combat such ideas is an obsession of the book as a whole. It is as though Wittgenstein felt human beings in jeopardy of losing touch with their inner lives altogether, with the very idea that each person is a center of one, that each *has* a life. There is no better evidence of this than the way Wittgenstein is interpreted on such matters. . . . I mean the sense his readers get that in denying that we know (say) our sensations and in denying that our words for the sensations of others refer to objects, something or other, inside that other, he is denying that we *have* sensations and that there is anything going on in the other. If one shudders at the thought, perhaps that comes from a surmise that what it feels as if Wittgenstein is denying may be true, that we have nothing inside, that we are empty. If one fails to shudder, that may be because one does not allow one's desperate idea of hidden somethings to come to light and become questioned. [*Claim*, 91.]

It is part of Cavell's aim in revising the stakes in Wittgenstein's work that he deepen our sense of the privacy of language at the same time that he is combating false ideas of privacy. Both currents of his thought will tend toward ideas of the voice, but it is not always the same aspect of the voice that he has in view. The details of the struggle against false ideas of privacy emerge more immediately. It will take a while before Cavell delineates in similar detail the view that a false idea of privacy is generally in the service of a certain inward falseness. The falseness in question is a sort of fault line within our various capacities for privacy and for true expression—a fault line for which insincerity is far too moralistic a term.

Speaking about those critics of Wittgenstein who responded to the views of the publicness of language that had become standard in accounts of the *Investigations*, Cavell remarks:

> I find my general intuition of Wittgenstein's view of language to be the reverse of the idea many philosophers seem compelled to argue against in him: it is felt that Wittgenstein's view makes language too public, that it cannot do justice to the control I have over what I say, to the innerness of my meaning. But my wonder, in the face of what I have recently been saying, is rather how he can arrive at the completed and unshakeable edifice

of shared language from within such apparently fragile and intimate moments—private moments—as our separate counts and out-calls of phenomena, which are after all hardly more than our interpretations of what
occurs, and with no assurance of conventions to back them up. [*Claim*, 36.]

Cavell's remarks build on his earlier reflections on the Austinian practice
of recalling "what we would say when"—with somewhat more emphasis
on the "when" than was perhaps current among Austin's other followers.
A page back, Cavell writes:

> In Wittgensteinian (and everyday) cases, *whether* to say it out is as
> much a problem as what there is to be said (as much a problem in the
> intelligibility of what is said). [35.]

He takes this thought somewhat beyond what we have seen in *Must We
Mean What We Say?*:

> Whether to speak (proclaim) has two aspects: determining whether you are
> willing to count something as something; and determining when, if ever,
> you wish [to], or can, enter your accounting into a particular occasion. . . .
> Grant that the predicate ". . . is in pain" is in our grammatical repertoire,
> that we know generally how to predicate it. To proclaim it here and now
> you must be willing to call out ("-claim") just that predicate on the basis
> of what you have so far gathered (e.g. you must be willing to count that
> wince as pain-behavior, or perhaps we should say, count that behavior as a
> wince); and you must find it called for on just this occasion, i.e. find your-
> self willing to come before ("pro-") those to whom you speak it (e.g. de-
> clare yourself in a position to inform or advise or alert someone of some-
> thing, or explain or identify or remark something to someone). [35.]

The latter necessity of coming before others—of confronting them—
Cavell associates with some work of Austin's and to some extent that of
Searle and Grice. Here, to say something is to do something specifiable
(inform, advise, remark, notice) in a specific situation of speech with others. These are, among other things, investigations of conditions under
which we can voice something. (The half-rhyming of "claiming" and
"clamoring" may indeed mark a valid etymological connection. But in
any case it is surely relevant to the aspects of voice that link "calling out"
[proclaiming] to the possibility of calling something, e.g., a chair or a
toothache. Cavell would surely have welcomed the suggestion that human calls must be called out, that claims must sometimes occasion a
clamor. It is the kind of coincidence of sound that can provoke further
reflection.)

Along with his earlier uses of "call" and "proclaim," Cavell's use of
"out-call" suggests that this region of the inwardness of language is also

the region of the voice. At the same time, it is the region of yet further and perhaps even falser privacies than are made explicit amid the "nothings" and "somethings" of Wittgenstein's investigations.

THE VOICE AND ITS HISTORIES

It is time to take a look at the sixth of the themes of voice in *The Claim of Reason*. In the passage quoted at the beginning of this chapter, the idea of my taking a "leading voice" in my own history is intimately associated with what Cavell there calls "my acceptance" of criteria. This will elsewhere be described as my living in the face of my disappointment in those very criteria. (As I have suggested, this sort of reflection gives rise to the idea that Cavell is *recommending* that we "live our skepticism.")

The idea of having a "leading voice" in one's history harks back to the finding of one's voice in politics, love, sex, and work. The idea suggests achieving a kind of harmony between the leading voice and the other voices. But the sense of a potential harmony occurs against a background of what is more likely to be a *dis*harmony of voices. More than that, there is a clear sense that mostly what those voices do is *dictate* to the one who has them. This crucial idea emerges in a lengthy parenthesis about Freud:

> If, for example, one is convinced that one is known through the concepts and procedures of Freudian psychology, that Freud's insights precipitate shapes of thought in which the human is, if still without sufficient refinement, genuinely known—that the human being must be whatever it is required to be if those shapes of thought are valid (in particular that the human individual, to win freedom, must be something that can fight for recognition, which now means, vie with its incorporated interpretations of itself for a voice, for the leading voice, in its history)—then it is *pointless* to discuss learnedly with the unconvinced whether this psychology is scientific (though courtesy might require conversation; and so might some as yet undefined form of intellectual shame). [*Claim*, 474.]

Whatever else Cavell's elaborateness is in the service of, it is evident that he is sometimes using it to establish a kind of order or decorum of thought, within a single sentence.[7] This sentence, for all its elaborateness, is almost a cry of exasperation. We could hear it, flattened out to its essential impatience, like this: "Freud? Science? *Again?*" But this voicing of exasperation is combined with Cavell's sense that he is demonstrating something: the emergence of exactly the philosophical refinement that the good doctor should have ordered. And that turns out to be exactly, if parenthetically, the voice.

The idea of having a leading voice in your own history contains a sense of freedom that oscillates between evading the dictation of past voices and listening to those voices as attentively as possible, in order to disobey them more perfectly. By the end of *The Claim of Reason,* Cavell has begun to form the idea that the self is composed not of private objects but of private voices. The privacy of these voices is not metaphysical but empirical, the sign not of necessary human separateness but of self-imposed isolation.

It is a refusal to let those voices *become* public—hence known to others as well as to us as the residue of past invasions of voices. This invasiveness is inseparable from the self's own sense of its origins: "parental" is too reassuring a word for the power of these voices. Our current sense of privacy covers over our fear that these voices really dictate our access to the public world, to our very idea of publicness. A "private object," as such, is no threat to the possibility of the public. The privacy of the voices that I have heard—that I continue to hear—threatens the very possibility that I will know of any access to words or deeds beyond what those voices have instructed me about. The voice thus reveals itself as the primary entity that is incorporated by the self in the moments of the self's formation. But the voice also thereby obliterates the signs of its having been incorporated.

This thought contains the germ of Cavell's later ideas of moral perfectionism. Above all, we can begin to see the relation of the idea of voice to the idea that the perfection in question is achieved through the continual undermining of a false ideal of wholeness, imposed by the self on the self, for the sake of evading the anxiety that is awakened by the voicing, or prompting, of the self's next step, its unattained perfection. But this idea also points to the notion of a self as made up of incorporated selves—of the dictates and sagas of ghostly voices. Abutting the apparent optimism of perfectionism's voices, there is a vision of the self as all but exhausted in the play of such voices. (Cf. Rothman's remarks, discussed above, contrasting Hitchcock with something like the "optimism" of Emerson's perfectionism [*Images in Our Soul,* 80].)

One side of the self is seen as aspiring to a perfection that is already outlined, however obscurely, within the self's constitution. The other side feeds on the breath of others, in order not to know if it can live on its own. If a nearly inaudible voice is the only sign that I might still achieve integrity and wholeness, it is painful to remember that I must listen for this voice within a universe of public selves and public voices. Even if we could learn to listen for these inner signs of change, the public universe is scarcely hospitable to such change. (Indeed, perhaps it is least hospitable when its official approval is loudest.) Our only chance to avoid becoming the ghostly counterpart of our ghostly voices is to become the auditor of a still less audible voice.

Not too surprisingly, Cavell finds this problematic to be under investigation in *Hamlet*. Somewhat more surprisingly, he locates a related set of concerns in the *Philosophical Investigations*.

> The voices, or sides of the argument of the ordinary, do not exhaust the space of the *Investigations*, or the task of its prose. There is the space not party to the struggle of the sides (I do not think of it as a further voice) often containing its most rhetorical or apparently literary passages. . . . The turning of my spade is part of such a passage.—By now it is becoming clear that each of the voices, and silences, of the *Investigations* are the philosopher's, call him Wittgenstein, and they are meant as ours, so that the teacher's and the child's positions, among others, are ours, one I may at any time find myself in. How else would the *Investigations* form its portrait of the human self . . . like Plato's and Freud's visions, a self that incorporates selves. [*Conditions*, 83.]

Here the emphasis has shifted slightly. The idea of taking a "leading voice" in my history suggests another picture of what the self must continue to overcome in order to keep itself in existence. The self exists as a plurality of voices vying for attention, and in their clamoring, they overwhelm my ability to listen. I overcome their dictation by finding a place for my own voice amid the clamor of the others. (Some of these other voices articulate my needs or wishes, some betoken various parental demands or prohibitions. These other voices will not generally seem to come from "outside" me, and so they will not normally seem to be "other" than me.)

When the emphasis shifts in this fashion to incorporation as the medium by which these voices become internalized, and in that sense mine, the path beyond dictation becomes correspondingly difficult. For we do not get entirely beyond the range of these voices, but we must somehow learn to get *over* their sound and their impact. We might think of this effort as one of disincorporating the voices. But if they have somehow constituted the medium in which my inwardness came into existence, I must manage to get free of their grip without losing my sense of my own inwardness and privacy. This would mean losing the possibility of making sense of my own utterances. I do not lose the meaning of the words so much as the point of making them in these very circumstances, to just these people.

Losing the point of making these utterances—of making something public—would be to lose the sense of one's inwardness. One would not necessarily lose all feelings of inwardness or secrecy or unknownness:

those feelings might well intensify. One would instead be losing the sense that a particular utterance can make a difference. And one might lose the sense that different utterances are *already* different acts, before they make the differences they are going to make. Not hearing these differences is to enter on a path of loss, a way of almost guaranteeing that we will lose touch with our capacity to make sense.

In Cavell's understanding of the self as incorporating selves and of the voice as incorporating voices, it is a little unclear what state I will be in when I get over these voices or when I get to the bottom of them. If I manage to get over all of them—or get them disincorporated, externalized—will there be anything left of my voice? This is not a fear that comes up in everyone, certainly not in philosophy and, at least in this form, not perhaps in psychotherapy. One possible vicissitude is that I will become once and for all voiceless, which is not the same as becoming mute. Statements perhaps get made, questions get asked and answered, even certain feelings and values might get expressed. But nothing is voiced. The point of saying anything in particular has been lost.

This is another reason for Cavell's focus on the fear that Wittgenstein provokes, the fear that the "private objects" that he wants us to relinquish will turn out to be hiding our secret nothings. Here the possibility of hearing voices when there is no one there can no longer be taken as merely a sign of madness. It is relatively easy to externalize this condition as a fate befalling others. And unless this fate is actually befalling you, it is also relatively easy to conceptualize this condition as something external to the core of your self, something that happens to the self from the "outside." These are still fairly reassuring ways to take the possibility of such voices. In Cavell's understanding, however, to acknowledge that you might be hearing voices when there is no one out there could also be a sign that you are entertaining a possible arrival at sanity. To wish for a sane relation to the voices that compose your mind and its dictates is not the same as taking yourself as essentially sane—awaiting some further possible symptoms or vicissitudes. It is rather to acknowledge the unsecured access to the voices of the mind, the impossibility of telling from the outside whether the path that one is taking will arrive at wholeness and health. The only wholeness lies in the sincerity of listening to what is there to be heard and in following the indicated paths.

For Thoreau, or for that part of us that knows how to respond to Thoreau's writing, it may still be possible to maintain the confidence that no one ever follows the faintest suggestions of her genius to the point where it betrays her. For most of us, most of the time, it is harder to feel we have a warrant from the world for spending so much time listening to something in us, which is also more than us and points beyond us. At such times, the possibility of madness and the possibility of sanity are separated by a couple of deep breaths, the space of reflection. Though we are not as inspired as Thoreau, or as comfortable with our inspiration, we may still discover that this is a place in which to stop and think.

CRISES OF VOICE: WALDEN'S WITHDRAWAL AND RECOVERY

Just beyond the accomplishment of *The Claim of Reason,* Cavell begins to make explicit that book's efforts to recover the voice. Near the middle of "Politics as Opposed to What?," Cavell speaks of the intimacy and the abyss that lie between the upheavals of deconstruction and the Anglo-American revolutions in philosophy. He characterizes the intimacy in terms of their analogous ways of inheriting the Kantian critique of metaphysics. He then goes on to characterize the abyss as defined by the difference between thinking that metaphysics has come to the wrong conclusions or turned itself in the wrong direction, and, on the other hand, the Anglo-American idea that metaphysics has come to nothing at all and that its conclusions are something like nonsense. He continues:

> A symptom of this abyss is Derrida's sense, or intuition, that the bondage to metaphysics is a function of the promotion of something called voice over something called writing; whereas for me it is evident that the reign of repressive philosophical systematizing—sometimes called metaphysics, sometimes called logical analysis—has depended on the suppression of the human voice. It is as the recovery of this voice (as from an illness) that ordinary language philosophy is, as I have understood and written about it, before all to be understood. [*Themes Out of School,* 48.]

In "Aftermaths of the Modern," I commented on some of the complexities of trying to relate a Derridean problematic of writing to the various things that Wittgenstein, Austin, and Cavell are up to.[8] The present investigation does not directly pursue these relationships. But the pressure of Derrida's writing, along with that of Lacan, seems to be operating on Cavell's work in that period. My reason for not explicitly addressing Derrida's work at this juncture is twofold: (1) It would take almost a chapter of its own to do justice both to Derrida's work and to the great differences between him and Cavell, even at the points where their paths cross or seem to cross. (2) What I am engaged in doing seems to me an important prior step to any comparison between the problematics of Cavell and Derrida.[9] In particular, I am pursuing and radicalizing the idea of the voice throughout Cavell's work, and specifically in the appeals to ordinary speech. Without this more radical problematic of the voice and a deeper sense of its conviction to Wittgenstein, the comparisons between Derrida and Cavell, or, for that matter, between Derrida and Wittgenstein, are bound to be pretty flat.

It is worth acknowledging that it is at least in part from reading Derrida that one becomes sensitive to the more metaphysical potentialities of the voice. The idea of voice can indeed be used to suppress and to redistribute the values of "difference" and of particular differences. Furthermore, as Cavell acknowledges in the crucial passage from *A Pitch of Philosophy*, quoted near the beginning of chapter 1, the impulse to metaphysics certainly draws us to make use of an idea of voice as a source of the meaningful differences of language. No doubt this voice is thought of in the first place as a kind of ideal inner voice, the organ by which the mind inwardly articulates its meanings to itself and assigns them to the hitherto meaningless word-sounds.

If the voice is thus conceptualized as the source of these differences of sense, then it is being understood as an aspect of the mind's capacity for a unified understanding of itself and its place in the world. Such a capacity must be ideal and it must exist prior to any differences of meaning within an actual language. The demand that the mind be intelligible to itself, before the existence of any actual language, is a metaphysical demand. The corresponding demand for a voice that is prior to any actual voice using any actual words is also part of this metaphysical conception of language. Inevitably, the actual voices and actual uses of words will be compared unfavorably to the ideal voice and its perfect intelligibility to itself.

The idea of an ideal organ that assigns meaning to its words is an idea of something that does not need words to understand itself or converse with itself. This is also the direction in which a philosophical mind is inclined to find any actual words to be imprecise, crude, or otherwise insufficient. Within what we call the Anglo-American tradition (including Frege and the early Wittgenstein), the response to this sense of the insufficiency of language has often been to point toward the possibility of constructing an ideal language. And the precision and fixity of that ideal is usually found approximated in the idea of a kind of writing or, anyway, a kind of notation. It has been some time—perhaps more than a century— since the idea of the voice *explicitly* captured for the Anglo-American tradition the metaphysical aspects of the mind's relation to language and the world. This is precisely part of Cavell's point in relation to the Derridean problematic: to put it in the form of a crude but still useful reminder: Frege is not Husserl. And working to overturn the metaphysical residues and inheritances in the one will not look or sound the same as similar criticisms aimed at the other. (These remarks do not yet touch the question of what becomes of the voice in earlier metaphysical traditions or impulses—for instance, in the question of how we imagine the work of Descartes' *cogito*.)

Looking in a different direction, I note that for sympathetic readers of Cavell, the ideal voice that metaphysics conjures up is uncomfortably close to the voice of the lyric poem that I singled out for attention in chapter 1. There Cavell's discussion associated the voice with the possibility of voicing something, of summoning the resources of the self and its situation in order to *mean* some passage of words as a passage of a particular mind. Indeed, one might feel that the picture invoked is of the voice breathing life into the otherwise dead words on the page. And this picture does indeed run a kind of metaphysical risk. Perhaps, however, it is the power of the lyric that engages us in this adventure.

Like certain kinds of philosophical thought about limits, the power of certain lines of poetry releases us from at least the sense of our confinement in the conventional structures of language. We find ourselves delivered over to what are apparently the most individual possibilities of meaning something, the bare possibility of saying something not backed by our ordinary resources. If this reception of poetry releases us from the holds of private meaning, it does so by leaving us more completely and transparently where it finds us: in the straits of our deepest privacies and solitudes.

No doubt the breath of difference between the lyrical and the metaphysical is a cold breath indeed. Thinking one is in a position to tell such differences is to come close to what one might call the metaphysical sublime. But there can still be differences between the metaphysical voice, which presents itself as *assigning* its transparent meaning to the syllables it will henceforth use, and the voice of the lyric poem, which does not assign its meanings but rather finds them. In finding them, the voice finds itself, in the specific syllables on which it has already been disposed. Cavell is bound to maintain our access to an idea of a source—some empirical origin of some aspect of meaning—that will be characterized as a "function of the voice."

Thus at the moment in which the idea of recovering the voice is coming to the fore as an explicit characterization of the goal and practices of Cavell's philosophizing with ordinary language, the idea of voice is beset on several sides at once. Derrida's emphasis on his version of the metaphysical voice and its suppression of something called writing seems to me to have undeniably provoked reminders and anxieties about the misuses and distortions of the voice, even as deconstruction proposed an analysis and a therapy for metaphysics that was not obviously usable within English-speaking philosophy.

But this encounter came at a moment when Cavell was still not quite ready to claim a perspicuous knowledge of the ways in which the voice functioned:

> I am prepared, or prepared to get prepared, to regard this sorting out [of the voice and of writing] as a further stage of intellectual adventure, for certainly I do not claim [it] is amply clear *why* the procedures of ordinary language philosophy strike me (and not me alone, I believe) as functions of voice, nor clear what voice is felt to contrast with; nor do I claim that this function cannot be interpreted as an effect of what might be seen as writing. What I claim is that no such interpretation will be of the right thing from my point of view unless it accounts for the *fact* that the appeal to the ordinary, as an indictment of metaphysics, strikes one, and should strike one, as an appeal to the voice. [*Themes*, 48–49.]

I don't insist on the exact dating of this stratum of Cavell's thought, but I know of no moment earlier than this in which he so nakedly lays out the idea of the philosophical appeals to the ordinary as aimed at recovering the voice. It is an important piece of confirmation of the story that I have been telling.

Cavell was struck by the sense that the appeals to ordinary language appealed to his voice *before* he could say why those appeals made just that impression. The impression created by these appeals was at work in him before he was able to characterize it. This may also say something about how, in general, those appeals to the ordinary come to have their effect on us. But in any case, the passage from Cavell confirms my sense of the difficulty we have in describing precisely how it is the *voice* that we invoke when we appeal to ordinary speech.

I mentioned Cavell's encounters with Derrida's work (and with his enormous influence in American departments of literature) as a source of pressure on Cavell to make more explicit the ideas of voice that he was relying on. But there is a danger in underestimating the inner pressure of Cavell's long preparation and gradual elaboration of the practices and the idea of the voice. Even in this study, I have traced only four or five of the strands that were thus elaborated in the course of the twenty years between the publication of his dissertation and the publication of its descendant *The Claim of Reason* in 1979. These internal elaborations and progressions released pressures of their own, which may well have been part of what precipitated Cavell's encounters with Derrida. As we shall shortly see, Cavell's progress toward the voice was already leading him to confront certain questions about the writing of philosophy and what he would come to call the problematic of writing "as such."

One type of pressure seems to derive from his efforts to locate Emerson and Thoreau as "underwriting" the procedures of Austin and Wittgenstein. What their writing underwrites, however, turns out to be most immediately not the appeal to the voice or to the ordinariness of our speech. What Emerson and Thoreau are in search of is rather the proximity or neighborhood of the ordinary world. But to speak of the ordinary world in this context is just to speak of the world that our ordinary speech is getting away from. The ordinary world is not one world among the possible worlds but the one aspect of the world that ordinarily shows itself to us, the one we grasp or fail to grasp in our words. The therapy of Wittgenstein invites us to lead an utterance "back" to the ordinary use that is its home, back to the world as it is for the most part touched by our words. In such ordinary uses, our words recover the life that they lose in the act of philosophizing.

Emerson and Thoreau exhibit an orientation somewhat different than Wittgenstein's toward the life of our words and toward the "home" that our words are bound to. Their writing dramatizes a different loss, or a different sense of that loss. If Wittgenstein enacts the moments in which our words begin to get away from us in the act of philosophizing, Emerson is more likely to be found dramatizing the moments in which our words withdraw from us. Or perhaps it is some nameless others who have withdrawn our words from the circulation we had wished for: So, as in "Self-Reliance," "Every word they say chagrins us."

Wittgenstein invites us to accept the rebuke implicit in discovering that we have to get our words "back" from their metaphysical flight. It is at least analogous to a classical philosophical rebuke, directed both to our ignorance of a threat to the meaningfulness of our words and, at the same time, to our false sense of knowing the ideals to which our words are tending. Thoreau and Emerson dramatize their sense that we have gotten away from what is worthwhile in any of our utterances. We are equally out of touch with the value that our words point to and the value of uttering these words, of talking with one another, and of speech itself. For Wittgenstein it is our failure to acknowledge the flights of philosophy within us that makes us deaf to the emptiness in our words. Philosophers no longer have to do much to escape the messiness of ordinary words. Nor do they seem to experience much of a trauma in the necessity of repressing the fact that our words must be *spoken*. Most philosophers nowadays seem to *begin* with a reasonably successful achievement of that forgetfulness. On the whole they have managed to forget that there was anything of interest in our words to be forgotten.

In Thoreau and Emerson, we can perhaps still talk to each other, but our expressions of the things we most ardently profess have become dull to us: "There are such words as joy and sorrow, but they are only the burden of a psalm, sung with a nasal twang, while we believe in the ordinary and the mean."[10] Thoreau claims that by withdrawing to Walden he has gone far enough away to be able to hear and read words that are uttered in sincerity. This implies pretty directly that we cannot hear such words from where we are now living. Indeed, Thoreau seems to suggest that we cannot even understand the words that express the life of our own needs:

> It would seem as if the very language of our parlors would lose all its nerve and degenerate into *palaver* wholly, our lives pass at such remoteness from its symbols, and its metaphors and tropes are necessarily so far-fetched, through slides and dumb waiters, as it were; in other words, the parlor is so far from the kitchen and workshop. The dinner even is only the parable of a dinner, commonly. [*Walden*, 220.]

To say that this insight implies that we are out of touch with our words would be to put it mildly. One of the defining functions of language, in Thoreau's vision, is the translation of need into the possibility of its satisfaction. This vision stands next door to the vision of language as the introduction of the unappeasable demands of our desires. Beyond this, Thoreau understands the very volatility of our words as furthering our craving for reality. The feast of words (as Thrasymachus called it) is neither the means of an ultimate satisfaction nor the grounds of a necessary defeat. In Thoreau's more apocalyptic moments, the question of language becomes still more urgent: If we cannot say what we are consuming, how shall we find the words by which to grasp what is consuming us?

Given the extremity of Thoreau's vision of what is happening to us and our words, why does he imagine that his words will reach us or touch us? His solution is not so much to bring words back from their metaphysical awayness as to bring them down from their metaphorical aloofness. He wants to summon some portion of the reader to some other kind of awakening. The first step of our awakening will be to realize that Thoreau is continually withdrawing his voice from his text, that is to say, from his readers. He will not contribute the life of his words or his life in the woods to the degenerative politeness of what we call our living rooms. He withdraws from our "withdrawing" rooms.

Cavell puts it like this:

> Thoreau's withdrawal is more elaborately dramatized [than Emerson's], its rebuke more continuous. In my book on *Walden,* I find that the writer who inhabits it asserts the priority of writing over speaking (at least for the present) in order to maintain silence, where this means first of all to withhold his voice, his consent, from his society. Hence the entire book is an act of civil disobedience, a confrontation which takes the form of a withdrawal. But silence has many forces, as in such a sentence as this: "You need only sit still long enough in some attractive spot in the woods that all its inhabitants may exhibit themselves to you by turns." [*Themes,* 50.]

I take it that Cavell has rightly discerned Thoreau's equation of sitting still in the woods with maintaining a kind of silence in the words of one's text. Then the final sentence suggests a path from the immediate context of withdrawing the voice and withdrawing to Walden to a still more radical sense of textuality. The implied point of the withdrawal is a kind of seduction, a seduction of stillness. Here "stillness" implies not only a kind of silence regarded as a withholding of speech but also silence as quietness. Such stillness is what we might characterize as the absence of unnecessary movement in our words. The withholding of false activity in *Walden* is a version of arriving at his true necessities or necessaries of life. Overcoming the bustle and clamor of human neediness in word and deed grants *Walden* a kind of temporary peace, a truce within its restless strife with language. Provoked by this self-restraint and lured by the promise of this quietness, it is the latest inhabitant of the woods— the reader—who does the turning and undergoes the exposure and the exhibition.

In *The Senses of Walden,* Cavell put the point about Thoreau's withdrawal like this:

> The writer keeps my choices in front of me, the ones I am not making and the ones I am. This makes me nervous and wretched. My choices appear as curiosities, and to be getting the better of me. Curiosity grows with every new conjecture we find confirmed in the words. It seems all but an accident that we should discover what they mean. This becomes a mood of our act of reading altogether: it is an accident, utterly contingent, that we should be present at these words on which he had staked his presence; and we feel this as the words' indifference to us, their disinterest in whether we choose to stay with them or not. Every new clarity makes the writer's existence obscurer to us—that is, his willingness to remain obscure. How can he apparently so completely not care, or have made up his mind, that we may not understand? This feeling may begin our almost unbearable sense of his isolation. Did he not feel lonesome? We are asking now. And then we find ourselves, perhaps, alone with a book in our hands, words on a page, at a distance. [*Senses,* 49–50.]

The passage from *Senses* is less explicit than the later essay about the seductiveness of the writer's withdrawal. But Cavell is more explicit about how the writer of *Walden* accomplishes the turning away of its words from the reader. What he is about to characterize as representative of the stillness and self-containment of a text (indeed the stillness in the very nature of a certain kind of textuality) is here characterized as the writer's obscurity. The writer's obscurity is not a matter of propounding obscure thoughts in obscure words. By means of his words, he withdraws his *need* to be understood by us. In our devotion to the kind of author who courts our favor, we read this withdrawal as the author's obscurity. What is obscured, according to Cavell, is the writer's *self*, most especially its need of praise and of being understood.

Cavell's later amplification suggests that we experience Thoreau's absence from his words as a *withholding* of his voice. This withholding is not an extirpation of the voice, and the result should not be characterized as being voiceless: Keeping still is not the same as being mute. The withdrawal of voice is achieved by means of the voice: it occurs as a mode of the voice's detachment from things and people. Such writing must manifest a particular mode of not caring whether it is being read, a mode that is very close to antipathy. The writer's voice must somehow exhibit not a lack of desire that we read his words but a lack of need. The text affects not to need this specific mode of reception at the moment of the initial textual encounter, and especially not at the moments when the reader most manifests a desire for the writer's complicity. What the reader really wants is not to possess the voice of the text but to be *needed* by that voice. The wish to cling to that voice and to preserve it is a thinly disguised version of the wish to be its indispensable audience.

Overcoming this mode of the reader's attachment to the text and, most especially, to the voice within the text is a major goal of the methods of reading discussed in chapters 4 and 5. These themes will get taken even further when Cavell takes up the question of the text's countertransference to its readers, an explicit development and inversion of his constant theme that we learn to read by accepting our exposure to being read. I might anticipate this particular reversal of the reader's need to work through and to learn from his or her transference to the text by remarking that the text has to learn to recognize its wish to be needed. In a modern or belatedly Romantic age, this wish will most often be apprehended as a wish that the voice in the text be *welcomed* or otherwise greeted by a grateful voice. But there is little reason to think that such corresponding voices will be immediately forthcoming.

C avell takes seriously Thoreau's antic remark, "I do not suppose that I have attained to obscurity" (*Walden*, 290). A little later in his commentary, Cavell will take this remark to refer to the obscurity—i.e., to the darkening and disappearance—of the "I," relating it ultimately to the paradox of self-knowledge: "I must disappear in order that the search for myself be successful" (*The Claim of Reason*, 352). Why should someone who knows this about the self and its obscurities choose to enact so unceasingly the appearance and disappearance of the writer's self?

Most immediately, Cavell stages this disappearance as the disappearance of the writer from the page. At one level, he depicts the reader's anxiety about understanding Thoreau's words as the other side of Thoreau's own willingness to be misunderstood, or to be understood only as the consequence of a kind of happy accident. How can Thoreau live with the knowledge that the reader encounters his words as a series of contingencies? Cavell wants us to see that Thoreau experiences his reception of his *own* words as just such a series of contingencies (which Thoreau, however, calls opportunities). But then Cavell wants us to go on to ask: How does anyone manage that fate as a writer or reader or speaker of words?

At another level, this distance and coolness toward the reader—a certain willingness to leave her alone—bespeaks one form of a writer's confidence, a willingness to let the words do the talking. (Still later, Cavell will take this coolness as a version of what Emerson and Nietzsche call the writer's neutrality, describing it as a state one must somehow return to.) At a third level, however, Cavell points to a risk within the withholding of the author's voice. Since the achievement of this voice was the very means by which the author's presence is felt and by which the author's work becomes knowable as the accomplishment of *that author*, the withdrawal of the voice is sometimes experienced as its disappearance. And surely it is not merely the reader alone who experiences this potential disappearance as the possibility of a crisis.

Recognizing these possibilities about Thoreau's work creates a sense of alarm in me, one that seems to emanate from the heart of Cavell's own project. I don't find it to be particularly comforting that Thoreau is also one of the inhabitants of the woods, and one of the first readers of *Walden*. Why should I expose myself as one of the company that this misery apparently seeks? What is the gain? What gets us beyond the mutual exhibition of our private anxieties or other discomforts? Again, I am not sure how to take it, when Cavell discovers that Thoreau appears to have anticipated me in my reluctance to grant him too much:

> I believe that what so saddens the reformer is not his sympathy with his fellows in distress, but . . . is his private ail. Let this be righted, let the spring come to him, the morning rise over his couch, and he will forsake his generous companions without apology. [*Walden*, 70.]

It is one thing to learn not to confuse the exchanging of gossip about our personal pain and discomfort with a genuine sharing of sympathies. It is quite another thing to abandon the hope that the book we are reading will contain some moment of genuine sympathy. And surely we are sometimes entitled to the writer's sympathy for the condition we are actually in, as opposed to the condition he hopes to wake us up to.

It seems to me that Cavell is deliberately cultivating our feeling of alarm at *Walden* and at *The Senses of Walden*, thwarting the search for sympathy and comfort that might be found in Thoreau's voice. The crisis Cavell discerns—and to some extent undergoes—is not merely a personal crisis and not merely cosmic and not purely political. In a long passage whose rhythms show more than a slight acquaintance with the Christian side of the Bible and the literature of the sermon, Cavell writes:

> We have heard it said, "We shall all stand before the judgment seat of Christ . . . every tongue shall give account of himself to God" (Romans 14: 10–12). But *Walden* shows that we *are* there; every tongue has confessed what it can; we have heard everything there is to hear. [*Senses*, 30.]

The mood in which we feel that we have heard everything there is to hear is not the same as the mood in which we claim to have heard everything there is to say.

Most particularly, when Cavell is emphasizing that we have heard what there is to hear, he is not claiming to have heard it all, certainly not to know it all. He is claiming, or getting ready to claim, that no one is in a position to *tell* anyone anything about any of this. Here we recognize a descendant of our friend the old mole of the Wittgensteinian burrow. How can we tell anyone what everyone already knows? When, if ever, are we in a position to announce such general facts of nature or history? At this moment, Cavell's position should generate more anxiety than Wittgenstein's. For Cavell is questioning not merely whether something could get told (e.g., as a piece of information or in the form of a proposition) but whether anything of this nature could ever get *taught* at all. It is not just that if we tried to advance a philosophical thesis, everyone would agree. If we try to teach what needs to be taught, everyone will have heard it before.

The stakes seem to get even higher: How are we to learn to read a book

s as an "accounting," as opposed to a recounting or a narrative, and he
o calls it a kind of scripture. We need to guard against the possibility
assimilating too seamlessly the idea of composing a scripture with
avell's later idea of a kind of redemptive reading.

Cavell may have discovered descendants of this idea of scripture in
e idea of a therapeutic text, or a therapeutic reading. But the composing
e idea of a scripture cannot be translated, without remainder, into a model of
f a scripture cannot be translated. Cavell's interpretation of the return of the voice to
herapeutic reading. Cavell's interpretation of the return of the voice to
philosophy as a *recovery* of the voice, as if to life, has misled some good
eaders. (I take this up at greater length in chapter 1 and in chapter 4, in
elation to Stephen Mulhall's *Stanley Cavell.*) Where the idea of writing
nation's scripture goes beyond the idea of enacting the possibility of a
herapeutic text, of redemption from the kind of bondage that is enacted
nd emblematized in a text, Cavell is quite clear that the power to compose a nation's scripture in Thoreau's sense contains not only a power of
ife and freedom but the power of prophecy and death.

Such indecorous and unsecular moments in Cavell's work are good-
humored and chastened compared to what Thoreau permits himself. Cavell catches him out enacting something very like the circumcision of the
heart, carried on by something like a natural fact ("glinting on both surfaces"). Thoreau depicts the moment as a kind of death: "and so you conclude your mortal career"—or at least as a willingness for death. But he
exhibits the moment as a kind of return to life.

To follow Cavell's path away from *Walden* will be to follow him in
relinquishing that dream of writing a scripture. But the residue of that
dream, of possessing the power of life and death in words, will remain
even after we have taken our path away from *The Senses of Walden.*

> Writing—heroic writing, the writing of a nation's scripture—must as-
> sume the conditions of language as such; re-experience, as it were, the fact
> that such a thing as language exists at all and assume responsibility for it—
> find a way to acknowledge it—until the nation is capable of serious speech
> again.

This is a little closer to home, and this aspect of the scriptural is a little
more amenable to life after the woods. The phrase "as it were" is meant
to leave room for something like a Wittgensteinian reminder that we can
only use language "full-blown." There is a fairly straightforward and important sense in which we cannot use words "literally" to place ourselves
at the origin of language. So, too, we cannot use our current capacities for
meaningfulness to arrive at a criterion for meaningfulness that would
operate, ideally, in advance of the existence of any empirical language.

about a book that tells us there is nothing left to *say* to one another? How
are we to learn to read a book by a writer who already thinks that philosophy contains the craving to inform someone of something that no one
is in a position to inform anyone of (e.g., that the world exists and that
other humans exist in it)? It is therefore not so surprising that throughout *The Senses of Walden* these two questions are deeply intertwined:
What now remains for us as writers to work on, and what now remains
for us as philosophers to question?

For Cavell these questions are also a kind of figure for the further
question of what remains to us as citizens. How are we to prepare to leave
this book, where that turns out to mean both the book that Cavell is reading and the one he is writing?

The passage just cited continues:

> There were prophets but there is no Zion; knowing that, Jesus ful-
> filled them, but the kingdom of heaven is not entered into; knowing that,
> the Founding Fathers brought both testaments to this soil, and there is
> no America; knowing that, Jonathan Edwards helped bring forth a Great
> Awakening, and we are not awake. The experiment of man ("We are the
> subjects of an experiment" [v, 10]) has failed. Not that any of man's dreams
> may not come to pass. But there is absolutely no more to be *said* about
> them. What is left to us is the accounting. Not a recounting, of tales or
> news; but a document, with each word a warning and a teaching; a deed,
> with each word an act. [*Senses*, 30.]

That the hopes and fears of Christianity, of the Enlightenment, and of
religious and social revolution are met in the experiments of a single text
and the voices of a single writer is evidently not a fantasy confined to
Thoreau alone. Still, the fact that certain books are deeds and that certain
deeds are testaments does not require that we take the authors of such
books as imagining that they are composing a gospel.

Here the fact of composing a deed or a testament does not imply, all
by itself, that Cavell takes himself to be composing a scripture, in addition
to Thoreau's. What *testament* means first of all is a promise made in view
of the death of the promiser. What is at stake—or what is about to be at
stake—is the linking of the issue of the author's withdrawal from the
reader to the author's departure. Such an idea of an account, like Cavell's
idea of a scripture, links the idea of objectivity to the idea of death.

Getting ready to end the book, Cavell writes this:

> Leaving *Walden*, like leaving Walden, is as hard, is perhaps the same, as
> entering it. I have implied that the time of crisis depicted in this book is not
> alone a private one, and not wholly cosmic. It is simultaneously a crisis in

the nation's life. And the nation too must die down to the root if it is to continue to recognize and neighbor itself.

Since it is, at that moment of writing, Cavell himself who is engaged in leaving *Walden*, the passage extends the crisis at Walden to the time and even perhaps the structure of Cavell's book. If the book is fairly muted about Cavell's private anxieties, the sense of connection between his crisis and the nation's is all but ubiquitous.

Moreover, the book's account of its own crisis sustains an intensity and a passion that is only rarely equaled in his other books. Those who take it for granted that Cavell's voice is pretty much always full of a sense of seriousness and crisis are unlikely to hear how singular these passages are. The passages I have in mind—including a handful from *Must We Mean What We Say?* and *The World Viewed*—were all composed in the late 1960s and the early 1970s. I doubt that one can separate Cavell's sense of his own genesis as a writer from his awareness of the war in Vietnam or of Nixon's efforts to stay in power at the expense of the American Constitution. Whichever way you turn, toward philosophy or toward literature or toward politics, part of the crisis that becomes audible is Cavell's anxiety about the nature of the voice.

Should anyone wish to confirm my specific conjecture that Cavell found himself representing a certain crisis about politics as a crisis of voice and voices, I cite the following passage. It comes from the cover letter to Alceste, another in the series of retrospective glances at the situation in which he wrote the essay on *Lear*, which was itself completed only a few years before he began teaching and studying *Walden* in the summer of 1969.

> Evidently I was going around in those days, as one did, subject to fits of hearing screams in my ears. Others sometimes may have thought me mad; I sometimes thought they were driving me mad. [*Themes*, 104.]

That the ear was occupied, in those days, with the cries and screams and whispers of political pain and rage is hardly news. And neither is the fact that we are often still thus occupied or preoccupied. I leave open the question whether Cavell's thought of madness stems primarily from the fear that he cannot hear himself think or from the sense that he can no longer distinguish his own voice from the screaming.

There might be various reasons and causes for such anxieties on the part of the empirical Stanley Cavell. That these fears are becoming some kind of an issue for the writer that Cavell was becoming is better discerned as the fears are filtered through a passage from *The Senses of Walden*:

> . . . [A]s once before, there is an unprecedented din [   ] world. Everyone is saying, *and anyone can hear* [my e   ] is the new world; that we are the new men; that the e   ] again; that the past is to be cast off like a skin; that we   ] children to see again; that every day is the first day   ] America is Eden. So how can a word get through whose   ] do not understand a word of it all? Or rather, that the   ] understand it is insane, and we are trying to buy and bu   ] heaven; that we have failed; that the present is a task and   ] period of America's privileged history . . . [*Senses*, 59].

These are some of the reasons why the writer of *Wald[ ]* taken a greater than normal burden of patience and of "[ ] sion." This passage adds to the echo of the failed voi[ ] Founding Fathers, and Jonathan Edwards, the cacophon[ ] rary prophecies—presumably closer relatives to the cr[ ] Cavell was hearing. Again, the passage suggests the fear [ ] voice will be drowned out, lost in the din of voices or i[ ] prophecies. And, again, I discern the writer's sense of t[ ] exposing his voice to the voices of others. How the need fo[ ] points us toward the question of writing by way of withdra[ ] is a good question.

In our present circumstances, the presence of the voice [ ] ambiguous or unmitigated good. My arrival at my voic[ ] (necessarily, methodologically) to the voices of others. A[ ] withhold my voice will suggest my complicity in the voices [ ] exposed to. This danger is something like the reverse of [ ] that my expressing an inner voice will implicate those read[ ] spond to it.

This complicity may also be created by the sheer fact that I [ ] to speak in a certain voice, that I am speaking at all. Thore[ ] desire to speak somewhere without bounds, like a man speakin[ ] Did someone imagine that this was a harmless desire, perhaps a[ ] a more human intimacy or a greater openness of expression?[ ] tainly a human enough desire, this wish to speak to humans [ ] declare that I desire to speak to humans, or for that matter that [ ] speak *for* humans, to brag for humanity, it surely does not fol[ ] I am feeling entirely confident of my own humanness, much [ ] humanity.

As I have been suggesting, Cavell depicts this withdrawal of [ ] the other side of a certain ambition in Thoreau's prose. Cavell chara[ ]

Why does Cavell want to act as if it could be otherwise?—as if we could do mythically, in writing and reading, what the skeptic in us wants to do literally? Or, if this is an accurate reading of Thoreau, why is Cavell drawn to a writer who is drawn to such projects?

Cavell goes on to cite three features of language that such writing must, as he puts it, "assume responsibility" for. It is as if the writing is paying off a debt to the language it lives upon.

> . . . 1) that every mark of a language means something in the language, one thing rather than another; that a language is totally, systematically meaningful; 2) that words and their orderings are meant by human beings, that they contain (or conceal) their beliefs, express (or deny) their convictions; and 3) that the saying of something when and as it is said is as significant as the meaning and ordering of the words said. [*Senses,* 34.]

Given the phases of Cavell's writing we have been working our way through, we can characterize the second and third of these features of language as functions of the voice. The first feature, the systematic and total meaningfulness of language, is not thus readily nameable. The various related tensions between voice and the appeal to voice, between voice and criteria, and between voice and method, here become extreme. The sense of our unsystematic approach to a perspicuous, if irregular, insight into the meaningfulness of words and grammar becomes a vision of the systematic potential of our language to mean something rather than something else, at any time and, essentially, in any place. There is a match between this capacity for the systematic meaningfulness of a written notation and the possibility that a writer will use some stretch of these marks of difference to express or to deny the differences that he or she has come to comprehend.

Here again it is not that hard to see that some aspect of voice is on Cavell's mind in this passage. He goes on to speak in these terms:

> Until we are capable of serious speech again—i.e. are reborn, are men "[speaking] in a waking moment, to men in their waking moments" (XVIII,6)—our words do not carry our conviction, we cannot fully back them, because either we are careless of our convictions or think we haven't any, or imagine they are inexpressible. They are merely unutterable. . . .
> Until we can speak again, our lives and our language betray one another; we can grant to neither of them their full range and autonomy; they mistake their definitions of one another. [34.]

Cavell's vision or fantasy of the total meaningfulness of marking is meant to create a place for withdrawal and recovery. We are to marshal our resources of conviction and expression, and locate, if possible, the requisite human circle in which these resources will be appreciated. Such writing is meant as a prelude to our awakened capacity for serious utterance, and also a possible cause of it. The deferral of speech in such writing can now be described as a withdrawal of voice to a place or text of recovery. Presumably, the hope for the withdrawal and recovery of the voice is a significant part of what produces the hope and the fantasy of a transparently meaningful prose—of a mode of writing that can assume the debts of language, in the absence of a responsive circle of human voices and companionship.

It is also a fantasy of writing as giving an account in a perfected notation, and perhaps also a fantasy as the process by which the notation gets perfected:

> This is what those lists of numbers, calibrated to the half cent, mean in *Walden*. . . . [T]hey are emblems of what the writer wants from writing, as he keeps insisting on calling his book an *account*. . . . A true mathematical reckoning of the sort he shows requires that every line be a mark of honesty, that the lines be complete, omitting no expense or income, and that there be no mistake in the computation. Spoken words are calculated to deceive. How are written words different? The mathematical emblem embodies two ways. First, it is part of a language which exists primarily as notation; its point is not the fixing of a spoken language, which had preceded it, *but the fixing of steps, which can thereby be remarked*. Second, the notation works only when every mark within means something, in its look and in its sequence. Among written works of art, only of poetry had we expected a commitment to total and transparent meaning, every mark bearing its brunt. [*Senses*, 30–31. The second emphasis is mine.]

That a notation that enables the systematic meaningfulness of marking is also a notation for the taking of steps associates writing *as such* with the idea of method. When the idea of "writing as such" is understood as taking on these burdens of language, we have reached one of the crucial junctures of Cavell's work. Here the work of the writer crosses over into the workings of philosophical method. The concept of a writer's inmost exploration of the capacities of language constitutes the clearest and most open path on which he may be followed.

Much later, in "Declining Decline," Cavell picks up such an idea of method as part of Wittgenstein's ambition for the "perspicuousness" of a presentation. He characterizes Wittgenstein as harboring a wish that his writing should capture certain features of a mathematical proof. Most particularly, Cavell is depicting a sort of "movement" that takes place in front of our eyes, wholly open to view. In both Wittgenstein and Thoreau, one might characterize a certain wish that the voice, with all its potential undertones and obscurities, should give way to the openness of method. (*This New Yet Unapproachable America*, 16.)

Here is a last indication that the crises of voice are on Cavell's mind. These issues of voice are not quite the same as the issues of "cacophony" that led Cavell into his first pronouncement about "writing as such":

> America's best writers have offered one another the shock of recognition but not the faith of friendship, not daily belief. Perhaps this is why, or it is because, their voices seem to destroy one another. So they destroy one another for us. How is a tradition to come out of that? [*The Senses of Walden*, 32.]

This little passage occurs in the midst of reflections that continue to blossom in Cavell's later work. Not only does the passage stand at the gate of the questions of writing as such and of writing scripture, but it helps lead him to the question "Why has America never expressed itself philosophically?" (33).

Other readers have commented, with varying degrees of hopefulness and self-congratulation, on the proximity of the doubt about philosophy to the question he goes on to ask about the philosophical potential in other forms of American writing: "Or has it [expressed itself philosophically]—in the metaphysical riot of its greatest literature?" (33). Some may even find in this concatenation of questions an anticipatory echo of the now nearly legendary parting question of *The Claim of Reason*: "Can philosophy become literature and still know itself?"

But these particular questions of Cavell's occur in the text as if prompted precisely by an experience of the mutual destruction of American voices—an experience, moreover, apparently set off by Cavell's having noticed that Thoreau was engaged in the "nameless marking" of Emerson. That is to say, Thoreau's withdrawal of voice is meant to load his writing with the power of life and death, in particular the power of life and death over the most powerful voice he knows—whether that voice is to be taken as literary or as philosophical or as a token of some other region of connection. On a more prosaic level, Thoreau's willingness to mark out Emerson (and presumably Emerson's voice) for safekeeping also bespeaks Thoreau's unwillingness or inability to name Emerson *explicitly* anywhere in *Walden*.

Expressing one's hopes and wishes cannot provide a satisfying answer to such questions about voices and generations and about the mutual voicing of philosophy and literature. For how else could an expression of hope for the survival of my voice exist, except as a further exposure of my voice to the risks of being ignored or damaged? Is there another, perhaps safer, way to find one's voice in philosophy? I mean, for instance, other than by getting out of earshot of at least the more disreputable voices of literature?

I will come back to some questions about philosophy and literature and about the destruction or damage to the voices in chapter 4. For the moment, I take it that I have sufficiently exposed the darker edges around Cavell's project to recover the voice. Indeed, I have pushed the question of voice as close to the question of Cavell's private crises of voice as I feel justified in doing.

What I want to pursue now is the suggestion that Cavell goes on to make in "Politics as Opposed to What?," immediately following his depicting the philosophy of ordinary language as aimed at recoveries of the voice and his depiction of Thoreau as withholding or withdrawing the voice from the words and other matter of his pages, and from the grasp of the reader. It is the idea and the practices of what Cavell calls the "containment" of voice within a certain representative kind of text, a containment that the text enacts as a way of enacting its own textuality.

With this notion of containing the voice we have arrived at another crossroads, related to the place where a certain mode of writing crosses over into the possibility of a method. Investigating Cavell's depictions of Thoreau's withdrawal of the voice has led us, at least on the surface, away from the questions of skepticism and of *that* path to the banishing of the voice. Correspondingly, I had earlier been investigating the voice in Cavell as the source and goal of the philosophical appeal to what we say in ordinary words. Here the voice is a kind of doppelgänger of the concept of method, containing the thought that for a method to exist it must be employed. And if a method is well employed, then surely the method and its employers are motivated and interested, and the fact that the method exists to be employed can come to have its own not quite autonomous interest.

I have been following Cavell into a different region of the voice, drawn there by the different registers of voice that he explores in *The Claim of Reason;* by his characterization of Thoreau's alignment of voice and consent; and by the overlapping alignment of voice as the twin of writing. Cavell lands hard on the idea that if the voice is something a writer knows how to produce, it is also something he knows how to withdraw. Here the voice begins as the medium of a speech that we can no longer tolerate, and then turns into the shadowy appeal of a writing that has withdrawn the voice in order to preserve it from further harm.

Whether we have in view the voice as the goal and medium of the methodical appeal to the ordinary or the voice as the path to a kind of stillness in a written text, Cavell's sense of the voice has drawn us into a crisis. It seems to me that this crisis of voice was also affecting the project of undermining skepticism's repression of the voice. Indeed, the crises of voice, whatever the exact etiology, seem to have been precipitated internally precisely at the moment where the process of revising and concluding *The Claim of Reason* became deferred by the inspiration of the voices that produced *The Senses of Walden*.

I mean this claim to depend on nothing more than textual evidence. Whatever the private crises that Cavell was undergoing in those years, they were transposed into *The Senses of Walden*, into the revisions of *The Claim of Reason*, and into the blue guitars of film. Anyway, as Cavell put it:

> The writer has secrets to tell which can only be told to strangers. The secrets are not his, and they are not the confidences of others. They are secrets because few are anxious to know them; all but one or two wish to remain foreign. Only those who recognize themselves as strangers can be told them, because those who think themselves familiars think they have already heard what the writer is saying. They will not understand his speaking in confidence. [92–93.]

Cavell is doubling back on Thoreau's special gifts for friendship and his special demands on his friends. He is also indirectly commenting on the passage where Thoreau identifies his readers as fellow-travelers, strangers bound together by the crossing of their paths and by their ability to share in each other's anxiety and sense of loss.

These pages of Cavell's run criss-cross over the routes on which he and Thoreau have been tracking their (own) anxieties. At this stage of the book, Cavell goes beyond speaking *for* Thoreau and seems sometimes to speak from within the pages of *Walden*, even in Thoreau's own words. He is certainly not the first critic to reach the point of speaking for the text that he is writing about. And he is also not the first to insert his own voice among the voices that his acts of criticism have activated or animated. And we have seen already that Thoreau is quite capable of invoking a kind of confusion of identities or confusion of tongues between himself and past philosophers.

Cavell's crossing of Thoreau's tracks still awakens in me a sense of alarm, an alarm that does not seem to be merely an echo of *Walden*'s various efforts to get me going. The alarm that Cavell reawakens in our response to Thoreau becomes an alarm at Cavell's text. I think it is more than just the fear that one might still lose some sleep over American literature and politics. The careful circling of friendship and familiarity, the

strangeness in having to depend on the confidence of strangers, draws me
further into the circling of words and withdrawals. It does not so easily
relinquish me. Of course, such voices have their dangers. But there are
also dangers to philosophy and criticism that stem from the absence of
the voice, or even just from the unacknowledged wish for that absence.
The failure to find a way of speaking for yourself, within a field or within
a life, will also present its share of problems to the aspiring student.

My alarm is derived rather, it seems to me, from a sense of Cavell's
exposure in his voice and therefore throughout his writing. It is an exposure that was perhaps already present in the earlier essays, but his
writing now insists on it. (This is perhaps another side of what he calls
his being "unguarded.") I imagine I am not alone in having felt called
upon—and not all that obscurely—to protect this voice. Sometimes this
wish to protect takes the form of a kind of imitation, hence sometimes of
inadvertent parody. It can take the form of a wish to cover up the voice,
sometimes by defending it to others and sometimes by hiding it away
among a circle of like-minded and devoted listeners. Sometimes the circle
may get very small indeed.

Whatever private wishes are expressed in this need to protect or to
cover up Cavell's voice, the need creates some further issues about writing
and philosophy. Do I wish to cover the exposure of his voice because I am
contributing to philosophy's rejection of the voice? Or am I afraid of the
costs of the writer's exposure by means of his voice? For if I am exposed
to the writer's voice then, in Cavell's understanding, the writer is exposed
to my voice. And my voice is likely to be but half-expressed, and I will
probably feel for the most part inadequate to respond to my sense of what
I have heard. I am also likely to be unaware of my countervailing rage to
order, my wish to be the only singer of the world that I am learning to
behold. But where else has the voice learned of this wish, if not from
Cavell or Thoreau, or from a writer very much like them?

Without the work of *Walden*, these thoughts of voice would merely
be self-aggrandizing or mad. After the work of *Walden*, they seem dependent on *Walden*—or on Cavell. The philosophical suspense here lies not
in wondering whether these voices will drive us to distraction, but in
wondering whether we will manage to recover. There is little to be gained
in going mad for the sake of philosophy or for the sake of some continued
possibility of balancing private and public sanity. But there is a great deal
at risk in the path one takes back to the realm of more ordinary activities
and more balanced minds.

Someone might say, consolingly, "Never mind, we are not mad. We
are only doing philosophy." (I seem to remember a cartoon to that ef-

fect—drawn from one of Wittgenstein's minor aphorisms—posted on the door of the Philosophy Department library at Harvard.) Others might say, less ruefully and with somewhat greater distance, "These voices exist after all, primarily as modes of *writing*, as some kind of literature." It is relatively easy to keep these voices from spreading their contagion. You merely have to stop reading the books that contain them.

Suppose one thinks that what makes the voices into voices of philosophy is very nearly the same thing that makes them, potentially, voices of madness: an unlimited desire for the knowledge of others and of the world. Then in backing away from the brink that such reflections have led us to, we had better not deny the power of the voices that we have been led to hear. But can these voices (of humanness and inhumanness, politics and transgression, freedom and dictation) be linked back up to the ordinary voices that philosophy has turned away from and suppressed? Can these crises of voice really respond to the therapy of the everyday?

4

THE MODEL OF
READING

As if certain paths for philosophy . . . are always in danger of falling
into obscurity.
—Cavell, foreword, *The Claim of Reason*

From the Recovery of the Voice to the Model of Reading

I now turn to examine a central set of issues that attach to reading in Cavell's work. I begin by giving an account of the issues
that led to this emphasis on reading. The first sections of this chapter
continue the account presented in chapters 2 and 3. They also start the
process of reorienting the questions of skepticism and the voice toward
questions of reading and its various audiences. I then proceed to abstract
from Cavell's considerations of reading a model of philosophical method.
This model, constructed from elements of his various accounts of reading,
consists primarily in a series of what I call reversals: between the philosopher and the subject matter that he or she is engaged in reading; between
the philosopher and the actual, empirical readers encountering the text
that he is engaged in producing; and between the active and passive aspects of reading itself.

In the next chapter, I examine how this model of reading emerged
from within Cavell's own activities as a reader, especially as a reader of
Thoreau and Emerson. I then proceed to show how the workings of this
model have drawn Cavell into the exploration of unfamiliar regions of
philosophical writing, which are in turn connected to his conception of the
risks of philosophizing, not least the risks to the reader or the audience of
philosophy. These philosophical risks have implications for Cavell's approach to skepticism and for his appeals to the ordinary. Along the way, I

outline some of the consequences of the failure of most commentators to appreciate the presence of this model of reading in Cavell's work.

Turning my investigations toward questions of reading is partly a response to the explicit and thematic importance of the issue of reading in the work of Cavell's that follows the publication of *The Claim of Reason*. But partly I am responding to the increased range and power of Cavell's authorial voice and to some radical developments in his anatomy of skepticism. In these developments he found the freedom to pursue his interests, and those interests took many forms. For these and other reasons, the thread of Cavell's appeal to what we ordinarily say is no longer sufficient to guide us through the forests of his critical readings and philosophical reflections. A new way of modeling his approaches to philosophical method has become necessary.

The appeals to ordinary language remain active and vivid in Cavell's work in this period. But the philosophical force of these appeals is in effect more often than Cavell will now make explicit; there are fewer explicit appeals to what we ordinarily say, and fewer examples. For almost a decade after *The Claim of Reason*, until *Conditions Handsome and Unhandsome*, Cavell tends to subsume the appeals to ordinary language within a wider-ranging invocation of the ordinary and the investigation of its significance. The force of his ability to present such samples of the ordinary was inevitably somewhat diminished in this period.

Moreover, when we follow out Cavell's projects in this period, we see that he is involved in thinking through the nature and the authority of the appeals to ordinary speech. Previously his questioning of these central appeals had led him to question the significance of the fact that our ability to mean what we say is dependent on at least two quite different features of our situation: it depends on the ordinariness—the commonness—of the meanings and other resources of speech at our disposal, and it depends on the fact that it is we who are using those resources and managing to mean those words in those conditions—or failing to.

We could put it like this: The first thing that interested Cavell about the ordinary speech in which our criteria show up is that this is where the criteria we possess actually do show up. In a certain sense, going after ordinary speech to elicit our criteria was like robbing the banks because that is where the money is. There was nothing especially interesting about banks, and nothing especially to be made of the fact that ordinary language was ordinary. It was important because it was not "philosophical" language, and it could be assumed to embody, as Austin once put it, something better than the metaphysics of the Stone Age. Of course, Wittgenstein was always more complicated, or at least more explicit, on the subject of what was ordinary in our language. And even in the early essays of *Must We Mean What We Say?* Cavell was becoming philosophically restless on the very question of the methodological grounding of the "ordinary."[1]

Nevertheless, the criteria do make their appearance, and the philosophers of ordinary language can go about their business. Or rather, the criteria show up when the samples of our speech are recorded and arranged in some particular array, at some particular moment of perplexity or unclarity. And they show up when our philosophical attention is open to the hints and reminders that can be produced by the appropriate handling of our words and a particularly perspicuous arrangement of what we say. Not everyone can activate this exhibition of our criteria in samples of our ordinary speech. But everyone who speaks depends on the fact that our criteria are active in what we ordinarily say and that we are normally attuned to this fact.

But in his later work, we can see that Cavell's attention is being drawn to the very ordinariness in which these crucial features of our speech show up. What gives the ordinary the authority and, indeed, the power to provide a home for our words? (Cf. *Investigations*, #116.) What gives the ordinary the power to sustain or restore life to our signs, to provide work for our concepts and sense to our speech? Why must the voice of a human being (who has, perhaps, so many extraordinary things to say) begin with the speech of the everyday world—and perpetually return to that world?

When we follow Cavell in trying to understand the nature and authority of the appeals to ordinary language, we will end up thinking about the nature of the ordinariness. We are likely to be drawn into thinking about Romanticism, more frequently those late Romantics, Emerson, Thoreau, Nietzsche, and Heidegger. And we are likely to bear in mind the prophet and antagonist of Romanticism, Immanuel Kant. These writers all have an interest in securing a human being's access to something like the ordinary world—or, indeed, the world. This is the sense of the ordinary that Cavell comes to regard the appeal to ordinary language as depending on.

No doubt, these thinkers all have something to teach us about language. Perhaps, therefore, they also have something to teach us about the ordinariness, or at least the naturalness, of language—at least if the ordinariness and naturalness of language are features that must be preserved in any philosophically adequate understanding of language. But even if these writers are necessary to a more adequate understanding of the appeal to ordinary language, when we attend to them we are, *eo ipso*, interrupting our attention to any specific passage of our ordinary speech. It is difficult, if not impossible, to explore the authority and scope of a philosophical method at the same moment that one is trying to learn the method well enough to put it into practice.

Such a difficulty with regard to procedures is certainly not unique to philosophy. Many, perhaps most, procedures and methods do not readily allow us to practice them and to reflect upon them at the same time. But in the case of philosophy—at least as Cavell invites us to practice it—the problems are doubled up. For Cavell keeps insisting that it is part of how he is treating the subject of philosophy that there is no such thing as metaphilosophy. There is no place *outside* one's philosophical activity in which to think about that activity or gain perspective on it. And one of the corollaries of that insistence is that there is no obvious way to get outside a philosophical procedure in order to describe it. There is no description of a philosophical practice (e.g., as an appeal to ordinary speech) that is not itself part of the philosophizing that the practice is meant to advance. The relevance for my project is the implication that there is also no model of a philosophical procedure or practice that is not part of some further philosophical practice.

Whatever the precise causes of this development, Cavell's explicit appeals to ordinary speech in this period of his work are far less visible than they had previously been. The appeals also seem to me less of a *guide* to his conception of philosophical practice, and perhaps also less guiding for the readers who followed along the path of that practice. My perception of the situation is this: After the period of work best represented by *The Claim of Reason* (and already in part 4 of that book), the appeals to what we ordinarily say no longer function as the primary *model* of philosophical method. However important those appeals continue to be in Cavell's work, they no longer constitute the model that most directly epitomizes and illuminates his philosophical procedures.

Throughout this period of Cavell's work, we can glimpse the development of a new model of philosophical method. I will call this "the model of reading." But the reader should bear in mind that it is intended not in the first place as a theory of reading but as a *model of philosophical method*. Since this model is drawn from Cavell's experiences of reading and the accounts he gives of these experiences, one should perhaps not make too rigid a distinction here. Nevertheless, I will argue that the intent of the model is clear and significant: a new look at the elements of reading is to guide us to a new understanding of the practice of philosophy.

There are, I think, a number of reasons for the emergence of a new model of method at this moment in Cavell's intellectual career. It is important to bear in mind that this is only one aspect of what amounts to a sea change in his perspectives and procedures as a philosopher. But to follow out this shift in Cavell's conception of method is to be on the track of the central development of his thought in this period.

The shifts of method and perspective that his work was then undergoing—shifts whose consequences are still being worked out—constitute one of the critical events of Cavell's philosophical life. They signal the advent of new modes of writing and productivity that are continuing to unfold. This advent is as significant in Cavell's development as his initial encounter with Austin and the philosophy of ordinary language; the revision and completion of the work embedded in *The Claim of Reason;* the discovery of ways in which he could write usefully about the movies; and his encounter with Thoreau and Emerson. Indeed, it seems to me that the shifts I am describing are involved in all of these encounters and discoveries.

To understand the place of reading and of the resultant model of philosophical method would be to go a long way toward understanding this period of Cavell's writing. In order to appreciate the shift toward this new model of reading, we need to know more about the philosophical tensions that produced the need for such a model. This means backing up a step or two. I begin by considering a passage from the mid-1970s in which Cavell registered his own explicit sense of a shift in his methods and procedures. I then show the connection of these issues of method with some of the issues of voices and writing that I have been exploring in chapter 3. Appreciating these issues will put us in a better position to appreciate the emergence of reading into the central place it came to occupy and still occupies in Cavell's work.

M ore of *The World Viewed"* is an elaborate review and supplementation of the issues and arguments of *The World Viewed.* Near the beginning, Cavell characterizes the earlier book as marking a radical shift, and even a rupture, in his procedures as a philosopher. Acknowledging a certain level of difficulty in the original *The World Viewed,* he goes on to characterize his "feeling that [the book's] difficulty lies as much in the obscurity of its promptings as in its particular surfacings of expression." The passage continues:

> Given the feeling that a certain obscurity of prompting is not external to what I wished most fervently to say about film and hence cannot have been

cleared up before I commenced writing, nor at any time before I called the writing over, the commitments I set myself as I wrote were, first, to allow obscurities to express themselves as clearly and as fervently as I could say, and second, to be guided by the need to organize and clarify just these obscurities and just this fervor in the progression of my book as a whole. These procedures would be pointless unless the obscurities I allowed myself were accurate responses to the nature of film and unless the expressions I found for them were accurate to those responses; and unless I did in fact manage in the progression of the book, to bring some order and to do some justice to these expressions. [*The World Viewed*, expanded ed., 162–63.]

Some readers may find it difficult to see how such remarks can describe anything like the book's "procedures." It is therefore worth guarding against a particular misunderstanding of this passage: Cavell is not arguing that the obscurity of the subject justifies the difficulty of his prose. He is saying something much more particular, something akin to Wittgenstein's remark about putting a certain "indefiniteness" into words—but without falsifying the indefiniteness.

Cavell is suggesting that the topics of film contain difficulties and regions of darkness that invite expression—that give him the sense that there is something to express—but without granting an equally clear sense of where the need for such expression is coming from or of what intellectual or emotional progress such expression may advance. Thus what he calls the ordering and progression of the writing of the book itself will have to clarify something of the impulses and the promptings that lie at the origin of the book. The book's "ordering" of such expressions will have to do justice to their "obscurity": that is, I take it, the ordering will have to demonstrate the correspondence of the obscurity of the expression to the obscurity in the subject of film itself. And beyond this, the progress of the writing must demonstrate that there is a possible movement from obscurity to illumination, or, as he will shortly formulate it, from privacy and perversity to a public and satisfying resolution of the problems of film.

In part, this means that Cavell's use of the ideas of "obscurity" will now move beyond the idea of a certain type of unclarity. From here on out, obscurity in Cavell will also refer to the edges of thought that have been pushed into darkness and kept from public view. Such obscurity need not be thought of as a consequence of "repression." For repression is, at least on an orthodox reading, an intrapsychic event—or one that occurs *en famille*. In the case of film, and in other cases of expression that we have already been exposed to, the "obscurity" in question seems to be a kind of transaction between something at least initially "outside" of our psyches and something that goes on within us.

In any event, we are, once again, in the region of the mind's relation to the world where what is hidden from our direct view is something that we have somehow kept ourselves from viewing. In the case of movies, it is the engulfing and engrossing presence of what film presents us with that keeps us from thinking about the disparate privacies and obscurities of our responses. As the presences of film tend to conceal the absences they refer to, so the immediacy of the responses that film elicits tends to conceal (and of course might still reveal) the depth of our craving for those vivid absences and for the anxious privacies that they console.

As with the word *obscurity*, Cavell draws the word *privacy* out of the closed circle in which it is supposed to refer to a sheerly philosophical disorder—attributable perhaps to Descartes. Cavell goes on to use these words explicitly to explore the region of communication between our misleading philosophical pictures and the hidden human fantasies that dictate our responses, whether to art, or to philosophy, or to the world.

Already in this paragraph, accordingly, there are signs of a shift from Cavell's earlier work. But the next paragraph drives home the possibility of reversal in the heart of his procedures:

> Such procedures differ from, almost reverse, the procedures I had fol-lowed in my previous philosophical writing. There my hope for conviction from the reader was placed in my ability to motivate assertions, and objec-tions to them, and to voice them in such a form and at such a time that the reader would have the impression that he was himself thinking them, had been about to have said them—not just about to have said something gen-erally along their lines, but as it were to find himself thinking those specific words just when and just as they were appearing to him. (Naturally this need not, even when done well, occur on a first perusal. Then what in a first should encourage going back?) Whereas in writing about film I felt called upon to voice my responses within their privacy, their argumenta-tiveness, even their intellectual perverseness, on their face; often to avoid a thought awaiting its voice, to refuse that thought, as if our standing re-sponses to film are themselves standing between us and the responses that film is made to elicit and satisfy. [*World*, 163.]

This is a passage that remains startling and instructive long after we begin to appreciate the radical nature of the claims Cavell is making. It contains a nesting of claims, entered almost casually, about the shifts and the con-tinuities in his philosophical procedures. It seems to confirm at least some of what I was claiming about the relative disuse that overtakes the ap-peals to what we ordinarily say. But Cavell is also making some claims about the goals of ordinary language philosophy that had never before been made.

This moment has been very largely neglected, even to some extent by Cavell himself. Here again, my claims do not depend on capturing a privileged authorial perspective that Cavell might be supposed to possess on his own work. Therefore the fact that he does not refer to this particular backward glance in his later moments of retrospection does not count against my sense of the significance of this passage. At the very least, it would be foolish or hasty to ignore the hints and glimpses of the methodological that I have been pointing to. We have been offered a kind of laboratory for testing our readings of Cavell, a kind of before and after pair of snapshots of the footpaths that lead up to and away from this moment of self-reflection. As with any such snapshot, the gesture of offering them is as crucial to the meaning of the moment as what the snapshots contain.

Here are some things I find worth noticing in this passage:

(1) The idea of "voicing" assertions and objections, and then again the idea of voicing a response and of avoiding a thought that is "awaiting its voice," enters Cavell's account at two crucial stages. But these procedures of the voice—if it is not too much to call them that—are not quite linked, and not quite expressly compared or contrasted. Nevertheless, it is tempting to imagine that we are being encouraged to draw out these connections concerning the voice and its relation to philosophical methods. And it is also tempting to think of this passage as a partially achieved moment on the way to Cavell's fuller calculation of the centrality of the voice.

(2) The voice does not quite emerge as a theme in the first quotation that I was considering: Instead we have such thoughts as the one about "allowing obscurities to express themselves"; "bringing some order and doing some justice" to these expressions; and, finally, the idea of a kind of accuracy: an accuracy of the responses to the film, and of the expression of the responses. These notions allude to issues of the voice, but they also point in other directions. For instance, having to assess an accuracy in one's expressions is not obviously a procedure that can be cast in terms of the voice. We can say: A voice might be right for a role or a part in a movie or an opera. But we would not normally say that a voice was *accurate* to a role or a part. Somebody might be capable of an accurate imitation of some movie star—but it is the imitation that is accurate or failing to be; the voice is rather the vehicle or the medium of the imitation.

For this very reason, these passages give us some way of locating the kinds of work that are being done next door to the problematic of the voice. Hence, they give us a better chance to locate the kind of work that

Cavell wants from the voice and the idea of the voice. Despite what some have thought about Cavell's description of his methods, voicing such experiences (of the movies, or of art or of some stretch of philosophy) is not enough. Or, if voicing them is enough, we will need a richer account of the voice and of the expressions appropriate to it than is yet available to us.

This issue might be used to raise the crucial issue about both film and literature: What is the relation between my finding words to voice my experience of a film or some other text, and the idea of "giving a reading of a film"? What is the relation between Cavell's idea of bringing some order and doing some justice to his expressions and the idea of following out the order that a text may be thought of, variously, as concealing or displaying?

(3) Cavell is taking a further step in his description of the very procedures of ordinary language philosophy that he is, at least temporarily, leaving behind. Given what we have seen of his way of taking a new step, this should not be so surprising. But I think the description is nevertheless quite startling. For Cavell presents his version of the procedures of ordinary language as, in the first place, the procedures of a certain mode of *writing*. And the ambition that motivates this mode of writing goes radically deeper—at least as an ambition for one's writing—than anything that Austin ever formulated.

Most specifically, I mean the ambition to create for the reader a decorum of prose, in which a reader might find himself or herself on the verge of thinking a certain thought, in certain specific words, just at the moment that the words appeared on the page. This idea casts the fate and fortunes of philosophizing from ordinary language together with the fate of a kind of writing.

Cavell once described Austin as thinking he had to choose between teaching and writing, and as having chosen teaching (*Must We Mean What We Say?* 113). Cavell's account of his writing here betrays the wish not to have to choose. And it betrays a further wish to capture the voicing of our ordinary language in written words. Much of this ambition may well be shared with Wittgenstein. But Cavell twists the practice up a notch.

The sense that you were about to think something, about to have just these words occur to you, in just this order, is not necessarily a pleasant sensation. When it works, the sense of the words hitting home can set off a wide range of reactions. (The arrows of this prose fit more than one wound.) But even when the method keeps precisely within a certain willingness for the appropriate reception, this procedure seems to have designs on the reader's voice as well as his ears. For if the voice is to exist in writing, it must be found precisely here—in the exact order of the precise words. (As in Wittgenstein, it is "something that is expressed only by these words, in these positions" [Cf. *Philosophical Investigations*, #531].) I would go so far as to say that this early writing of Cavell's bears some of the hallmarks of an Emersonian theft of our words and voice. At its best, a reading of those essays allowed us to return to our words, appreciating a measure of ecstasy, precisely in the ordinary routines of our speech.

As he was getting drawn beyond the methods of the ordinary, Cavell depicted those methods as themselves the principal agency by which we are drawn beyond them. In this passage from "More of *The World Viewed*" we can see something of the radical shift in procedure that Cavell was undergoing. But we can also appreciate his perception of a radical edge to those earlier procedures of appealing to what we ordinarily say. The newer direction in this shift of procedure raises such issues as this: How do you voice obscurities in a way that allows some readers to move from an obscurity they have not yet recognized to an illumination they have not yet felt the need of? More therapeutically or clinically put: How do you give voice to repressed material without ruining another person's chance to find his own access to that material?

Radicalizing the appeal to ordinary language increases the need to investigate the source of the authority of the ordinary and the everyday. We have already caught a glimpse of this investigation, but this radicalization of the appeals to what we say goes even further. In voicing the ambition to be the voice of the appeal to the ordinary, Cavell raises a principal question about these appeals: Who speaks first? If, in his retrospective glance at these procedures, Cavell now finds the writer coming *before* the reader with words that the reader will find himself in need of, this will soon raise the question of what justifies the writer in making this appearance. The sheer fact that you can write philosophy like this successfully—making a given succession of words appear in front of a given reader at a given moment—will not be enough to establish the authority of the philosophical writer.

In his depiction of his earlier procedures, as in his depiction of his newer directions in writing about film, Cavell raised issues of method that could not be solved entirely in the terms in which he raised them. The radical instabilities of philosophical authority that were uncovered by these shifts of procedure drew Cavell toward the work of a past master of such questions of authority, namely, Emerson. Under the sign of this question of philosophical authority and in the terms forged in his encounters with Emerson, Cavell brought the issue of reading into a new prominence—and also into a state of crisis.

Having encountered the shift in relationship between the appeals to ordinary language and the audience for those appeals, we are in a better position to follow out some of the issues and crises of writing. We have already tracked some of Cavell's steps toward recovering the voice through the appeal to what we ordinarily say. At each stage, I have insisted that you cannot accurately attend to the voice that Cavell achieves as a writer without at the same time seeking the voices that he invokes in our ordinary speech. There are of course many types of voice and many tones of voice to be found within our ordinary forms of speech: there are different voices to be located in cries, complaints, pleas, conversations, speeches, and warnings. I have suggested some of the consequences of letting our grasp of the philosopher's voice become too isolated from our comprehension of the voices that he is invoking. And I singled out the special dangers of hearing the singularity of Cavell's style apart from hearing the ways his writing calls upon the unnamed harmonies of speech that any speaker of a language might employ.

Midway through chapter 3, I isolated the moment in "Politics as Opposed to What?" where Cavell puts a new name on the accomplishments of *The Claim of Reason*: "It is as the recovery of this voice (as from an illness) that ordinary language philosophy is, as I have understood and written about it, before all to be understood" (*Themes*, 48). It is a crucial moment in the development of Cavell's work: Cavell exhibits *The Claim of Reason* as engaged in the philosophical recovery of the voice. But that project was carried out in advance of an explicit description of the work of recovery in terms of the voice. Naming the voice as what was expressly excluded from philosophy and naming the philosophical resistances and repressions that performed that exclusion would have accomplished very little, apart from *The Claim of Reason's* detailed working-out of the methods and therapies of ordinary language.

We must continue to explore this double movement of the recovery of the voice and of the explicit characterization of that recovery. I have, in effect, described this delay in naming the recovery as a kind of displaced continuation of the work of recovery. It will help us to understand the situation that Cavell found himself in if we take a few more steps with the essay "Politics as Opposed to What?" In this essay, Cavell works to provide a new perspective on earlier work, which in turn would allow him to keep in touch with that work. He thereby establishes his right to reopen the case of the skeptic's suppression of the voice without dragging himself through the entire bill of indictment established by his preliminary labors of analysis.

Or else we might say that Cavell has acquired the freedom to regard as "preliminary" the labors of analysis and diagnosis that left him exposed to the inconclusiveness of the struggle with skepticism. He has been engaged in a struggle to wrest the skeptic's self-interpretation away from him. But he realizes that if this struggle for the interpretation of the skeptic's claims and procedures is reappropriated as an argument that leads to a conclusion (whether for or against the skeptic's claims), the skeptic wins out after all. For the triumph of skepticism lies not in the particular solution proposed but in getting us to pose the question of the presence of the world as, fundamentally, a problem about our knowledge of the world's existence.

Over and over again, we have to arrive at the perception that the resources of ordinary language cannot be converted into an *argument* against the skeptic. To do so is to give over the ground of the ordinary, and to pervert the appeals that were meant to keep us in touch with that ground. Perhaps it would not be an exaggeration to say the appeals to ordinary speech are meant to maintain our ability to hear the ordinariness of ordinary speech, or to listen for it. Constantly listening in these ways and constantly refusing to counter the ways of skepticism with an argument is a good method for arriving at a new species of intellectual isolation. And it is also a method designed to exacerbate any anxieties a writer might experience in relation to the problem of how to conclude.

The struggles between skepticism and the ordinary left Cavell in a region he calls "Nowhere" in *Conditions Handsome and Unhandsome* (35). He associates the inconclusiveness of the struggles with skepticism as part of what drew him to texts of Shakespeare, Romanticism, and, above all, Emerson. From the standpoint of the shift in methodology that I am outlining, this is a critical moment. Any reader who followed Cavell up to this point of his work would have needed some way of dealing with the question of the validity of the appeals to ordinary language. The question of our access to the world of the ordinary and the everyday—the world in which our language is at home—was hardly likely to be on anybody's front burner.

Indeed, in those days philosophers were more likely to be raising methodological issues about how we arrive at a genuine sample of ordinary speech. That is, the focus was on whether there was some representative "we" who could be imagined saying the thing that philosopher was claiming "we" said. That something was said to be a piece of "ordinary" speech meant, first of all, that it wasn't technical or "philo-sophical" speech. And, second of all, that it was said to be ordinary meant that it was "common" and likely to be widely shared. But the emphasis was clearly on what there was to be learned from what "we" said, and much less on the relevance of the fact that what we said was a portion of "ordinary" speech. By the end of *The Claim of Reason*, Cavell is taking the issues about the appeal to ordinary language in a fundamentally dif-ferent direction.

"Politics as Opposed to What?" may be taken both as a kind of con-solidation and as a further employment of the philosophical—and thera-peutic—achievement of *The Claim of Reason*. In signing off on *The Claim of Reason*, Cavell was also taking steps to stay in touch with its projects. In making explicit the idea of the recovery of the voice, "Politics as Opposed to What?" was moving to occupy new regions of subject mat-ter and of method. And one of the first regions Cavell moved to occupy was precisely the region of texts and textuality.

We have already taken a first look at the moment in this essay where Cavell refers us back to the earlier maelstrom of crises and losses, the ones that I associate above all with the composition of *The Senses of Walden*. These were crises of consent and withdrawal, of citizenship and injustice, of friends and strangers, and of voice and writing. In my efforts to arrive at a usable assessment of these crises, I saw them as threatening to engulf *The Senses of Walden* even while they presided over its engendering. I also cited some of the connections between these crises of voice and the central revisions of the work on criteria that became *The Claim of Rea-son*. I have been arguing that there are still unfathomed links between the crises of consent and withdrawal in *The Senses of Walden* and the crisis of self-revision that allowed the emergence of the voice in *The Claim of Reason*.

One such link emerges strikingly in "Politics as Opposed to What?": Cavell sketches a path from a particular idea of textuality to a particular understanding of skepticism. The withdrawal of the voice that is con-ceived as a kind of withdrawal of consent, hence as a response to political crisis, is here shown to be affiliated with the withholding of assertion in the face of the world of objects and others.

> Of all the problems that beckon and seem to me worth following from the sketch, the one that is perhaps paramount in terms of my work on skepticism that I have mentioned . . . is one I only mention here, namely, why or how the same silence, or rather the stillness of the text, the achieve-ment of which perhaps constitutes textuality, or a text's self-containedness, should be interpretable politically as rebuke and confrontation and be

interpretable epistemologically as the withholding of assertion, on which I have found the defeat of skepticism, and of whatever metaphysics is designed to overcome skepticism, to depend—as if the withholding of assertion, the containing of the voice, amounts to the forgoing of domination. ["Politics," 199.]

What I depicted in chapter 3 as a withdrawal of the voice from the crisis of its implied consents is now portrayed as the path to a kind of textual "stillness." And this "stillness" in turn is somehow to be related to the withholding of assertion and the containment of the voice, on which the undermining of skepticism will depend. But the path that leads from the political and ontological stillness of the text to the silence that undermines the skeptic's words will soon lead us back to issues about reading.

We will need to know more about the relation of such textual containment to the withholding of the voice from the community. At the same time, we need to attend to the philosophical perspective contained in the phrases about the "withholding of assertion" and the "containing of the voice." Most immediately, these formulations seem related to the work Cavell had just completed for *Pursuits of Happiness*, which was published in 1981. In that book, he also takes a retrospective look at the enterprise of *The Claim of Reason*: "I have . . . cast skepticism as the wish to transgress the naturalness of human speech" (74). I take this to be one of the key formulations of skepticism for the whole of Cavell's later work. Skepticism must now be thought out as an expression of an anxiety that our words will not reach the world of objects and human beings that can be named, or addressed, or called upon. In our responses to this anxiety about the distances of people and things—in our responses to the surmise of skepticism within us—we abolish not only the appropriate distances of these beings but, at the same time, their appropriate intimacies. And this, in turn, abolishes the distinctive otherness of the other.

One of the sounds of restoring this otherness is the happy banter and other intimate distinctions established in the dialogue of the movies discussed as the "comedies of remarriage." Sometimes Cavell characterizes these movies as comedies of equality, which is surely partly a matter of the equality represented in the back-and-forth of the voices. These dialogues of difference are no longer available to philosophy, at least not in the prose of philosophical journals. By reconstructing and restoring the sound of the dialogue through criticism and reading, some aspects of the form of dialogue evidently became available again through Cavell's work.

The darker and more perverse side of skepticism shows up in these comedies as forms or hints of incestuousness. Cavell interprets these hints as pointing to features of life and language, which the comedies of remarriage are meant to overcome. The incestuous side of desire casts a shadow on the intimacy that imagines we have known each other forever. Cavell also takes the opportunity of this reading of the comedies to point us toward another aspect of his analysis of skepticism. Here he is inclined to see, first of all, the issue of narcissism, which is perhaps always in the wings when the skeptic seeks to establish his connection to the world from within his private resources.

Cavell reads these issues as not merely a matter of the psychological risks attendant on a particular form of philosophical project. He interprets the philosophical edges of narcissism as more or less made to order for certain regions of the skeptical problematic. The narcissist uses the world to stage a reflection of his own existence, a maneuver that manages to confirm both the independence of the world and its ultimate dependence on the self. The skeptic uses the world to confirm his isolation and powerlessness as a knower, at the same time that it confirms the integrity of his efforts to know. His integrity as a seeker of knowledge is the ground of his integrity as a self: Descartes' unsuccessful effort to doubt the existence of the "I" is all it takes to confirm the temporary necessity of that I.

In the register of language, Cavell reads the skeptic not just as tolerating but as *requiring* the transgression of the naturalness of speech (*Pursuits*, 74). He presents the wish for this transgression as more than analogous—but never quite identical—to the wishful expressions of incest or narcissism. Both skepticism and incest are interpreted as efforts to abolish a certain breach of naturalness, itself interpretable as breaches of innocence and immediacy. But our efforts to restore an earlier condition of immediacy end up abolishing the very otherness that we had meant to preserve. The effort to link ourselves to the world by knowledge or by marriage is incessantly threatened by a disfiguration of the other—in language or by other means.

At a slightly later stage of reflection, our words seem to reach the rest of the world as signs that we have already turned away from it. This sort of "turning away" has perhaps its most common form in the pervasive tones of irony that many adults employ as their normal mode of commenting on the passing scene. (This tone is not to be confused with the sarcastic irony of adolescents, though it would be worth studying more closely how the two modes of address are related and how they interact.) Sometimes the tone presents itself as a kind of knowingness or sophistication. It is more likely to be a protection against exposure to the world of others, which is also the world of everydayness in all its boredom and repetitiousness.

It is around this time that boredom and a lack of interest in the world become a subtheme of Cavell's writing, most immediately connected to the issue of boredom in *Walden* (and at Walden), and to Wordsworth's preface to the *Lyrical Ballads*. But within the issues of irony and boredom, Cavell often discerns a very human—and not an especially philosophical—defense against being exposed to the implications of the words and tropes of our address to the world. In Cavell's reading of Wittgenstein and Emerson, the lack of an immediate connection between our words and the world is not a fault in language but in the way we live with words. Our speech is constantly revealing our indebtedness to the world. We would rather turn away from the world than acknowledge this indebtedness.

If the undermining of skepticism promises the recovery of the human voice, it cannot—all by itself—teach us to turn back to the world. And the recovery of the voice from its skeptical denial does not make our voices immune to the wish for transgression. The therapies of withholding and containment will continue to be part of our philosophical battery of possible treatments. Accordingly, Cavell's treatment of the threat of skepticism does not mean finding some new ground of a maturity that consists in accepting the limits of human knowledge.[2] The drive in part 4 of *The Claim of Reason* cannot be read as moving toward some set of recommendations that we adjust our lives to live within more reasonable limits, accepting that there will be limits to our knowledge of others.

To put it briefly: to accept the limits of our knowledge of others, as we currently exist with one another, is not to overcome skepticism but to withdraw from the only realm in which our most authentic struggles with skepticism can be conducted. Nor is there any reason to be confident that we are accepting just those limitations in our knowledge that have to be accepted as the "given" (as Wittgenstein sometimes puts it). We are more likely to be accepting, in a disguised form, our disappointment with our criteria and our knowledge. It is as if the skeptic's way of testing the limits of our attunement in those criteria was, after all, the right way: since criteria don't deliver knowledge with any certainty, we should conclude that therefore criteria fail, or else that they have nothing to do with knowledge.

This conclusion that we should learn from skepticism to live within reasonable limits will tend to keep us from considering that we are at least as disappointed with the successes of our knowledge as we are with its failures. Such disappointment casts its shadow on the everyday occasions of knowing. Our awareness of the shadows should not be mistaken for maturity. Especially about other human beings but also, I think, about the world, the real disappointment and anxiety can begin only when we realize that we *do*, after all, know—and that we will go on knowing. But something in us had wanted knowledge to be more than this. Something keeps alive in us an image of knowledge or, perhaps, an image of a kind of knowledge that is now lost or somehow forbidden. (This possibility is introduced in *The Claim of Reason*, 440ff.) To live within the limits of a reasonable knowledge of others will do nothing to elicit these images. Here, again, we do not know whether a sense of limitation in our knowledge of others is informing us that we have reached the limits of what we can know or is promising us a better way of knowing.

Cavell is, of course, arguing that the impulse to skepticism feeds on our disappointments with knowledge. Skepticism in Cavell's account is more of an effect than a cause of this disappointment. But images of knowledge that skepticism feeds on must be construed as more than merely the sources of skepticism. When Cavell speaks of what "knowing another, or being known by another, would really come to," he pictures such things as "a harmony, a concord, a union, a transparence, a governance, a power . . . " (ibid.). The list gets a little obscure—or perhaps poetic. But it is scarcely a list of images that we should seek merely to be rid of. In Cavell's work, the study of such images leads him further into the regions of tragedy and of psychoanalysis. Perhaps it is also one of the stimuli for his study of perfectionism, one aspect of which is to further our knowledge of the images of perfection, both false and true.

The acceptance of limitation does not begin to diagnose the perversities in our efforts to get outside our limits, to live outside our skin. These efforts can be tragic or neurotic or Romantic, as well as skeptical. If we treat the itch to produce such efforts as itself a product of our sense of limitation, we will never know what the itch might have become. Just as significant, we will be living within a sense of limitation and disappointment that seems to dictate that we live in such a way as to forestall any further question concerning our ideal of knowledge. We put the crisis of knowledge behind us, and suggest that we live as best we can in the aftermath of our disappointed discoveries. But this is beginning to sound like the course that skepticism itself is inclined to take, and not the course of its overcoming.

With the completion of *The Claim of Reason*, there was evidently a general liberation of Cavell's voice. This newfound freedom permitted him to widen the scope of his analysis of skepticism and the voice and to find analogies to the skeptic's problem in entirely new territories.

From the concluding essays of *Must We Mean What We Say?*, there had always been for Cavell a haunting sense of connection between the problem of tragedy (especially Shakespearean tragedy) and the question of skepticism (especially in its formulation by Descartes and, to some extent, by Hume). The sense that some connection between tragedy and skepticism remained to be worked out is part of what drives the concluding sections of *The Claim of Reason*. (Cf. *Claim*, xviii–xix; 476–94.) He there explores a number of different and perhaps even competing formulations of such a connection. Central to his reading of *Othello*, he exhibits the play as "epitomiz[ing]" "the logic, the emotion, and the scene of skepticism" (483). It is important to Cavell's argument that this work of epitomizing—and implicitly of situating and dramatizing the movements of skepticism—is not just a matter of the psychology of the character Othello but of the structure of the play *Othello*. Cavell is not always very explicit about how this is supposed to happen. But it is clear enough that when he speaks of the precipitous "rhythm of *Othello's* plot" as matching the rhythm of skepticism, he is not just making a psychological claim.

Once that fact of Cavell's account is understood, we can start to wonder what sort of entity skepticism turns out to be, that it can possess the structure and the rhythm of a Shakespearean tragedy. And that is precisely the sort of question that Cavell will urge on himself and on his audience in the decade following the publication of *The Claim of Reason*. The sense of analogy and relationship between the philosophical skeptic and various works of literature and film (ultimately even of opera) is omnipresent. But somewhere in this period, and no doubt drawing upon the formulations of the question in *The Claim of Reason*, Cavell begins to put forward a picture that goes beyond even the deepest sense of analogy.

He begins to refer to the philosopher's version of skepticism as an "intellectualization" of some other, deeper skeptical condition. Out of this more radical, or anyway, more human condition, Descartes and Hume for instance fashion their problems and their arguments. Henceforth, the relation between philosophical skepticism and tragedy is to be explicitly more than analogical. They stem from something like the same source. And, as if matters were not complicated enough, that primordial skepticism is itself to be characterized in two different ways: skepticism as a modern consequence of an ancient wish to know beyond what human beings are given to know; and skepticism as the wish to substitute knowledge for what Cavell calls acknowledgment.

And skepticism is also Cavell's name for the historical accentuation of these wishes in the European response to the rise of Protestantism, the death of kings, and the dissolution of the boundaries of the closed universe. In this view, skepticism is the other side of the birth of modern subjectivity, unhinged from itself by its consciousness of itself, and interposed between itself and the world. (We block our own sight.)

At the very least, the different domains in which skepticism shows up are henceforth not to be conceived as *mere* analogies, but as various ways of working out the same underlying skeptical problematic in different forms. The various domains in which we can glimpse this skeptical problematic are, generally speaking, domains of art and representation, and each problematic must also obey demands of form and genre. Indeed, Cavell's sense of skepticism as showing up in a wide range of writings and works of art ought to have raised in his audience an acute sense of the question of form. For if we are to make comparisons of these different skepticisms, we have to be able to make allowances for the contribution of the forms and the genres within which these versions of skepticism take shape. Apart from Cavell's own remarks on such subjects (especially on Shakespeare and on film), this critical work concerning form has tended not to happen.

B eyond what we have already looked at, the new domains of Cavell's explorations include film, Shakespeare, Romanticism, and Freud (in particular, his essay "The Uncanny"). Along with the further developments in his anatomy of skepticism, Cavell was also drawn to think further about the status and authority of the "ordinariness" of ordinary language. It seems likely that it was precisely the successful release of the voice through the appeals to ordinary speech that gave Cavell the philosophical room in which to worry about the nature of our access to those ordinary voices.

The most visible manifestation of the liberation of Cavell's voice was an enormous release of productive energies. One might well imagine that this had to do with Cavell's resolution of at least some of the crises of the voice that I have been exploring. Whatever the precise causes may be, the extent of his productivity and the range of his interests in this period are staggering. As Cavell emerges from the shadows of his prolonged encounter with Wittgenstein's *Investigations*, he enters on a season of fruitfulness and virtuosity. In little more than a decade, in half a dozen books and in still-uncollected essays and reviews, Cavell turns his hand to pretty much anything he likes: Shakespeare and Wordsworth; Coleridge, Kleist, and Poe; Keaton, Sturges, Hitchcock, Hawks, Bergman, and Makavaev; Emerson and everybody (but especially Nietzsche); Jacques Derrida, Julia Kristeva, Melanie Klein, Jay Cantor, and Eve Sedgwick; Emily Dickinson

and Svengali; Henry James and Richard Nixon; Groucho Marx and E. M.
Forster; Jewishness and Jerusalem; feminism and film; castration, melan-
cholia, and the maternal voice; Beethoven, modernism, jazz, and quilting;
television, end-time theology, and Japanese puppets; baseball, exhilara-
tion, boredom, and whistling.

Even this list is not complete. It stops short before the explicit engagements with opera and with what Cavell calls "moral perfectionism." More
immediately, it leaves out his continued involvement not only with Austin and Wittgenstein but with the Anglo-American precincts of philosophy, most notably with John Rawls and Saul Kripke. But the list at least
suggests how far we are from any accurate sense of the unity of Cavell's
work. And it points to the danger that readers who feel themselves at sea
with this outpouring of work will find themselves grasping for a perspective that will seem to provide some unity. Such attempts to unify Cavell's
work have proven to be premature and unhelpful.

The Model of Reading

The issue of reading has already come up for discussion. Reading is
clearly a major theme in *The Senses of Walden*. The other side of what
Cavell characterizes as the writer's withholding of the voice from the
reader is the question of the reader as the one from whom the voice is
withheld. (Not every reader is in a position to know that it is the voice
that the writer is withholding.) Furthermore, I have argued that some
idea of reading will have to enter into the methodological upheaval that is
made explicit but left unresolved in "More of *The World Viewed*." And
without some investigation of reading, we will have little chance of pursuing what *The Claim of Reason* means by its wish to understand philosophy as "a set of texts," rather than as a contribution to "a set of *given*
problems" (*Claim*, 3). Whatever else a text may be, it exists as something
to be read. The idea and the practices of reading play a correspondingly
dominant role in Cavell's later work.

I am going to be arguing that the role of reading is even more significant than has so far been publicly and usably articulated. For in the
work that follows *The Claim of Reason*, Cavell uses the idea and practices of reading as elements in a new model of philosophical method.
The first and perhaps most surprising fact about this use of reading as
a model is that it can be attempted at all. It is difficult to absorb the idea
that an activity as multiform and apparently irregular as reading should

illuminate our sense of philosophical procedure. My goal is to make this account of reading more available, in part by guarding against its assimilation to a certain image of a theory of reading.

My initial claim is still more specific: Cavell constructs his account of reading as a model of philosophical method from a series of *reversals*. I will present three such reversals, without claiming that my list is exhaustive:

(1) The reversal of the one who is producing a philosophical text into the position of one who is reading a (prior) text. That is, the philosopher turns from the position of one engaged in the business of producing a text or discourse to the position of one who is engaged in *reading* or receiving a previously existing text. This reversal is already a reversal from an idea of thinking as a type of production (whether of an argument or a text) to an idea of thinking as a kind of reception. I mention two brief points concerning this first reversal: (a) the posture of philosophical reading cannot be reduced without remainder to the posture of the philosophical commentator; (b) the prior text, in the face of which the philosophical writer turns into the philosophical reader, need not be a text *in words*. These two points go together in ways that will require further exploration.

(2) The second reversal radicalizes the thinker's turn from a certain kind of activity to a certain kind of passivity. This reversal converts the philosopher from the position of *reading* the prior text into the position of one who is, as Cavell puts it, *being read by* the prior text. This reversal is, I think, the region of the model most in need of illumination. But it is also the point of Cavell's most consistent application and elaboration of the model and his most sustained productiveness in his use of it. Not too surprisingly, this is the feature of the model that points most directly toward the analogy of reading with psychoanalytic therapy.

(3) Finally, the resultant text of the philosopher-turned-reader must put forward some form of invitation. This will not be, for instance, merely some special access to the words: it must also offer the empirical reader some point of access to the role of reader that is already being enacted within the text. Something in the text must enable me to assume the role of the reader of the prior text and to take on the activities and the responsibilities that such a role implies.

From a more literary or more Continental side of things, some will say that the important thing is not that reading can *model* philosophical activity but that it just *is* a philosophical activity. That reading can be construed as a philosophical activity I am happy to acknowledge, but such an acknowledgment does not solve one of the most intractable problems: reading has always been construed as an activity with some sort of relation to philosophy. But it is generally construed as secondary, or ancillary, like the activities of commentary or interpretation. And if we wanted to argue that reading should be a primary mode of philosophical activity, like interpretation in some versions of Continental philosophy, we would have to guard against the charge that we have merely changed the subject.

Cavell will sometimes say that reading is a matter of caring about texts and hence a matter of finding out what allows you to stay with the text (*Pursuits of Happiness*, 14). He distinguishes the mode of philosophical reading that keeps you connected to a text in the appropriate way from the mode of philosophizing that wants to take something *away* from our reading—whether an argument or a moral. This formulation is valuable, but it is also, I suggest, provisional. Cavell is not very explicit about how we are to characterize the philosophical value of staying attached to these texts. It is clear enough what he has in mind at this stage of his reflections about film and philosophy. It is in the act of criticism—or rather in the act of giving a reading of these films—that the attachment to the work is best manifested and best accounted for.

Rich as these reflections about criticism, reading, and philosophy may be, there was more work to be done. Cavell would soon go on to articulate certain questions of interest—my interest in film and in the world, the reader's interest in my words of criticism—as themselves bound up in questions of skepticism and reading (*In Quest of the Ordinary*). In a book about films as pleasurable as the comedies of remarriage, one can afford, mostly, to suspend the question of the audience's interest. Or rather, the interest of the audience in the films and their interest in Cavell's criticism tend to become merged with one another. And when Cavell describes the point of taking an interest in a film as the same as the point of learning to take an interest in your own experience, he has already invited us to merge our *own* acts of taking an interest in Cavell's words for his experience with *his* acts of taking an interest in the film.

This is the kind of merger I discussed in the introduction, in connection with Arnold Davidson's review-essay of *Themes Out of School*. It is just the sort of moment that calls for an investigation of the relation between the author depicting himself as reader-critic, and the reader understanding himself as responding in a kind of unison with the author's reading of (for instance) a film. However good this is as an act of critical reading, it calls for distinctions—further acts of philosophy. And it calls for what I am characterizing as the model of reading as a series of reversals.

The level of central importance that I am ascribing to reading in Cavell's work should not in itself seem surprising. It should also not be very surprising that this model and the practices it is meant to illuminate inherit problems and invite suspicion about the status of anything like an audience for philosophy or for philosophical writing. Already in the foreword to *Must We Mean What We Say?* Cavell was raising issues about the questionableness of any "audience" for philosophy that is not engaged in the same enterprise as the author. Even more surprising are the ways in which the sheer idea of reading yields usable methodological results. But staying close to this idea is not always so easy.

What makes it worth pursuing this account of reading as a series of reversals is, I hope, already apparent. What makes this account into a model of how philosophical work gets done is not yet apparent. Generally speaking, the answer will have to appear in relation to specific acts of reading. (I also suppose that an account of argumentation as the essential activity of philosophy would have to prove itself in at least some specific acts of argumentation.) Some of my general answer, however, can be set out in advance of the specific acts of reading that will be required: the feature of philosophy that I want most immediately to locate and to emblematize in the reversibility of reading is this: *the steps of a philosophical method can, in principle, be taken by anyone.*

Whatever has brought someone to the point of taking the next philosophical step—whatever special knowledge or ability or feeling or special sense of the existence of a problem or of something to be questioned—it must not be anything *further* that is special about us that leads us to take this next step.

The first thing that reading and its reversals is meant to emblematize is this feature of *nobody special* or *nothing special* in the position of the one who is reading or the one who is taking the next step. Nothing special, I mean, beyond the fact that the person in question is already engaged in some activities of reading. This is meant in part as a kind of gloss and in part as a continuation of Cavell's remark on Socrates in "An Audience for Philosophy": "No man is in any better position for knowing it than any other man—unless *wanting* to know *is* a special position" (*Must We?* xxviii).

The actual, empirical reader is encouraged to step into the shoes of the (depicted) philosophical reader and begin to engage in the process (and the reversals) of that reading. This reversibility of the steps of the reading challenges us to see what we have in common with the position of the reader we are changing places with. That we have stepped into the middle of someone else's activity of reading invites us to examine what we find representative about that reading. In turn, we are invited to extend our reflections in order to see what is representative about our ability to take the steps—and to try out the results of taking those steps.

Beyond the issue of the representativeness of reading, there is something else to be accounted for. The spirit of these reversals of reading is not exhausted by these ideas of "No one special" or "no special position." Indeed, one crucial element in the spirit of the philosophical reader must be expressed in terms rather more like these: "Until I came along, this text had not found its reader. And until I found this text, I had not found the thing that makes me the reader I now am." Without the spirit of such encounters, I am not sure that the best reading, or the best hours of reading, would ever occur. But as it stands the relation of such reading to the philosophical reading that Cavell is characterizing has not yet been secured.

Something about the sense of possessing a text in part precisely because one has become possessed *by it* is certainly in the spirit of the reversals I am trying to characterize. It points again to the significance and the difficulty that attach to the second of these reversals. For Cavell's continuing efforts to formulate the relation between reading a text and being read by that text are surely a variant of his Emersonian perception that we learn to possess only what we have already been possessed by. To put this insight in terms that can be followed *methodically*, we will have to say more about the spirit and manner in which this possession occurs. Indeed, we will have to find a way of possessing a text that is not itself possessive or exclusive. As we shall see, that is exactly one of the themes of reading that Cavell most assiduously follows out.

At various moments, Cavell is quite explicit about the fact that these reversals form a major part of his model of philosophical method. Nevertheless, the presence of this model has proven difficult to bear in mind. This model of reading as philosophical method contains much that is continuous with the appeal to ordinary language. Some of what is discontinuous can be usefully mapped back onto the earlier work. But the new model cannot be simply characterized either as merely replacing or as amplifying the older model. For one thing, the model of reading sometimes obscures the appeal to what we ordinarily say, or renders its procedures and results somehow less obviously usable.

The model of reading as a series of reversals points explicitly to certain aspects of psychoanalytic therapy. And the appeal to therapy is in turn designed to illuminate certain features of reading, not least of which is precisely the sense of reversal. Here Cavell presents the reversal of reading as a version of the turning around from the position of offering an interpretation to the position of the one who is being interpreted (if only by a certain silence). This perception points to Freud, and emerges in connection with reflections on psychoanalytic therapy. However, we must be very careful not to imagine that, because Cavell is borrowing a feature of psychoanalysis for his model of reading, he thereby intends to be giving a psychoanalytic account of reading.

Cavell's use of psychoanalytic therapy as a central element of his model of reading is incomprehensible apart from his use of a certain idea of reversal—a certain image of turning back the need for interpretation onto the one who first offers it. But this use of psychoanalysis is still not the same thing as giving a psychoanalytic account of reading or of philosophy. In Cavell's understanding of the situation of reading, we could equally turn the question of explanation back onto the situation of psychoanalysis. Cavell has added a challenge to those efforts to understand the epistemological and ontological commitments of psychoanalytic therapy. He insists on some understanding of how the patient and analyst "read" each other, and how that reading itself can undergo reversal. Of course, psychoanalytic theory had already raised these issues in some form, but mostly under the heading of transference and countertransference. (Cavell, in fact, addresses these issues of transference in *Contesting Tears*, most notably in the chapter on *Letter from an Unknown Woman*.)

Within these issues of psychoanalytic therapy and of reading as a model of philosophical receptivity, we need to examine more closely the relationship between listening to a voice and reading a text. The reversibility of a certain kind of reading can help us understand how and why our speaking out loud in therapy is also an effort to listen. We are, I take it, supposed to be learning to listen to ourselves. But part of what we learn from is our efforts to listen to the therapist as the therapist is listening to us. (An account of transference would be incomplete if it didn't provide at least some account of how it is that the transference attaches to the image of someone who listens. For among the archaic images out of which the transference is constituted, there are presumably more voices than there are listeners.) To adapt a remark of Thoreau's that Cavell is fond of citing: We are learning to listen in this other way, from this other position.

Finally, the account of reading as a series of reversals points toward Cavell's more recent engagements with the writings of what he calls perfectionism. It contains specific room in which to develop certain images and models of perfectionist writing, most specifically the aspect of such writing that proposes to exhibit (mostly in words) a kind of human exemplar, confronted with whom the reader is enabled to recognize certain features of his or her situation and aspirations. Not the least of these aspirations is the one that brought the reader to the pages in question.

This model that I am proposing may seem cumbersome and more than a little opaque. What seems especially to call for more attention is the business about converting the condition of reading into the condition of being read. But without some such version of this account of reading as a model of philosophical method, a great deal of the philosophical value of Cavell's work is likely to be lost amid gestures of philosophical ambition or smothered in high-sounding hopes for a philosophical recovery of the human world. The aim of the following section is to point out some of these dangers, as well as some means of recovery.

I am not arguing that you can experience Cavell's critical or philosophical insights only by coming to appreciate the model of reading that I am investigating. To put it analogically: You do not need to possess a model for Freud's various approaches to a literary text in order to appreciate the timeliness of his insight that sometimes an uncle stands in for a father. But the possibility of such sporadic access to Freud's work does not mean that a more methodologically oriented search for the various models that govern his interpretive labors would be of no use.

A clearer account of Cavell's model of philosophical reading would be of practical use in applying his interpretive insights more methodically. To establish this more effectively, we need more examples of the actual use of Cavell's insights. And I need to provide some instances of a reader—in this case, myself—actually being guided by Cavell's model of reading. To some extent, each of the investigations that compose this book is intended as such an example. But it is becoming more critical to make this relationship between his text and mine more explicit.

In the meantime, I am indeed trying to focus attention on some familiar patterns and perhaps also on some less familiar patterns of reading Cavell. Certainly, Cavell's emphasis on reading has not gone unnoticed. Elements of what I am calling the model of reading have shown up in various discussions of Cavell's procedures, some of which are very useful. Yet the model as such has remained in the background, and its mechanisms have been obscured.

From the perspective of those who are interested in Cavell's literary and film criticism, the willingness to leave Cavell's model of philosophy in obscurity can lead to something like the following picture of his work:

A philosopher with a certain literary sensibility is also, as it happens, a gifted literary critic. Sensing—or hoping—that criticism and philosophy are relevant, Cavell binds them together in a story about the overcoming of skepticism and the recovery of the voice, and about the importance of human acknowledgment in the knowledge of others and in the acceptance of human limitation.

One thing that is missing from this picture is the fact that Cavell is drawn to certain specific works of literature and film, works that present us with the shapes and significances of human events in some of the same ways in which the philosophical skeptic enacts the connection of the human being to the world. The full analogy between tragedy and skepticism has to be between the tragedian's play and the philosopher's textual work. The analogy works in part because for the skeptic the stakes are nothing less than the world—our presence to the world and its presence to us. The skeptic finds that the bare possibility of knowledge—our presence to something real, something well founded—requires that we forgo the world in which we had thought that this connection was secured. The attachment to the world, or the failure of such attachment, cannot be reduced either to the psychic events of a single character or to the play of social forces that the characters are shaped by.

We will also need to examine the relation of this model of reading to the model of philosophy that it succeeds: the model founded on the appeal to what we ordinarily say. The model of reading bears a definite, but to some extent inexplicit, relationship to the model of ordinary speech: it cannot be said simply to replace the earlier model, since the earlier model continues to function, if somewhat less visibly. And it frequently surfaces again to play a striking role in Cavell's work, for instance, in the first two chapters of *A Pitch of Philosophy*. But the new model cannot be simply said to amplify the older model, since sometimes it renders obscure and unstable what had seemed secure among the results of ordinary language philosophy. Like skepticism itself, the idea and act of reading exploits the givenness of language to its own ends. Reading can at least give the appearance of repudiating the givenness of speech. The relation between these two models of philosophical method continues to provoke philosophical reflection in Cavell's writing. An account of his work should neither minimize the tension between these models nor overstate their discontinuity.

On the other hand, if an account of Cavell's work remains unaware of the emergence in his work of this new model of philosophizing, it is unlikely to register any usable awareness of Cavell's methodological insights. Since Cavell offers, however piecemeal, an astonishing range of such insights, and since the secondary literature on his work does not appear to be overflowing with any corresponding appreciation of these insights, I plan to dwell on this model of reading for a while. Readers of Cavell who have worked out these issues of method for themselves will perhaps nevertheless find some use for my formulations.

We can begin studying this model of reading at any of the three moments of reversal: (1) with the act of turning away from the actual reader to become the reader of the prior text; (2) with the action (or passion) of letting oneself be read by the prior text; or (3) with the effort to embody one's transactions with the prior text in a text that exhibits those transactions of reading in a new text, one that is in its turn usable and encouraging to a new set of readers, who are thereby invited to take on the position of the philosophical reader.

This model is capable of illuminating some features of the activity and passivity of reading that good readers from throughout the humanities will be familiar with. At its best, the model draws us further into the region of the transactions, and does not spare us the textual labors that are therein described. Moreover, versions of these features of reading and reversal have been studied by critics such as Northrop Frye, Harold Bloom, Jacques Derrida, Jacques Lacan, and Shoshana Felman. In practice, the readers of the present book are more likely to be engaged with Cavell's transactions of reading, in varying degrees of entanglement and explicitness. It is more specifically to these transactions that I will address this model and from which I will abstract further details and modes of the model's operation.

In many ways, what I am calling the third reversal is the most difficult place to try to begin understanding the series of exchanges between yourself and the text. For this reversal is made up of the exchanges we are most immediately absorbed in: the point of primary access to this model must be acts of actual, empirical reading. There are general difficulties about trying to study the activity one is currently engaged in, and there are some special problems about reading and self-consciousness. Studying the acts of reading that you are now engaged in is likely to be at least as problematic as studying the nature of consciousness by examining the headache you currently suffer from. (Cf. *Philosophical Investigations*, #314.)

A more promising start can be made by examining the other two reversals. Such a study would make clear something of what enables or impedes the flow of insight and energy between the position of the prior text and the developing position of the philosopher-reader. In a sense, the third reversal—that of empirical reader into philosophical reader—invites us to reenact the first two reversals on my list, and to do this as representatively as possible. That is, we are invited to take on the posture of the text that is in front of us: You have to try it out on yourself, as Cavell is constantly saying. But what sounds like a democratic-Thoreauvian invitation to see for yourself, or read for yourself, soon becomes more complicated. For what we are supposed to be trying out for ourselves is, first of all, the present text's conversion of itself into the role of the philosophical reader of some prior text.

There are two dangers that attend fairly closely upon our acceptance of this invitation to read. The first is that we take the invitation to read as an invitation to read the prior text *directly*, without the mediation of the philosophical reader. The second danger seems at first to be opposite to this one: If you have accepted the invitation to read in the posture of the philosophical reader—call him "Cavell"—how will you tell the difference between a reading that puts his insights to a new use and a reading that contents itself with imagining that it has merged its position with his? And in either case, a further question will arise: How are we to do the thing that Cavell keeps telling us we are supposed to learn from Emerson and Thoreau: How do we stop reading? This raises the issue of how we are to dispense with the intermediary and go on to read something on our own.

This wish to dispense with the intermediary is an admirable pedagogical and philosophical goal. But the model contains no immediate hint of how this is to occur: How are we to dispense with the text that is teaching us to read, and go on with our reading? The text contains no further hints beyond what we can discern from the activities of the philosopher-reader. It is from these activities that we have to figure out how the reading he is engaged in will come to an end and how our own reading will supervene.

Cavell's sketches for the model of the philosopher-becoming-the-reader text almost invariably contain a moment where the reader stops or checks himself. At such moments, reading may continue again in a moment, or another theme of reflection may take over, if only as a sign of the need to relinquish reading. I will be dealing with these various dangers in the course of my investigations, along with Cavell's own suggestions and depictions of this sort of reading and of its remedies.

It may seem as if I have neglected the most important question about this model, the question of what makes it a model of philosophy. How can this model show us something of the steps by which a piece of philosophical work can be accomplished? It is true that I have not yet tried to say explicitly what makes this model of reading into a model of philosophy. The answer to this must appear in relation to specific acts of reading. (As indeed we would not know the role of argumentation in philosophy unless we knew some good arguments and could also perhaps produce some.) Some of my answer will have to wait until the next sections, when I try to give some readings of Cavell's engagements with Emerson and Thoreau. But my account of those engagements needs this preparatory work, precisely because I am trying to pry loose Cavell's model of reading from at least some of his versions of the story about the emergence of that model. So I need to retell that story, but from a series of different vantage points. What those differences amount to will show up more clearly later on.

In the meantime, it should be clear that focusing on these reversals is meant to be faithful to Cavell's own accounts of reading. But my continued insistence on this focus is intended to initiate a kind of commentary on his accounts. Moreover, it is precisely my portrait of these reversals that is meant to capture the philosophical center of Cavell's model of reading. Without this idea of reversal, it would be much more difficult to think of the idea and the practices of reading as providing a model of philosophical method.

I want to discuss further the feature of philosophy that I have already mentioned as emblematized in the reversals of reading. This is the requirement that *the steps of a philosophical method can, in principle, be taken by anyone.* Whatever specialized knowledge of the nature of a problem has brought us to the moment when we have to take the next philosophical step, it must not be anything special about us that leads us and enables us to take this step.

This feature of *nothing special* about the one who takes the next step will seem too weak or perhaps itself too specialized to count as part of a characterization of philosophical method. What gives content and pertinence to this characterization is precisely the characterization of what is excluded. We know what counts as "nothing special" by looking at what falls under the heading of "special" knowledge or ability.

It will hardly be doubted that it was a fateful and formative moment for philosophy when it excluded the declarations of religion or revelation as forming the condition from within which a new step is authorized. More controversial but more recently decisive is Descartes' exclusion of expert testimony—or indeed of any of the traditional philosophical modes of inheritance that he could get his hands on. It is still unclear how far the exclusion of other modes of inheritance contributes, in itself, to the sense of inevitability attaching to the steps that lead Descartes into the cauldron of doubt. What is interesting is that the prohibition against any inheritance of philosophical testimony remains effectively in force when the author emerges from that doubt to take the remaining steps of the *Meditations*. Dialogue with others is no longer an intrinsic part of the prosecution of philosophical method.

Whether or not Descartes' cogito succeeds as an act of methodological self-grounding, it is an outstanding example of the kind of methodological step that must be open to all. Its substantive point is compromised if the assertion "I am" is not open to all who can speak. And the methodological point would be lost if any other authority or expertise were permitted to be relevant. There may or may not be specialists in the sui generis (as Austin joked). And there may or may not be those who can be described as having successfully specialized in the knowledge of their own existence. But there are no experts who have specialized in the *performance* of the *cogito*. (This is not to discount the expertise of the historian of early modern philosophy but to specify one of its limits.)

To speak of the steps of a method as open is not meant to cover everything that might be discovered to be a valid philosophical method. The other feature of method that seems most to require attention here is the idea that *the methodological step is not only open to all but is necessary to all who can see the possibility of taking the step.*

The idea of the reversibility of reading is meant to comprise both aspects of what might count as a methodological step. But it gives us an image of the necessity of the step only with an important difference. It is relatively easy to see how the idea of reversal gives us an idea of the openness of the method: If I can take over the position of the first philosophical reader—the one whose text is giving me a reading of some prior text—then I am able (at least under certain circumstances) to apprehend what enabled me to take this step. In turning around from my position of reader of the text in front of me to the position of actually performing the reading that this text is now performing, I have a chance to see what this reading depends on in me. Nothing ensures that I will take this step of checking what my reading depends on. Nothing ensures that I will not discover, for instance, that the points of my identification with the text in front of me are themselves too special to count as generally valid.

The kind of text that Cavell gravitates toward goes a step further: the ability to take on the position of the philosopher-reader depends on the ability to take on that reader's activity. As you find yourself addressed, you must be prepared to reverse directions along with whoever or whatever is addressing you. In particular, you are to orient yourself in relation to the activity of whatever is addressing you, as that text orients itself in relation to what it finds itself addressed by. You are to follow the author as she reverses direction from the stance of addressing you to the stance of reading and receiving the prior text. And then you are somehow still to follow along as the text you are reading turns back to the stance of authorship, making good on the receipts of reading. The ability of the empirical reader-student to engage the philosopher-reader is not so much an activity as it is the right kind of passiveness and the right kind of reception.

But from the vantage point of the kind of step that enables us to re-verse ourselves—and check our reading—we also come to see the need for taking the step we have just taken. Clearly not every kind of text will allow for this sort of self-reversal and self-reflection. And sometimes, of course, you won't see either the step forward or the step back. Or else you will wrongly imagine that you have taken the step along with the writer. Or you will wrongly imagine that you have taken the step back into your own position as a reader, and wrongly imagine that your perceptiveness was enlarged or enriched by what you have been reading. But a surprising number of texts and readers will succeed with each other on something like these terms. There is plenty of room to explore the possibilities, and, no doubt, plenty of room for improvement.

It is also the case that when you do not or cannot take the step, the problem may not lie with you. Perhaps you were offered a step that was not really a step, or offered an invitation that was only the form or the shell of an invitation. But reading is surely not the only aspirant to the status of a philosophical method in which there is a question about whether the problem lies with me or with the step that was offered to me. (Or perhaps there is a yet more grievous problem with the one who made the offer.)

The features of methodology that I have isolated as at least having counterparts in the model of reading are both primitive and so-phisticated. The primitiveness I have in mind is not necessarily a dis-advantage, and I want to pause for a moment to draw out a historical comparison. I think it will ultimately prove to be more than "merely" a historical comparison, but I will settle, at the moment, for some his-torical perspective on the origins and significance of method. I have in mind, in particular, the ways in which methods are depicted or dramatized as at the origins of philosophy. And I have in mind the relation of such depicted methods to our sense of what the philosophical text is or is capable of.

We can think of the difference between a methodological step that is open to all and a step that is not thus open as analogous to the difference between the way Socrates deflects the oracle's effort to single him out and the way in which the hero of Parmenides' poem accepts his heroic assignment from the goddess. I am not denying that there is philosophy to be found in Parmenides' poem. But I wish to make something out of the fact that the philosophizing in the poem comes as a dictate from the voice of the goddess. The steps *toward* philosophy, or *toward* thinking, are not themselves depicted as open to anyone other than the hero. At any rate, they are not open to us, unless we happen to have some divinely inspired animals to bear us toward the divine realm of truth.

My reading of the opening verses of Parmenides' poem takes seriously what is usually dismissed as a sort of residue of religious stage-setting. I am suggesting that the depiction of the hero's journey tells us something of how the hero came to be in a position to heed the call of the goddess. The members of the audience of the poem are, in effect, listening in on the transactions between the goddess and the hero.

Philosophical method begins not so much with a disclaimer of divine inspiration as with a willingness to open the methodological steps to all and sundry. Or to put it in terms of the difference between Parmenides and Socrates, the methodological steps are open to all those who desire to speak to Socrates and who are willing to go on subjecting themselves to his ability to listen and to gather in the various elements of their assertions. I am close to describing Socrates as *reading* the discourse of those he listens to. But I will settle for insisting that the point of Socrates' discovery of logic is the discovery of a method by which we subject ourselves to the implications of what we have already said. And the steps of this method must be open to all—though naturally only the one who has already spoken will feel the pinch of the method most acutely.

The precise timing of when you will see the necessity of the step that you are taking is more than a little up in the air. In the model of reading, we saw that the acknowledgment of the necessity of the step was delayed or deferred. In Socrates' step-by-step invitations to self-refutation, the victim sees that each step *must* be taken. After a while, he may see something of the intellectual self-cancellation toward which he is ineluctably moving. What the interlocutor tends not to foresee in a Socratic dialogue is the exact steps by which his assertions will destroy themselves. And he often does not see the casual moment of self-assertion in his words that gives Socrates what he needs to bring two incompatible assertions together. All Socrates needs to do, apparently, is to bear these assertions in mind until the moment when the incompatibility can be made evident.

And why shouldn't Socrates be able to do this? Since Socrates has freed his mind of all other cant and rubbish and has, above all, freed himself of the need to assert something, why shouldn't his mind possess powers of concentration that we can only dream of? We don't believe in this sort of thing anymore—or at least not in most frames of mind. But it is unclear what we disbelieve in more: that one could truly free oneself of this human need for assertion; or that freeing oneself of the need for assertion will effect a more general liberation and transformation of the character.

It is relevant to my argument that in this period of his writing Cavell finds the defeat of skepticism to depend on what he calls "the withholding of assertion." Before we could link this diagnosis and treatment of the skeptic to Socrates' practices of philosophy we would have to build some conceptual bridges. On the side of Socrates, one would first have to propose the sense that assertions always contain, if they are genuine, some elements of self-assertion. We might postulate a kind of myth of a Greek world in which the self is staked more clearly on the words that it asserts. Or we might imagine that somehow the selves in a Platonic dialogue are more invested in their words than seems to be the case in contemporary conversation, or indeed, in contemporary speech altogether. If Socrates managed to free himself of the normal human investments in a merely private logos, this would be a way of justifying his repeated claim that he is following the logos, wherever it leads.

Far from being a mere piety about the power of argumentation and his faithfulness to it, the idea of following the *argument* would be his way of characterizing his procedure as the reverse of that of ordinary mortals. For they make the logos follow them: they make their assertions express their desire and their wish to justify their position. But Socrates makes his own position obedient to the logos, to what has been said, whoever has said it. He follows the argument, the way the rest of us follow the crowd. That may be just as hard to believe as the idea that freeing the self of its need to assert will in fact free up its powers of recollection and, so to speak, collectedness.

I present this image of Socratic argument and methodology first of all as an image of the openness of the steps in a philosophical method. I have said very little about the relation of this openness to the more famous esotericism of philosophy. But my image of Socrates suggests at least one way in which a faithfulness to the apparently simple steps of a method can yield a path of thought that is far from the habitual thoughts of ordinary human beings. It is not the eventual distance from the populace that separates Socrates from the hero of Parmenides' poem, but the nature of the first steps that they find themselves taking.

Two other issues about reading bear mentioning: (1) It can seem as if this idea of philosophical reading is just a dressed-up—or dressed-down—version of the idea of a philosophical commentary, an idea at least as old as Aristotle. (2) The model of reading seems too complex to help illuminate the complexities of reading, as it was presumably meant to do.

The second issue raises an important point about models, namely, that the closer they get to whatever they are meant to be modeling the more they start to seem either unwieldy or irrelevant. In this case, when the model of reading is put to use—that is, when we are actually engaged in reading—the workings of the model should tend to simplify themselves. They will then be of greater help in elucidating the reading that we are engaged in. (Sometimes it is easier to perform a somersault than to describe one. But something like a description may still be part of teaching someone how to do a somersault.)

The question about the relation of Cavell's model of philosophical reading to the good old-fashioned model of philosophical commentary points us to the question of authority: the philosophical authority by which I offer a running commentary on a prior text is partly related to my skill at noticing historically and philosophically remarkable items. What counts as "useful" or remarkable may depend in part on how well the commentator can either illuminate a well-known textual or philosophical puzzle or else make the audience feel the existence of a problem where none had been felt.

As an instance of the former, we may take "What does Kant mean by pleasure 'without interest'?" or "Does Plato change the meaning of 'justice' from book 1 to book 4 of the *Republic*?" Examples of the latter are harder to come by and harder to state briefly. But consider in this light the efforts to understand Kant's conviction in the power of beauty to symbolize the good as something more than a faded neoclassical piety. Or consider the efforts to remove some of the sting of the prejudices against Aristotle's argument from the "function" of a human soul to its specific virtue. And against a different kind of resistance, some commentators got us to reread Aristotle on friendship as a virtue. Some of this work has helped to change the shape of modern philosophical ethics. A good commentator may alter our sense of what counts as a problem in a text and may even shift our sense of what, in the present day, can count as a serious philosophical interest.

Naturally, changes in current philosophical interests may also change the ways in which we read the past.[3] We might try to say that such changes are merely changes of intellectual fashion. But then one must remember that where these shifts in perspective are not merely matters of intellectual fashion they are likely to be the effects of significant intellectual work. Those who believe that the dictates of fashion are undetectable, or unavoidable, are unlikely to do the work that it takes to recognize this sort of philosophical accomplishment.

Surely a good commentator and a good reader (in Cavell's sense) are related. But the reader cannot count on a prior community of interest. This sort of reader must, indeed, actively strive to discount any prior agreement on the part of any particular community of scholars. No other interest is supposed to be present when we begin to read. In particular, there is supposed to be no prior philosophical authority deriving from the importance of the question or the problem, or the philosophical standing of the text. At the furthest reach of this image of reading, Cavell is willing to give up even the interest in the bare idea that a thought might count as philosophical.

No doubt his willingness to forgo all such authority in his activities of reading and writing has to do with his distrust of the pattern of interests around which philosophical authority has been organized since roughly the time of Descartes. This sort of authority implied, among other things, a certain picture of philosophical progress and interest. And within that pattern of interests, argumentation was already destined to be central, and reading was already destined to be secondary and derivative.[4] Cavell's image of reading is intended to offer a kind of incentive to give up the traditional vision of philosophical arguments and the interests they advance. Part of that incentive is the model of philosophical method that I have been presenting as contained in the practices of reading. But part of it is surely to be found in the anarchic pleasures of reading beyond the bounds that modern philosophy has set for itself. The method of reading no more guarantees that we will stay within the bounds of philosophical decorum than the method of doubting.

S uch willingness to read past our interests as they currently stand— including one's interests in philosophy as a path of thinking—can be exhilarating. (That it can be scary is surely no bar to its being exhilarating.) The image of such reading leads Cavell to some of his most elated encounters, especially with Thoreau and Emerson.

> [Emerson's] difference from other philosophical writing is, I think, that it asks the philosophical mood so purely, so incessantly, giving one little other intellectual amusement or eloquence or information, little other

argument or narrative, and no other source of companionship or importance, either political or religious or moral, save the importance of philosophy, of thinking itself. [*Senses of Walden,* 152.]

I could not say, offhand, whether anyone has ever actually read like this,
from scratch. The dream or the fantasy of arriving at such a mode of
reading seems important for something like the same reasons that "wonder" can still seem to be a cause and consequence of Plato's ability to phi-
losophize. In any event, the "purity" of this mode of thinking need not
be there at the beginning of a session of reading: the purity is the purity
of relinquishment. Its dangers are not, in the first place, the dangers of
going too far but the dangers of asceticism or of false purity.

Cavell identifies the mode of writing that calls for "thinking itself"
with a mode of writing that brings us to a certain mood, or fails to. This
is an image of thinking as arriving at—and no doubt as safely departing
from—a frame of mind in which one is willing to give up the need for
importance and companionship and the received forms of significance and
signification. Academic philosophy gave up thinking about the appropriate moods of thinking at roughly the moment it gave up thinking about
"wonder." So it is safe to say that this idea of philosophy as drawing us
into a particular mood is not likely to catch on.

In terms of my own investigation of Cavell's model of reading and its
various potential reversals and failures, it is worth noting that Cavell's
ecstasy about Emerson is introduced by a sense of its failure, or rather of
its deferred effectiveness:

> The idea of a mood to which philosophical thinking must bring us is
> still not quite enough to describe my inability for so long to get on with
> Emerson. His words did not merely strike me as partaking of a mood to
> which they could not draw me, and hence remained empty to me. They
> seemed to me repellent, quite as if presenting me with something for which
> I could not acknowledge my craving. [*The Senses of Walden,* 152.]

It is an old story, or at least a perennially Romantic story, that when you
start to read or to write you do not know whether you will end up with
sublimity or with embarrassment. (There is, of course, still a great deal to
learn about the nature and the sources of this embarrassment.) The sublime itself seems constituted, even according to Kant, as an alternation of
attractions and repulsions. Cavell clearly wants to find in just such materials the stuff of a philosophical reading.

It should be clear by now that my biggest problem with this enterprise
is not that Cavell will fail to accomplish it, but that he will succeed. Those
who find Cavell's words repellent are all too many, and they seem un-

likely to wait around for the eventual attraction. Those who find them attractive are inclined to find them too precious to want to acknowledge their intermittent emptiness. Must we find his words repellent before we really learn how to read him?

If you do not think these words about Emerson are meant to apply to Cavell—to be in this sense reversible—then you are very unlikely to believe that there is a method of reading at work in Cavell's massive productivity. You are also unlikely to think there is a usable relation between his moods of creation and reception and the specific paths of investigation that he is taking. If you *do* see that the words about Emerson's powers of repulsion apply to our reception of Cavell, then the next question is even tougher: Why should we want this diet of cravings for emptiness and fullness? Why go searching for this peculiar mix of significance and the undoing of false significance? How are you supposed to live—let alone hold down a job or get any reading done—on so strenuous a regime of thought?

Matters do not get much better when you start to appreciate that the text you are reading does not, according to Cavell, have to be a text of words or even a text of art. One might have felt liberated to discover that a philosophical reader could work on a poem by Wordsworth or Hölderlin or a novel by Eliot or a story of Poe's or a play of Ibsen's. Then there are those faces and physiognomies of human beings and their words, which are also becoming available for something that *The Claim of Reason* at least calls "reading." And Cavell also offers us an image of Thoreau contemplating the history he finds written in a railway carload of torn sails, more "graphically" and more "legibly" than in any book (*Walden*, 108–10).[5]

Cavell's first two books on the movies were so full of pleasure that many readers found it easy enough to put aside the question of how exactly his viewings and soundings of a movie were supposed to constitute a *reading* of it. He takes up the question in the expanded edition of *The World Viewed*, and thematically in the introduction to *Pursuits of Happiness*. In both places, a connection is getting made between the idea of reading and the idea of *having seen* something. This connection underlies his recurrent use of the history of the word *reading* as a word for "[being] advised," which in turn contains a root for "seeing." It may help to locate the significance of the etymology if we see the tension between reading as a current process and reading as gathering the significance of something that has already occurred. This displays more precisely the problem of how to characterize the "reading" of a film within a larger problem of how to locate the temporality of film and, indeed, the temporality of reading. (Cf. *The World Viewed*, xii–xvii.)

There is still a question whether we possess an adequate sense of the connection between the reading that philosophy represses and the neglect or derogation of film that philosophical aesthetics has perhaps engaged in. (There are by now significant exceptions to this rule.) In part this means that the neglect of film seems overdetermined. Intellectuals still routinely make remarks like the following, as if their significance for the subject were obvious: Film is a popular form, essentially mass-produced; it is an escape; the plots are silly and "unrealistic"; the dialogue isn't interesting enough to sustain serious commentary; Hollywood insists on happy endings. And so on.

But where exactly within these various causes of the neglect of film do we locate something that might be called the repression of film? And where within such an idea are the repressions of reading that Cavell discerns and the recoveries of reading that he encourages? This ultimately forces the question of the relation between the repression of the medium (e.g., of film, but possibly also of verse) and the repression of the methods of the investigator of that medium.

I note one other difference and one other similarity between what Cavell calls philosophical reading and what philosophy calls commentary. As commentators, we do not normally have to work to get some particular philosophical audience to accept Kant or Aristotle as serious philosophers. So we do not have the additional question of whether what is being dismissed or neglected is the subject matter or the medium of my investigation and argument. On the other hand, if my task is trying to get Aristotle on friendship or Kant on beauty as a symbol accepted as a serious topic, it may require a certain level of reflection about the contemporary philosophical means or media available to me for such a discussion.[5]

Cavell's understanding of the repression of reading ought to raise the issue of whether we really understand what kept us from reading such things, and what, from time to time, still keeps us from such reading. At first it may seem that if you have the taste for something you might as well go ahead and give a reading of it. Those who think that Cavell's discernment of a repression of reading has given us permission to read anything we like are not exactly wrong, but they are somewhat hasty. Like those who responded to Freud's announcement of the repression of infantile sexuality by striving to increase the quality and the quantity of their current sexual encounters, those who receive Cavell in this fashion are likely to miss the fact that the philosophical repression of reading is not going to go away just by increasing the number and kinds of texts that you are willing to try to read.

I do not mean to simply recommend against such an effort by philosophers to read a greater variety of texts. But this sense of what I might call polymorphous legibility is likely to affect our understanding of what Cavell means by inheriting philosophy as a set of texts. It is possible to feel at certain moments that philosophy's prohibition against reading drops away at Cavell's announcement that we are now free to read. But we must be careful not to conclude from this feeling that Cavell's idea of inheriting philosophy as a set of texts implies that we begin by *getting rid of* philosophical problems. Cavell is very clear that taking a problem such as other minds as a kind of text (or as embedded in a text, or as generating a field of texts) does not imply that the philosophical problem has suddenly vanished. The fact that a problem can become the source of texts does not abolish its status as a problem (just as the fact that philosophy can "treat" a question "like an illness" does not imply that the question-like character of the question is merely a symptom). Cavell's remarks about the relation of problems to texts are only the beginning of the discussion, and it would be harmful to reduce the complexity of the relationship.

We have already seen something about how the issues of reading form part of a still more encompassing set of issues about reception. Early on, Cavell connected these issues to questions about the reception and possession of philosophy. The fact that reading and reception are necessarily up for grabs in this model helps prepare the way for the question of who possesses philosophy—or more accurately, about what the possession of it is found to consist in. More recently, Cavell has explored these questions under the rubric of inheritance—strikingly in his readings of the story of Jacob and Esau. In the next chapter we will pursue some of these questions in connection to the problems of the audience for philosophy. Here I will just dwell briefly on the fact that some of these issues go back to the beginning of his reflections about the writing of philosophy.

As I pointed out above, the foreword to Cavell's first book had already raised issues about the questionableness of any "audience" for philosophy. What emerges in that foreword, titled "An Audience for Philosophy," is a question about the "possession" of philosophy. It is not hard to relate this question to the various reversals of reading that I have been characterizing. You do not need Cavell's writing as a guide to find the act of reading to be a struggle with the text—Harold Bloom, or Lionel Trilling, or Nietzsche, or even David Hume can tell you that much. (I am thinking of Hume's essay "Of the Rise and Progress of the Arts and

Sciences," admittedly not a very familiar piece of Hume among American philosophers.)

But Cavell's work forces the question about the nature of this struggle and of this "possession," a possession that, as he says, is not only not possessive but the "reverse of" possessive. In "Thinking of Emerson" he puts it like this:

> Such writing [as that of Emerson and Thoreau] takes the same mode of relating to itself as reading and thinking do, the mode of the self's relation to itself, call it self-reliance. Then whatever is acquired in possessing a self will be required in thinking and reading and writing. This possessing is not—it is the reverse of—possessive; I have implied that in being an act of creation, it is the exercise not of power but of reception. [*The Senses of Walden*, 134–35.]

Despite the somewhat gaudy, or Romantic, talk of creation, this passage seems pretty clear that the leading term is reception, and hence, when you get down to it, reading. The right kind of reception lies underneath (or is a form of) the appropriate mode of possession and creation. ("All I know is reception; I am and I have but I do not get . . . ," as Emerson puts it in "Experience.") As we shall see, Cavell develops the importance of "the right way of reading" or of "creative reading" as a kind of allegorical transition between the actual, literal activities of scholars and writers— their transactions with literal books and literal reading—and the kind of reception in which the self is conceived or reconceived.

Anyone taking seriously Cavell's first published encounters with Emerson is unlikely to miss the potential significance of reading. Once we see the links between reading and reception—and then a little later, between reading and abandonment—we understand that on this path lies the appropriate response to skepticism. Again, we are not to refute it but to "reconceive its truth" (133). Here the acknowledgment of the intimacy of ourselves to our words and of our words to our world becomes a kind of appeasement. We hang between our sense of having allowed some peace to supervene on the quarrels with our world and with our thoughts, and our sense of being unable to support our present settlements. In this vision of what Cavell calls "onward thinking," the time for departure might always be at hand. We are to live "undefined in front" (as Thoreau puts it), in a state of emergence that is difficult to tell from emergency.

More immediately, I want to go a step further with Cavell's idea of reading as a reception and a possession that is the "reverse of" possessive. This thought is a kind of clue that will take us beyond the idea that reading is the opposite of the possessive, the miserly, and the (merely) oedipal confrontation with a prior text. Indeed, I take the thought to confirm the point of my model by implying that good reading is arrived at by a process of *reversing* whatever is possessive and constricting in such confrontations.[6] And this piece of methodological advice reminds us that not every reversal of reading is equally valuable: the reversal that merely wishes to possess what the philosophical author possesses—to take over the hoard of precious insights—will not undergo the reversal that learns to disburse this insight.

Perhaps it is not so surprising that underneath the shifts in Cavell's procedures and within the tremendous productivity concomitant with the publication of *The Claim of Reason*, the idea of reading comes to provide a central point of methodological organization and perspective. It comes to epitomize Cavell's procedures. But these epitomes of his reading are not merely static pictures of foregone conclusions. The energy of these readings is the energy that is circulating throughout his work. Now we need to know something more about the sources of that energy. We must search for these sources within Cavell's own powers as a reader. We are not likely to find them apart from locating our own responses to the specific texts within which he encountered the model of reading and its reversals.

5

READING AND ITS REVERSALS

In chapter 4, I outlined a model of reading as a method for taking steps in philosophy. I want now to examine more consecutively the moments where Cavell first encountered these issues of reading and first began to offer us his sketches of this model. This moment will in turn help illuminate one of his central themes, the relationship between the successful achievements of philosophical reading and the dangers that such reading is exposed to. This model is meant, among other things, to help us locate and calibrate these difficulties: we are to learn to take the failures of reading less personally—though not less intimately, as Cavell once put it. This sort of defect in our reading is not so much a matter of our personal shortcomings, severe as these may be. Such failures are not necessarily inevitable, but they are inherent in the structure of the enterprise of reading and, hence, inherent in this way of doing philosophy.

These issues about reading will return us to the questions of Cavell's treatment of skepticism and point us toward some further issues about the risks that form a part of such philosophizing. Finally, I want to connect these questions of reading and skepticism to questions concerning the implication of the audience for such work. Those who become the audience for such procedures are often implicated as much by the work's success as by its failures.

Perhaps every interesting model of reading, like every interesting model of philosophical method, can be understood only in glimpses, in the course of its actual use. Cavell's own sketches of this model of reading emerged piecemeal, as I remarked above, mostly in the course of his engagements with Thoreau and Emerson. I will examine several of these texts at moments where the model emerges most strikingly. I will then draw out some consequences for a reading of Cavell and isolate a number

of misreadings. Again, reading and misreading lie close together, but not inextricably so.

The first fully thematic emergence of this idea and model of reading is to be found in "The Philosopher in American Life," delivered at Wesleyan as a commencement address and then revised as the first of the Beckman lectures at Berkeley in 1983. Cavell begins with an enactment of the kind of delay in naming a philosophical operation that I have characterized as typifying the work of *The Claim of Reason.* I note especially that Cavell introduces his understanding of the effectiveness of Thoreau and Emerson's writing *prior* to the naming of this effectiveness.

> The moral to draw here [from the failure to take up Emerson as a philosopher] may of course be the one [Bruce] Kuklick draws, that Emerson and Thoreau are to be comprehended as philosophical amateurs, toward whom, it would be implied, there is no professional obligation. But suppose the better moral is that Emerson and Thoreau are as much threats, or say embarrassments, to what we have learned to call philosophy as they are to what we call religion, as though philosophy had, and has, an interest on its own behalf in looking upon them as amateurs, an interest, I think I may say, in repressing them. This would imply that they propose, and embody, a mode of thinking, a mode of conceptual accuracy, as thorough as anything imagined within established philosophy, but invisible to that philosophy because based on an idea of rigor foreign to its establishment. [*In Quest of the Ordinary,* 14.]

Cavell goes on to show his awareness that he is delaying the release of the name of this foreign rigor, the thing that Thoreau and Emerson embody and the thing that "established philosophy" represses. Since his essay explicitly mentions "suspense" as one of the tendencies that Kierkegaard attacks in philosophy, and as a danger that Thoreau and Emerson successfully overcome, I take Cavell's delay to be deliberate.

> Before I go on to name this foreign rigor, I have at least to indicate some way to avoid, or postpone, a standing and decisive consideration that professional philosophers will have for refusing to hear out an articulation that Emerson and Thoreau warrant the name of philosophy—the consideration that no matter what one may mean by, say, conceptual accuracy, a work like *Walden* has nothing in it to call arguments. [Ibid.]

Written five years after the composition of *The Senses of Walden*—and not published for another five years—this passage feels like the other shoe of acknowledgment dropping.

It is not as if the author of *The Senses of Walden* was unaware of this

charge against *Walden* and against his own efforts to establish a philosophical access or beachhead at *Walden*. Indeed, one might well wonder what originally allowed him to pursue the idea of Thoreau as a philosopher, or the scarcely less controversial idea of Thoreau as next door to philosophy, as neighboring it. Cavell's pursuit of Thoreau and Emerson is so tireless and so antagonistic to academic philosophy's sense of appropriateness that one can also start to wonder whether all of Cavell's motives for this pursuit were equally evident to him.

I remember a small piece of instruction from the unofficial curriculum of my graduate education. One of the younger teachers that I admired had been impressed by something about Cavell's early work on Wittgenstein and had tried to read *The Senses of Walden*, which had just appeared. He sought me out to explain, with a restrained sense of urgency, that he could appreciate Thoreau as a writer who possessed great insight into human existence and an aptitude for powerful descriptions of nature. But he could never regard Thoreau as a philosopher. However much wisdom and brilliance *Walden* might contain, it contained no arguments. And the ability to put forward arguments in support of a position, while not the whole story, was so distinctive a part of what made something a work of philosophy that a philosopher couldn't really give up arguing without giving up philosophy.

It was clear that he wanted to say this to me before anything else got said, either about Thoreau or about Cavell's book on Thoreau. But once he had made these remarks, the possibilities of further conversation seemed constrained. I knew I needed to say something more about arguments, and he didn't seem to know how to say anything very consecutive about what he *did* like about Thoreau or Cavell. I gave some sort of response to the issues he was raising, but nothing sufficed to get that conversation started again. In fact, periodically I find myself wanting to add to my response. For instance, it seems to me that it is not quite right to say that there is *nothing* to call an argument in *Walden*. (The premises may be unusual, but then aren't some of Plato's premises a bit unusual—a bit myth-ridden, from time to time?) Thoreau, for instance, gives some fairly elaborate arguments in favor of reading the classics. But almost as quickly as I think of such points I come back to the realization that the argument about arguments is rarely advanced by further arguments. His point did not catch me completely off guard, but it left me, nevertheless, with a sense of being unprotected. And it continues to leave me so.

I was therefore pleased when "The Philosopher in American Life" picked up the thread of this quarrel. But my pleasure was muted. Underneath the disputes about Thoreau, there remained a series of unresolved

questions concerning what draws a writer to certain subjects and to certain treatments of those subjects. I still, from time to time, find it worth asking, Why did Cavell have to turn to *those* writers—and hence go to those lengths—to ask and answer such questions? Was there no book closer to home by which to challenge the strictures of contemporary philosophy and no way to avoid provoking the counter-questions ("How can this be philosophy?") that inevitably seemed to spoil any chance for a straightforward discussion of the issues?

It is not that there were no answers to the objections that flowed in on my efforts at discussion. It is rather that the answers seemed sometimes belated and sometimes premature. Either they came too late to change anything fundamental in the presuppositions of those who were making the objections, or, what is perhaps worse, it seemed necessary to arrive at a defense of Cavell too quickly. It wasn't just that I felt called upon to say things that I couldn't follow up (for instance, because they required a wider knowledge than I possess of the history of philosophy or of modern literature and the arts. Or perhaps I needed a more articulate way of presenting the issues of Kant's aesthetics in relation to Cavell's procedures).

Beyond this, I was being drawn into defending aspects of Cavell's work that should not, at that moment, have been defended. I do not mean that these aspects of his work were indefensible. But his own response was different. He rarely responded to the discussions of his work merely in order to defend himself (and almost never in print). His response to being attacked and feeling exposed was, generally, to bring what he could of the objections within the purview of his own procedures. More often he then found ways of converting something about being objected to into something worth learning from. A partial exception that tends to prove my case is "A Matter of Meaning It," which was a rejoinder to the responses of Monroe Beardsley and Joseph Margolis to the essay "Music Discomposed." Cavell's piece soon abandons the form of the rebuttal to objections and looks toward a wider context of modernism, of Romanticism, of intentionality, and of the poet's address to the reader. Cavell even ends up with his first sustained writing about the movies (Fellini's *La Strada*).[1]

It is in looking back at this period of his writing that Cavell begins to use the phrase "leaving myself unguarded." Somewhere he even calls it a point of philosophical pride. Whatever place such moments have in his *character* as a philosopher, I am suggesting that they also play a significant role in his *development* as a philosopher. But these tendencies have also had their effect on his students and readers. A student cannot appeal to the virtues of being unguarded precisely at those moments of a philosophical discussion when the best offense is a good defense.

The one feature of Cavell's work that he could not offer to his students by the example of his writing was the virtue of its patience. From within the imperatives that your own writing enacts and obeys, you cannot also exemplify your reader's need to find her own pace of self-development as a philosopher and a writer. There was therefore a certain accuracy in my sense of being drawn prematurely into a defense of Cavell's work. And under that threat of prematurity, there was also an obscure feeling that I needed to develop faster than the timetables of graduate school and teaching could allow for.

In later years, something seems to alter the relation between Cavell's writing as such and its more pedagogical relation to his students in philosophy. In any event, the economy of the exchanges between his work and his explanations of his work is a significant departure from Austin's way with these matters. As Cavell has pointed out on several occasions, Austin gave very few answers about the point of his philosophical practices, and perhaps even fewer answers concerning his radical departure from the traditional proceedings of philosophy. The answers he gave were interesting enough, but generally speaking, they were far less satisfying than the practices they were meant to explain. (For example, there is Austin's aphoristic remark that the appeals to ordinary language yield, if not the Last Word, then at least the First Word.)[2]

Cavell's reflections on method and on reading are built into the footpaths and highways of his work. But for that very reason they may occur to a student or reader of his, before the student has gotten far enough with the practices to catch anything more than the drift of the reflection. One price of these answers is the possibility that a student is able to defend a position or a practice, but without yet being able to withstand the rigors and isolation of that position. In other cases, one can see more immediately that steps have been skipped. And in a procedure founded on reading, the skipping of steps, like the skipping of sentences, is liable to cause problems.

I take the tendency to prematurity in answering questions about Thoreau and reading to be foreshadowed in the delay and deferral of Cavell's own answers. And these answers had to be bound up, I am arguing, in a conception of reading that needed to be, so to speak, exemplified before it could be conceptualized. By then of course, the answers available to his students were essentially limitless—but out of touch with the labor and example of reading that had produced these answers and these conceptualizations. The answers I had wanted to be able to give to such questions as my other teacher had challenged me with had gone from prematurity to belatedness. My present investigations and readings of Cavell can be

seen as an effort to restore the missing stages of my appointments with
Cavell's questions, no less than with his answers.

C avell's answer to the question about arguments in Thoreau had a
power and a suggestiveness that carried well beyond its ability to
take Thoreau under its philosophical wing:

> But suppose what is meant by argumentation in philosophy is a way of
> accepting full responsibility for one's own discourse. Then the hearing I
> require depends on the thought that there is another way, another philo-
> sophical way (for poetry will have its way, and therapy will have its way)
> of accepting that responsibility.
> This other philosophical way I am going to call reading; others may call
> it philosophical interpretation. [*Quest*, 14.]

In characterizing this path of philosophical steps as a way of "reading"—
a way of gathering the sense of something—Cavell goes about as far as
he can go in showing his hand about a conceptual rigor and accuracy in
responsiveness to a text. And in calling reading a "way" and in characterizing it as a kind of path, Cavell starts to suggest the methodological potential in the idea of reading. He will explore and exploit this potential
throughout his later work. Reading is explicitly introduced as in competition with argumentation for the custodianship of responsible discourse:
Both are ways of taking responsibility for what one says (and for what we
say). It seems to be difficult, if not impossible, to manifest one's acceptance
of both responsibilities at once.

Further questions start to emerge almost as soon as we have taken in
the answers. Let us grant the connection of this idea of reading to the idea
of inheriting philosophy as a set of texts to be dwelled on rather than a
set of problems to be argued about (as in the opening lines of *The Claim
of Reason*). Doesn't this just transfer the obvious question from the text
to the apprehender of the text? And, for a philosopher, the obvious question is: What is this reading for? What good is it? Or rather, what is the
philosophical good of it? For even those philosophers who pride themselves on reading well are not inclined to care very much *philosophically*
about the nonphilosophical benefits that we may obtain by reading.

Some readers will, I think, be surprised to learn that for Cavell the
benefit of philosophy has something to do with the way in which it carries
on its distinctive business. As far back as *Must We Mean What We Say?*
he writes this: "My assumption is that there is something special that
philosophy is about, and that [the] procedures [of ordinary language phi-
losophy], far from avoiding this oldest question of philosophy, plunge us

newly into it" (99). Cavell's task is not merely to show that it was in some vague sense a good thing to read true books in a true spirit, or to read great books in a heroic spirit, or for that matter to watch some fantastic movies in a spirit of ecstasy and creative responsiveness. His task was to demonstrate that reading and its reversals could be central to the special business of philosophy. Moreover, he had to demonstrate this at a level of detail that could be *followed* or could even prompt succession.

Like Austin in *How to Do Things with Words* and "A Plea for Excuses," Cavell aimed to provoke the collapse of our current ways of being interested in the preoccupations of philosophy. And almost in the same breath, he had to allow a new path or new possibility of making progress with our interests and occupations in philosophy. This effort would be complicated by his efforts both to modify Austin's revolution—especially about skepticism—and yet somehow also to retain Austin's capacity for listening to ordinary speech. I make this last point with some sense that Cavell may not have directly experienced this tension in the shift of models from ordinary language to reading. So I cannot be certain about the connection in Cavell's mind between the shift in models of methodology and the related shift in priorities about the "business" of philosophy and language. The latter shift was a part of a series of events that even Austin was willing to call a "revolution in philosophy."[3]

As an emblem of the kind of self-interruption that is bound to afflict anyone trying to pursue this investigation of Cavell encountering his teachers of reading, we should let our suspicion of his appeal to reading unfold a little further. Why should a philosopher allow himself or herself to be drawn away from the obvious benefits of the philosophical focus on problems and argumentation? With an argument at least you know where you are, even if you fail to make much forward progress. (Thus one side of my philosophical education argues back.) At least you know when you have committed an error, and by that knowledge you also know that you have stayed within the boundaries of the business of philosophy. Granted the sclerosis of so much of our philosophical education and its modes of argumentation, isn't Cavell's proposed alternative more radical than is justified?

Here a more sophisticated objection emerges: If our training has been precisely designed to repress reading and to render its discipline invisible from the standpoint of philosophy, then how can one even go about adhering to a set of philosophical procedures whose very existence seems at best obscure and distant? This objection emerges from a region somewhat outside of my philosophical training, a region informed by certain considerations that are partly psychoanalytic and partly methodological.

Accordingly, I do not know how to locate the methodological considerations within any familiar field of work in the humanities, or for that matter in psychoanalytic writing. The effort to respond to Cavell's characterization of reading as a philosophical method runs the risk of forcing us outside not only traditional philosophy but the very fields of reading he means to be keeping track of.

The most convincing answers to such questions will not come by way of arguments but only on the path of further reading. (I have elsewhere tried to characterize some of this idea of further reading as the activity of "reading on.")[4] To answer a principled philosophical question by encouraging the questioner to keep reading will certainly seem circular—at least if you are not already reading. The responses do indeed presuppose that the questioner is in a sense, or somewhere, already reading. As in the case of the repression of the voice, the repression of reading as a discipline does not mean that the activities and effects of reading are entirely absent. Reading may make its appearance within the study of philosophy as something merely auxiliary and inessential. That is, the practices of reading may appear as something pretty much external to the central business of philosophy. Reading is invariably conceived as a means to an end and never as one of the ways in which genuine thinking occurs.

To encourage reading as a response to doubts about the philosophical validity of reading will seem circular to those who are not engaged in reading or who have succeeded in repressing it. Such encouragement may well seem beside the point to someone who has begun the process of lifting this internal censorship. In any event, repressions are rarely overcome by telling someone that repressions ought, in general, to be overcome. If the encouragement of reading—Cavell sometimes speaks of "recommending" it—goes beyond the telling of such a tale, it is bound to meddle in the most private mechanisms of a philosopher's intellectual equipment. The fact of reading may disrupt the ability to concentrate and to focus on essential things; the ability to take some steps rather than others; the ability to turn back. If you start in on such a therapeutic revision of what counts as thinking—not to mention what calls for it—you had better be willing to stick it out, through some pretty messy intermediate stages on the way back to consecutive thought. (Numbering the paragraphs is likely to seem positively decorous by the time these processes of reeducation are under way.)

If such encouragement of reading is to be effective in such a therapy, the encouragement must itself be subject to a philosophical reading. This aspect of the process is no more circular than the fact that we begin teaching students how to argue by giving them arguments—and then perhaps by arguing with them. But if this process is not necessarily circular, it is still risky. For while you are arguing with someone, it *can* become clear to her that she is capable of arguing on her own. It may even become clear to her that when the discussion is over, she is capable of writing the argument down. (At any rate, this is the sort of thing that philosophy teachers like to tell themselves.) But if you are offering yourself as an example to practice reading on, you are not necessarily offering the student a path on which the student can learn to read without you. And this is true even when you offer yourself as an exemplar of the reversals of reading that I have sketched in. That is, even when you offer a text of yourself as a reader of a prior text, your encouragement of reading is likely at times to overwhelm the newly emerging capacity to read in precisely the best students of your reading.

In the very success of such writing-as-reading, you run the risk of compromising the students' ability to stop reading the text in front of them and go about the business of their own thoughts. And if you have presented yourself as the exemplar of philosophical reading as such, then you have compromised the students' ability not merely to read you but to read, period. (Of course, there remains plenty to read and plenty to talk about it. So the lack of exits from such reading into a student's own territory may not show up for many years.)

The philosopher's specific objections to reading are beginning to seem less pertinent and less powerful than the objections that stem from reading itself. That seems fair enough. But before I turn to this new region of difficulty, I want to follow out Cavell's own response to the conception of philosophy as devoted to argument. This is part of his way of staying in touch with the present constitution of philosophy, and it is necessarily intermittent. There is a kind of oscillation between the moments where Cavell addresses the English-speaking tradition of philosophy and the moments where he is responding to the immediate demands of his own way of reading. This alternation helps to account for the piecemeal emergence of reading as a model of *philosophical* method. A philosophical method cannot adopt the terms of its competitors wholesale, nor can it simply go off in search of its own questions and its own answers. However satisfying it might be to contemplate the latter course of action, a new method must keep in touch with the traditional alternatives. It cannot assume from the outset that the goals of the old methods are merely *different* from the goals we will now set for ourselves. For instance, the method of reading cannot assume that the conception of philosophy as a set of texts exists in what is flatly a different region of the intellectual world than the conception of philosophy as a set of problems to be addressed.[5]

Cavell's sketch of an answer to the philosopher begins with a sense of responsibility toward one's own discourse, a responsibility that must be discharged in the searching out of the hidden implications or presuppositions of what one has said. Somehow the achievement of this responsibility is furthered, or facilitated, by the prior discourse that one is engaged in reading. Such philosophical reading must be faithful both to the spirit and to the mastery of the details of the prior text. The primary responsibility of such reading seems to be to the spirit and details of one's own text. But these responsibilities need not always conflict, at least to the extent that the spirit and details of the prior text have been incorporated in your own.

There is a more startling reason why one's responsibility as a reader is expressed primarily in the care of one's own text, and specifically in a responsiveness toward the terms one is learning to mean. For here we arrive at the most paradoxical and thought-provoking moment of Cavell's model of reading, the moment where he interprets Thoreau's vision of reading as a vision of being *read by* the prior text.

> Having praised the written beyond the spoken word and finding that the "heroic books . . . will always be in a language dead to degenerate times," the writer of *Walden* interprets "the noblest written words" by a startling identification. "There are the stars, and they who can may read them" (iii.4). This is an interpretation of nature as a text, of course, but it is one of Thoreau's clearest interpretations of what reading itself is. It interprets reading (dangerously invoking, to revise, the idea of the astrological) as a process of *being read*, as finding your fate in your capacity for your interpretation of yourself. [*Quest*, 16.]

The idea of a reversal of the one who reads into the one who is being *read by* the stars is put forth as if it were just waiting to be discovered in the passage in question. But it is far from the obvious reading of that passage, and Cavell's version requires a twist or a trope of its own. Here are Thoreau's words in a slightly larger context:

> However much we may admire the orator's occasional bursts of eloquence, the noblest written words are commonly as far behind or above the fleeting spoken language as the firmament with its stars is behind the clouds. There are the stars, and they who can may read them. [*Walden*, 92.]

What will shortly become the contrast between the astrological and the astronomical (as Cavell rightly suggests) begins as a contrast between the realm of astronomy and something like the realm of the weather report. What obsesses Thoreau is the contrast between reading as a heroic act (appropriate to the "heroic books") and the kind of trivial and impoverished reading that serves as a convenient medium for our dissipation.

Indeed, when Cavell addresses this passage for the first time, in *The Senses of Walden,* he does not immediately take up the issue of the reversal of reading. He takes up the issue of the ontological status of the meaning of nature as opposed to the meanings of words. These two issues are related, but it takes a few steps to demonstrate the relationship. Thoreau takes the idea of the book of nature to such an extreme that he seems to characterize the heroic books—the classics—as part of nature. That effort seems to place at least some sorts of classic texts in an order—and at an altitude—of meaning and signification essentially beyond what we modern mortals are capable of.

Thoreau is certainly treading close to Matthew Arnold's ground in the sonnet that begins, "Others abide our question. Thou art free." This praise of Shakespeare also seems to place an author's capacity for making original sense in a fundamentally different realm from our ordinary powers of making sense. This is nowadays, of course, an easy region to mock. Moreover, it is a region that has come to seem primarily political, or rhetorical, in its nature. Some professors of literature and art are apparently ready to deny the existence of any works or regions of originality and to assume that any alleged experience of such works must be in the service of some prior ideological purpose. And there are those new ideologues of the old "high culture" who apparently wish to commandeer the very possibility of original work as a kind of buttress for their own political ideals.

If we hold off for a while on the politicized version of the controversy, then we might note that Arnold and Thoreau seem to be on different sides of a very particular, and somewhat specialized, aesthetic question. Arnold puts the work of Shakespeare into a particular realm of freedom, and Thoreau at this stage seems happy to put the works of the great poets into a particular realm of nature. I am less concerned to settle this question than to pose it accurately. It is not really that hard to understand why philosophers have resorted to such ideas of discontinuous regions in order to characterize the discontinuities in the human power to produce original work or, indeed, to make sense of it. Perhaps we do not need, for instance, the entire Kantian problematic of the discontinuity between nature and freedom. But perhaps we need more conceptual work than the recent decades of theory have tended to allow for. In any event, the apparently widespread perception that we have no special need for such a problematic of originality seems to block our comprehension of the aesthetic concerns of an earlier age.[6]

Cavell does not present us with this problematic, but he is making some conceptual room for it. Already at that moment of his reflections, Cavell inflects Thoreau's identification of the written word with the stars toward a different region. He continues to develop Thoreau's sense of the stars and of nature itself as providing us not so much with physical as with mathematical emblems of significance. "It is by a mathematical point only that we are wise." The context makes clear that the point in question is a star, and the North Star to boot. Given Thoreau's participation in a certain historical setting, the North Star is the primary point in nature by which we are to orient the idea of freedom in relation to the slave-holding regions of the century.

This little piece of history does not resolve the antinomy of nature and freedom, but it might show us a different way of looking at it. What is at stake here is the significance not solely of natural phenomena but of the *placement* of natural phenomena. This placement is something that could easily be characterized as at least partially a human construction or imposition—like the signs of the zodiac, degrees of longitude and latitude, etc. Except that we must not fail to remember that within these constructions of the earth and the sky we are somehow able to orient ourselves and perhaps to guide ourselves to a destination.

What Cavell wants from this picture of a mark made within a mathematical notation (as we saw in chapter 3) is the idea of the placement of a word. He wants us to remember that despite our sense of the arbitrariness in the formation of words and in our selection of our words, we can still locate ourselves within their networks. "[T]he occurrence of a word is the occurrence of an object whose placement always has a point, and whose point always lies before it and beyond it" (27). We can lay down whatever words we choose: Both the word and the placement of the word will tell us something about where we are and where we might be. We might think of this as a sort of regulative ideal of reading. It contains a little allegory of reading as mediating between what is natural to us and what enables us to take the path of our own freedom. Thoreau shows this path to lie not so much *against* fate or nature as within them (*Walden*, 107). To see reading in this way, we must learn not only to read what fate and nature seem to have written for us but also what we have written for ourselves. Thoreau's words contain a kind of injunction not to stop reading until you have learned what there is to learn from the location of a word and from your relationship to that location.

The other move Cavell makes is to draw this passage toward the passages where Thoreau describes nature as confiding in us, singling out the later passage "much is published but little is printed" (101). He takes these passages, together with other material, to suggest not a fundamental discontinuity but a fundamental continuity between the messages tendered by nature and those delivered by human beings. We can only print what we have already learned how to read. If the heroic books are written in a language that is dead to us, nature publishes a great deal in a language of which we speak only a dialect.[7]

Cavell's willingness to explore Thoreau's sense of being confided in by nature—which Thoreau cheerfully extends to the idea of nature's confidence in him—takes us a step closer to the topic of Thoreau's animism and the question of the reversal of reading. If nature does not just speak to you but confides in you—and perhaps delivers its daily news to you, express—then it becomes less of a step to the idea that we are being read by the books that we are reading. Thoreau has already taken the leap into animism. He has begun to discern the life we have in common with the natural world and not just the laws and the meanings that we find in it. Thoreau is outlining an understanding in which there is a continuity between natural law and linguistic significance.

Beyond these steps of Thoreau's, Cavell readies us to think of Wittgenstein as reanimating the life of our words. He chooses this moment of his book on Thoreau to cite Wittgenstein's reminder that "[e]very sign *by itself* seems dead" (*Investigations*, #432). It is as if Cavell already wants the sense—ten years before he goes public about Coleridge and Wordsworth—that there is proximity between a Romantic perception of our severed relations to nature and the Wittgensteinian perception that our words have gone dead. They are dead, first of all, because we become conscious of them and write them down only in isolation from our habitual use of them. We have left behind the requirement that we give voice to our words.

Thoreau's perception of our words derives from Wordsworth and Coleridge, who warned us that nature is dying from our inability to sustain connection with her. Our words are also dying because we have isolated them from one another. Perhaps we merely wanted to study them. Or perhaps we found ourselves wanting to withdraw certain words from circulation in order to protect them. There may now be many spirits who would rather not use certain words in public, preferring to keep them in some sort of private circulation. But these are stopgap measures, desperate efforts to keep a desperate culture from laying waste whole forests of significant speech. And there is no guarantee that when the occasion arises, we can reconnect the words to the contexts in which they have their best chance for coming alive.

Cavell responds to his perception that the isolated sign is dead by somehow reading the sign back into its element. That is to say, the solution is to *read* the sign, since reading is already a matter of gathering a significance and a context that is greater than the sign can ever provide on its own. We find the place or the region in which the sign was readable and, hence at least to that extent, alive. And we allow the sign to return to the stream of sense and life from which it had been severed.

The idea of reading as having something to do with reattaching the sign to its use and life doubtless requires more work. Some such idea that reading has to do with reanimation is an insight that Stephen Mulhall picks up on. But Mulhall's idea seems to be that what he labels as Cavell's idea of "redemptive reading" is a way of reading that must come specially equipped with Cavell's individual powers as a reader and as a perpetrator of something like autobiography. This conception runs deep in Mulhall's work. If we stick to it, it will block the way to an understanding of the question of the reanimation of our words as a *philosophical* question.

> [Cavell's] investigation of modern skepticism leads him to think of his Wittgensteinian practice of recounting criteria as a mode of thinking whose prosecution constitutes a reanimation of words, self, and world—a way of declaring and enacting one's own existence and that of others through the full acknowledgement of the life in (that is, our life with) words. [*Stanley Cavell*, 193.]

The question that has to be asked is this: by what route do we acknowledge in *writing* the life in our words? Mulhall tends to conflate the idea of the life *in* our words with the idea of our life *with* words. However hard it is to formulate them adequately and however close they are in practice, these ideas point us in very different directions. The life *in* our words is what the words possess in their ordinary use. (Cf. Wittgenstein: "Every sign *by itself* seems dead. *What* gives it life?—In use it is alive. . . . ")[8] This is the life that drains out of our words when philosophical reflection severs them from their common use.

Our life with words is a relation to language that is created or restored through the accomplishment of some particular writer's art. From the time of *The Senses of Walden*, Cavell has been interested in what he calls the writer's wording of the world. The restoration of this possibility in writing is both reanimation of language and a reinhabitation of the world.

The achievement of an intimacy between the world and the wording of the world brings with it, perhaps, an undoing of our skeptical distances. Cavell's later work depends very much on his reading of the connection between Wittgenstein's recovery of the ordinary language-game and the Romantic achievement of an ordinary commerce of word and thing— the "simple produce of the everyday." But this Romantic renovation of the realm of the ordinary does not obviously address the life that philosophical reflection drains out of ordinary words. (Cavell's treatment of Coleridge's efforts to reunite poetry and philosophy might be taken to demonstrate that Coleridge is a counterexample to this general rule. But it is a very specialized case.)

Our feeling for our words may range from the Romantic to the comical. I may have a great deal of feeling for the word *pillar*—or *Säule*. Perhaps it makes me think of the first time I read Wittgenstein, or Rilke. Perhaps somewhere I continue to associate the word with the character Pilar in *For Whom the Bell Tolls*. I might be able to communicate to a reader something of the intensity this word evokes in me, along with the oddly casual way in which it crisscrosses the peculiar landscape of my education. I might try to write down something of the way this word can seem to summon up and condense my relation to language in general.

Even if I could thus close the circuit of energy between the word and my responses to the word, this would not entail, for instance, the explicit recollection of the criteria for the words and concepts involved. (This might be a matter of distinguishing a pillar from a flying buttress, or from a pile of rocks.) So it is not yet part of the sector of philosophy that we associate with Wittgenstein, or with Cavell's reading of Wittgenstein. My ability to evoke something of myself in relation to the exact occurrence of particular words is, I hope, something of value. But the circuit between me and my ordinary uses of words has not been closed. I can exemplify how the energy of the word's occurrences flows through me. But I have not yet shown how the energy flowing into my portion of the common fund of words can reveal the commonness of that fund.

The writer may invoke the fact that words are held in common without illuminating the powers of revelation residing in the fact of commonness. Wittgenstein and Cavell may insist that words unshared are always potentially dead. And the way in which a writer makes a word come alive for us must always somewhere tap into some fund of common life and some potential common significance. But it does not follow that bringing a word back to life will *eo ipso* exhibit the route back to the common fund of uses. And it is even less likely that such a reanimation of the word will be able at the same time to represent to us the relation of its use of words to the "grammar" of the world. (Reading Thoreau or Wordsworth is not a substitute for reading Wittgenstein.)

These remarks should help to remind us that even if Cavell has taught us to trace the autobiographical edge to philosophical writing, autobiography is not, in itself, philosophy. All the autobiography in the world cannot alter this requirement of making plain the path you take to the common fund of significance. You cannot use the brilliant life of your words to circumvent the necessity of method: the voice of one who is writing philosophy must be able to invoke the voices that philosophy has specifically sequestered. This is the promise and the danger of Cavell's experiments with autobiographical narrative. Apart from the pertinence of his voice to the voices and repressions of philosophy, his voice cannot by itself reanimate the severed condition of our words or our world. The danger of hearing his authorial voice apart from the voices that it invokes is the danger of hearing his voice as even more isolated and powerful than it sometimes is. What Cavell characterizes as a kind of *cogito* is enacted by something that seems less like Descartes' bare "I am" and more like a text. (Cavell no doubt intends to suggest that, seen from this angle, Descartes' *cogito* reveals an "I" that is more of a text than we initially realized.) The text of this performance of the *cogito* must contain the willingness to let oneself be *read*. This means that we are willing to be exposed to what others will read in us—and no doubt sometimes read into us.

Mulhall conflates the specificity of a text that is composed under the aegis of a *cogito ergo sum* with the specificity of Cavell's acts of reading—that is to say, his acts of receiving the particularity of the past and allowing it to be inflected by his own reception. No doubt this receptivity helps to define Cavell as a writer as well as a reader. But if it also helps to define Cavell as a philosopher, the particularity of these thoughts and feelings and life and dedication had better not belong to Cavell alone. Again, we must look for the ways that Cavell finds to acknowledge the representativeness of his reading, its openness to being checked.

> In his writing on these particular texts, Cavell is acknowledging the absolute specificity of his particular experience of reading them; and—since reading is the most fundamental activity of his life, since it is that to which he has most deeply committed himself—he is thereby attempting to declare and to enact the specific texture of that life, the particular constellation of thoughts, feelings and experiences that go to make him up as a person. He is, in short, not only furthering a philosophical argument and engaging in a mode of cultural analysis: he is also attempting to enact his own existence as an individual by bringing his personal world of experience to our common words, and by acknowledging us, his readers, by asking us

to acknowledge his words, and so himself, through reading them in the spirit to which their writing aspires. [194–95.]

For Mulhall, it is Cavell's own existence that he bestows upon his words and exhibits to his readers. We acknowledge Cavell's words by coming to share the spirit in which they were uttered. And in this way we become aware of some new forms of life—the forms of life in which we read Cavell. This idea seems to fit the facts of other forms of life better than in the case of reading. For instance, it fits the forms of life in which religious feelings and thoughts are uttered, since learning to share in the spirit of the utterance is of the essence.

This sense of a kind of merger with Cavell's spirit in uttering certain words seems to me precisely to elide the questions of reversal that I have introduced. In particular and most critically, it neglects the direction that I characterized above as "reversing possessiveness." The spirit of Cavell's words must be accepted (or rejected) as a kind of supplemental life to our words, beyond whatever vividness we have managed for ourselves. In refusing to return to the condition of severance and isolation that characterizes the skeptical moment within us, this sort of analysis would end up refusing the relevance of Cavell's analysis of the perversity of skepticism. A reader in the grip of this view is inclined to receive from Cavell's writing the gift of his vividness, and is satisfied to think of this as a way-station on the path back to the life of our words. Such analysis severs the question of the perversity in our wish to know from the question of the perversity and transgressiveness in our grasping of the world in words. If adhered to consistently, this analysis would render itself incapable of connecting Cavell's work on skepticism and the voice with his work on reading and being read.

It may be useful to bear in mind several of Thoreau's own explicit terms for the relation of reader to writer. I take the following such terms from the pages leading up to the passage about reading the stars: "emulation"; "laboriously seeking the meaning of each word and line"; "conjecturing a larger sense than common use permits"; and "review" or "revision." (I offered a few others in chapter 3.)

> The student may read Homer or Aeschylus in the Greek without danger of dissipation or luxuriousness, for it implies that he in some measure emulate their heroes, and consecrate morning hours to their pages. [91.]

And a bit earlier:

> With a little more choice in the choice of their pursuits, all men would perhaps become essentially students and observers, for certainly their na-

ture and destiny are interesting to all alike. . . . [I]n dealing with truth we are immortal and need fear no change nor accident. [90.]

Thoreau declares explicitly that Walden was favorable not only to thought but to serious reading. By now, we should not need Cavell in order to add that *Walden* and the activities and passions that constitute the writing of *Walden* are also favorable to reading. We know that Thoreau was reading as well as writing at Walden, devoting "morning hours" to both activities.

Thoreau also implies that emulation is as much the business of a reader as of a writer. Thoreau construes the labor of emulation and the consecration of morning hours to a page as types of both reading and writing. Emulation is not just an activity occurring between writers engaged, for instance, in acts of anxious competition, or for that matter in confident acts of inheritance. Emulation occurs between the reader and the "hero," where the hero is somewhat closer to being Homer or Aeschylus than to being Achilles or Orestes.

The exchange of identity between reader and writer prepares us for more fantastic, or phantasmatic, exchanges. Here is the exchange of identities with the ancient Eastern philosophers, at the beginning of the chapter called "Reading":

> The oldest Egyptian or Hindoo philosopher raised a corner of the veil from the statue of the divinity; and still the trembling robe remains raised, and I gaze upon as fresh a glory as he did, since it was I in him that was then so bold, and it is he in me that now reviews the vision. [90.]

Cavell is drawing connections between Thoreau's changing places with the "Hindoo" philosopher and Cavell's own efforts to characterize the reversal of reading into being read. To follow these connections adequately, we need to know more about how the act of reading becomes represented as acts of looking, or gazing, at a statue. Both the presumed acts of reading (the chapter is after all titled "Reading") and the depicted acts of gazing are intended to characterize the sharing of thoughts—the sharing of what is called "the vision."[9]

This passage and similar ones are often taken as a kind of humanistic vision of the timeless community of great books and great truths. Thoreau's brief fable contains a more complex set of subtexts. Just under the question of "Who is looking at whom?" lies the question "Who is reading whom?" Thoreau plays with the exchange of identities of the one who views and the one who reviews and revises. He thus makes room for the idea that a past thinker's words can be construed as a revision of the present thinker. And this is only a step or two away from the idea that a past thinker's thought could provide a reading of its readers' own thoughts.

Grant for the moment that such exchanges of identity, along with a certain animism of the stars, help Cavell create the conceptual room for this idea of a reversal of reading into being read. What more does it take to get this reversal going at the opportune moment? How do we actually turn this somersault?

There are in fact several paths to Cavell's revision of Thoreau and to his location of his own idea of reading within Thoreau's constellation of depicted readings. The one I want to follow out most immediately is this: To get to the idea of a reversal in the exclamation, "There are the stars . . . ," Cavell draws the passage through the idea of the astrological. The image of astrology is indeed explicitly present, a page or so later:

> The works of the great poets have never yet been read by mankind, for only great poets can read them. They have only been read as the multitude read the stars, at most astrologically not astronomically. Most men have learned to read to serve a paltry convenience, as they have learned to cipher in order to keep accounts and not be cheated in trade; . . . yet this only is reading, in a high sense, not that which lulls us as a luxury and suffers the nobler faculties to sleep the while, but what we have to stand on tip-toe to read and devote our most alert and wakeful hours to. [94.]

The identification of the stars with the works of massive and fateful powers of significance is clear enough. The opposition of greatness to paltriness fits the earlier sense of the astronomical versus the meteorological. And the deadness of the words of poetry to our degenerate times suggests our own incapacity for creation and generation. The sort of reading we use for relaxation ends up making us too drowsy to enjoy anything else, and the limited excitement of such books just creates the continual craving for more of the same. Our habits of reading have dissipated the very energy we would need to raise our sights to anything higher.[10]

At this stage of circulation between reader and reading matter, Cavell requires only one or two more steps to arrive at his particular sense of reversal. The steps can be formulated like this: Those who read books astrologically, like those who read the stars astrologically, are entangled in something like a mechanism of projection. They take their own sense of fatedness—a sense of being taken down a path that is beyond their control—and they project this sense of fate and compulsion onto the stars. In particular, they take the exactness of the relation between our temporal existence and the precise position of the stars as an emblem of the necessity and the precision in the agencies that compel us. They then read this emblem as containing a specific announcement concerning what must come to pass.

The crucial connection for Cavell is now readily seen: we pass from astrology's idea that the stars enable us to know the necessities of our condition to the idea that the stars *harbor* such knowledge. Not for the first time, Cavell entertains the idea that there is a kind of truth in the fantasy that the stars know something about us. ("Their actions divine our projects," he says in *The World Viewed* [29].) He wants to hang on to this fantasy of what the stars know about us long enough to learn something from it. At the very least, Cavell wants to bear down on the idea that the stars give a reading of our conditions. He wants (a) to reverse the idea that it is we who give a reading of their position and (b) to express the fantasy that the stars are able to give a reading of our condition because they are aware of it. It is natural for a human being to harbor a picture of the stars as *overlooking* our condition. Why shouldn't they also oversee it? Cavell's version of the fantasy suggests that the stars are *advised* of our condition. Rightly conceived, they will help us reconsider what we have taken as given.

Cavell does not simply arrive at such a notion of astrological projection, carrying the unwelcome baggage of this animistic fantasy of what the stars know about us. He wants to evoke this fantasy, in order to isolate the mechanisms within our reading that correspond—at least allegorically—to the mechanism of astrological projection. We are to locate an unsuperstitious version of the movement by which astrology takes its (outward) sense of fate and projects this sense above us into the stars, where we are able to read it. It will take him a while to name this set of mechanisms, but this delay or deferral of naming should no longer seem surprising to us.

What he does go on to say immediately, however, confirms my sense of the general location of the problem. Let us look again at the sentence that I began with:

> [Thoreau's interpretation of reading the stars] interprets reading (dangerously invoking, to revise, the idea of the astrological) as a process of *being read,* as finding your fate in your capacity for your interpretation of yourself. [*In Quest of the Ordinary,* 16.]

We learn of ourselves by seeing our capacity for interpretation in action. We are to *turn around* our sense of ourselves as interpreting the stars into a sense of our (projected) capacity for interpreting ourselves. Mythically, this gives us a sense of the stars as interpreting us, reading us, confiding in us.

But the pivot around which we turn our picture of who is reading whom is our concept of fate. This is perhaps less surprising if we bear in mind that our concept of fate entails not only our understanding of necessity but also our understanding of the *location* of that necessity. That is, our concept of fate will normally dictate whether we apprehend necessity as coming from outside us or inside us. The concept will often include some sense of the origin of necessity—a sense of something as the *author* of fate. The concept may also include some image of the sorts of events by which the necessitated future is actually to come about. And the richest concepts of fate will also include an account of the development of the future from our present condition, whether as a fulfillment of our present necessities or, perhaps, as an overthrowing of them.

In Cavell's account of this reversal of the reader into the one being read, each of these features of the concept of necessity passes through the act of reading. When Cavell says that we will find our fate in our capacity for interpretation, he does not just mean that our sense of fate will show up best in our acts of interpretation. This is a good start, and perhaps it would be good enough to defend the humanities against its uncultured despisers. It can yield results that go well beyond the commonplaces of humanistic study. (For instance, if we insist on projecting our sense of fate outside of ourselves and into the stars, we are likely to view ourselves as underlings.)

Cavell means more than this. He means that reading is the way of proceeding that transfigures the text of your circumstances into the occasions of your activity. In this he agrees with Thoreau:

> Will you be a reader, a student merely, or a seer? Read your fate, see what is before you, and walk on into futurity. [101.]

This is the passage that is the most direct source of the link Cavell proposes between our ability to read a book and our ability to read our fate. What we still need, however, is a clear picture of the path on which our ability to read in general is able to reverse the mechanism of astrological projection and make something of it.

Once Cavell arrived at this depiction of what I am calling the second of the reversals—the reversal of reading into being read—the path to further encounters with Emerson and Thoreau opened up. However complex and potentially animistic it may seem to take oneself as being read by the text—as becoming the subject of the text's interpretive activities—such a moment can actually simplify the workings of the model as a whole. If I can imitate the moment at which the philosopher-reader becomes *read by* the text, then I am not simply taking the place of the philosopher-reader in a struggle to occupy the only position in the model where the action of reading is really occurring. If I submit, in turn, to becoming *read by* the text of the philosopher-reader (call it "Cavell") as that text is read by the prior text (call it, for instance, "Emerson"), I am submitting neither to an endless struggle for the position of reader, nor to an endless deferral of the moment when I actually begin to read.

However complicated Cavell's transactions with Emerson or Thoreau may be, and however mysterious the language in which he records those transactions, what comes to me, at a given moment, is a single text. Whatever contortions it may take to submit myself to being "read by" a text (which is in turn being read by a text, which is in turn being read, perhaps, by the stars), it comes down to the fact that I am presently engaged in an act of reading. For all those complexities can still occupy only the single space of my present reading. All the reversals are in me, or they are nowhere of interest. Only those reversals that I make good on will be the reversals of my reading. Conversely, the reversals that do not show up in my reading are, so far, irrelevant to that reading. (The therapy of my therapist may no doubt have an enormous impact on my therapy. But it is not, in itself, a part of my therapy.)

Confirmation for how well this model works, at least in relation to the reading of Emerson and Thoreau, comes quickly enough. When you are alerted to this possibility of reversal in reading these texts, you will not lack for examples. This side of Emerson has not gone unnoticed by other good critics and readers. It is, for instance, one of the major themes of Barbara Packer's *Emerson's Fall*. More generally, students of Harold Bloom, Jacques Lacan, or, for that matter, Lionel Trilling, are as well suited as students of Cavell to appreciate the reversals of reading implicit in a remark like this from "Self-Reliance": "To talk of self-reliance is a poor external way of speaking. Speak rather of that which relies because it works and is. Who has more obedience than I masters me, though he should not raise his finger." You do not really need the reference to "self-reliance" to remind us that Emerson is addressing the present reader of the essay called "Self-Reliance," but it helps to see that the next sentence is addressed precisely to that reader: we readers will speak—and speak more clearly—because we have been listening to the speaker and have been, in that specific sense, obedient. Then perhaps we will take in the fact that the exchanges between obedience and mastery and the exchanges between a reader and something like Emerson's text are indeed something that you can master without lifting a finger—with no admonition, and no other work than the effort to follow.

Somewhere along the line, we are better able to see that the opening

paragraph of "Self-Reliance" presents a standing challenge to readers of
a certain ambition. It begins with Emerson depicting himself as reading:
"I read the other day some verses. . . . " And it moves swiftly to the
climactic series of lessons that Emerson is trying to instill:

> In every work of genius we recognize our own rejected thoughts; they
> come back to us with a certain alienated majesty. Great works of art have
> no more affecting lesson for us than this. They teach us to abide by our
> spontaneous impression with good-humored inflexibility then most when
> the whole cry of voices is on the other side.

As with Cavell's allegories of the work of the text as a function of the
voice, Emerson's remarks are not meant to elide the labor of reading or
otherwise apprehending the work of art that teaches us, ultimately, to
dispense with that work.

In both cases, the power of the voice that inhabits the text is in some
sense a model for the working of that text. But the power of the voice
tends to efface the very textuality that engendered the voice in the first
place. Even a sympathetic reader can lose track of the reciprocity of the
voice and the text. The voice submits itself to legibility and the text demands to be received as a voice of admonishment and encouragement.
The text is a kind of lesson for the day, with no scriptural authority apart
from the possibility that it will somehow speak to us.

I will not present the evidence that this set of difficulties is embedded
in Emerson's most interesting work.[11] Cavell is acutely aware of the difficulties and of the consequences of losing the thread of this interaction.

> . . . "Self-reliance is [the] aversion [of conformity]." This almost says,
> and nearly means, that you find your existence in conversion, by convert-
> ing to it, that thinking is a kind of turning oneself around. But what it
> directly says is that the world of conformity must turn from what Emer-
> son says as he must turn from it and that since the process is never over
> while we live—since, that is, we are never finally free of one another—
> his reader's life with him will be a turning from, and returning from, his
> words, a moving on from them, by them. In "Fate," Emerson will call this
> aversion "antagonism": "Man is a stupendous antagonism," he says there.
> I can testify that when you stop struggling with Emerson's words they be-
> come insupportable. [*In Quest of the Ordinary,* 118–19.]

Perhaps what strikes us first in such a passage is Cavell's capacity to invest
the act of reading with yet another garment of thought. We see in reading
another posture of Man Thinking. But where Hölderlin had told us that
we are a sign that is not read, Emerson is informing us of the fate of
incessantly reading and being incessantly read. We never know how or

when we are to stop reading each other. And if we stop in fatigue or in despair, it is likely that we will never hear the end of it.

Surely Cavell meant to make us aware that these same possibilities apply to our struggle with his words (and no doubt, prospectively, his struggle with our words). With all this struggling and the struggle to stop struggling, what keeps us on the path of reading? If reading is so perplexing and so strenuous, why not take up a more convenient line of argument or discourse?

Sometimes what keeps us reading is no more than a kind of fantasy or picture. Sometimes we can formulate it as a wish to trace the origins of a particular fantasy and its consequences. Caring about a text is only the beginning. Faced with our current academic ideologies of reading and of textual production and reception, I might remark that caring about a text in certain ways is not a condition that one should overcome too quickly.

Cavell pictures the knowledge contained in a text as related to the way in which we are *drawn* to a text.

> So the question that Emerson's theory of reading and writing is designed to answer is not "What does a text mean?" (and one may accordingly not wish to call it a theory of interpretation) but rather, "How is it that a text we care about in a certain way (expressed perhaps as our being drawn to read it with the obedience that masters) invariably says more than its writer knows, so that writers and readers write and read beyond themselves?" This might be summarized as "What does a text know?" or in Emerson's term, "What is the genius of a text?" [*Quest,* 117.]

It is only a half-step from here to the idea that what we desire of a text is to possess the text's knowledge, and most particularly its knowledge of itself. We have already encountered the fantasy that I am being read by the text that I am currently reading. And if I can picture the text as reading me, then surely I can imagine that the text is learning something about me. It must, for instance, know at least this much about me, namely, that I am something that can be read, a kind of text. So the idea that a text can know something *beyond* the knowledge of the one who composed its words is not perhaps as fantastic or Romantic as it first appears. This fantasy of the text's knowledge of me is cognate with the understanding of genius as "creative." In particular, it is cognate with the understanding of creativity as due to the possession of more than ordinary powers of production. One middle ground between these ideas would be provided by the fantasy of genius as possessing special access to other realms of knowledge and vision, hence provided with particular possibilities of inspiration.

Neither Emerson's nor Cavell's ideas of genius or of guiding spirits or of knowledge quite fit the romantic mythologies and theologies from which they in some sense derive. Without entering on a full-fledged defense of their ideas here, I note a couple of themes that follow out the question of reading and reversal:

(1) Cavell's thought about the text's knowledge as going "beyond" the knowledge of its actual writer and reader can be understood as following out a remark of Thoreau's. Since the heroic books are in a "language dead to degenerate times . . . , we must laboriously seek the meaning of each word and line, conjecturing a larger sense than common use permits out of what wisdom and valor and generosity we have" (91). The bulk of our days, the way we habitually spend our waking and working hours, is exactly what Thoreau means by "degenerate times." They are "degenerate" in that they oppose or subvert our powers of generation. At the same time, such times are likely to dissipate our capacity for desire and thwart our wish for useful work. Our reading must become a version of the reading of philologists, canvassing the dead text of our days for some signs of awakening life.

(2) What we have to ask is why Cavell is drawn past the image of our ordinary lives and common sense as deadening us to what we might somewhere *know* and hence no longer need to conjecture about. It seems to me that he does not abandon the idea of reading as waking yourself up to some higher possibility, or as Thoreau puts it, to some "earlier, more sacred, and auroral hour" (80). He generalizes his sense of reading beyond the boundaries we commonly set to our reading (and thinking). Now it is the text that is capable of knowledge beyond the conditions of its production and reception; it is the text that draws us out of our knowledge into the pursuit of a knowledge beyond us. A knowledge we are drawn to, which is beyond ourselves but nevertheless pertains to us, can be construed as a knowledge of our possibilities. Here again Cavell is offering a claim to knowledge that is not exactly unfamiliar to philosophers. Of course, it is presented in a somewhat alien or even deliberately alienating form. Cavell's reasons or motives for doing so are worth pondering.

(3) What is required is an image of the text as possessing knowledge, not the kind of knowledge that is aware of certain facts but the kind of knowledge that presents us with certain possibilities. We are on the right track, at least mythologically, if we think of the text as containing the knowledge of a region of possibility. For Plato and Wittgenstein and sometimes for Wordsworth, it is possible to think of this knowledge as consisting in a kind of recollection. ("The work of the philosopher consists in assembling reminders for a particular purpose" [*Investigations* #127].)

Within the grip of this fantasy, it is not very helpful to deny that what we are seeking is a kind of knowledge. It would be especially unhelpful to deny that we are seeking knowledge on the grounds that we are only acting from within a fantasy of knowledge. Among other things, that would forgo the opportunity to learn of the knowledge that resides within the fantasy, the knowledge that is available only by working *through* the fantasy. This would also tend to deny that our relation to the text we are reading is of a kind to produce such fantasies of knowledge and its possession.

But it is also useless simply to *affirm* that we can possess a text's knowledge of itself. So far, all we can affirm is, precisely, our fantasy of what such knowledge consists in. This raises the difficult question of what Cavell calls the "shadowing" of reality by fantasy: Part of what counts as real for us, hence part of our concept of knowledge, must be reached through the tracings of the realm of fantasy. What enables the shadowing of reality by fantasy is not the existence of objects but the possibilities of objects (cf. "Psychoanalysis and Cinema," 245).

(4) The fantasy of the text as possessing knowledge is, among other things, a way of refusing the idea of the text as a structure or an object. This will turn out to mean that from Cavell's point of view, the question about the "objectivity" of interpretation is decidedly secondary. More immediately, this picture of the text's knowledge of itself suggests the nature of our relation to the text and, indeed, something of the hold it has on us. One need not entirely deny the currently fashionable idea that audiences help to constitute the texts that they read, in order to confront the more difficult idea that a text may constitute its reader. Cavell locates some of Emerson's effects on us within still another fold of textuality. For Emerson's words often implicate us the most when they declare that they do not need us. These words seem to know that they can live without us. The independence of these words from their reader is not the same as the independence of an object from human consciousness or perception. (Though surely the problem of the self-sufficiency of the words descends from Cavell's rather Kantian understanding of the problem of the independence of things. The task of knowledge is not to know things as they *are*, apart from any contact with our consciousness, but rather to be able to grant the autonomy of things from *within* our knowledge of them. Otherwise there is nothing there to count as knowledge, and nothing to count as the object of knowledge. The same condition holds for reading.)

Emerson's words draw us in by withdrawing into their own work, the work they are engaged in. They are supposed to teach us to abide by our own perception and hence to abide by our own work. But since our own work is, at the moment, reading Emerson, part of the lesson is going to be the need for a change of direction in our reading.

A round this time, Cavell was being drawn to a way of thinking about these reversals that relied more openly on the concepts of psychoanalytic therapy. Here he formulated such questions as: Where do these images and fantasies of the text come from, and what are they for? Can they really promote our understanding of some particular book or movie or poem?

In the same essay in which he first spoke of philosophy as aimed at recovering the voice, Cavell first broached a model of reading explicitly based on psychoanalytic therapy. However useful this model has proved to be, it has caused a great deal of confusion among certain of his readers. They are inclined to forget that to employ psychoanalysis—or, more exactly, to employ one version of the structure of psychoanalytic therapy—as a model of reading is not to offer a psychoanalytic account of reading. I am not saying Cavell would be averse to such an account, but his model will not by itself provide us with it.

One reason that I have been dwelling for so long on the model of reading is to show how the model of psychoanalytic therapy emerges from this preoccupation with the prior model. The tensions and lacks in the model of reading as reversal call for the psychoanalytic model, in something like the way that a reading of a work of literature may end up calling for psychoanalytic insight ("Psychoanalysis and Cinema," 238). As in the latter case, we have a situation in which one region of insight is coming to the aid of another, but we do not know what the result will be.

Given Cavell's early theoretical reticence concerning his relations with psychoanalysis, it is better not to claim that psychoanalysis as such elucidates the model of reading. It is true that an essay like "Politics as Opposed to What?" might be taken to suggest that the understanding of psychoanalysis comes first and is then used to elucidate the model of reading. But it is at least of equal importance to note that Cavell's development of the problematic of reading was already helping him to excavate some conceptual space for a treatment of the work of psychoanalysis.

It is true and important that in "Psychoanalysis and Cinema," therapy is introduced as a model of reading. This implies that we already possess some understanding of the situation of psychoanalytic therapy. But the fact that such therapy possesses this ability to *serve* as such a model of reading and of being read is also a significant feature of Cavell's understanding of psychotherapy.

When Cavell returns to the idea of reading as being read by the prior text, he provides us with a key to the actual operation of the model. As he puts it here, we are to turn our picture of interpreting a text around into a picture of our being interpreted *by* it. Here it should be noted that the notion of interpretation has already been inflected toward the idea of therapy: interpretation no longer means something like "offering a comprehensive view of a text or a person." Interpretation now refers precisely to a specific sort of moment, which is indeed best exemplified by certain moments in psychoanalytic therapy.

Cavell has in mind the moments where the analyst refuses the patient's first effort at interpretation and turns it back on the patient. Either by silence or by some other indication of refusal, the analyst declines to endorse the patient's interpretation. And this refusal is followed by a further indication that the patient has yet to interpret his or her own investment in the act of offering an interpretation. This might well be part of interpreting the patient's transference to the analyst, and, in particular, it may be an interpretation of the patient's wish that his words coincide with the analyst's perception of him. But it need not be so specific either as an interpretation or as a rejection. It is enough that the patient understands that the source of his need to offer a particular interpretation—and perhaps the need to interpret altogether—has not yet been reached.

These seem to me to be useful analogies, but they are certainly far from completely worked out. Part of Cavell's point is precisely that the usefulness and application of these features of therapy are not exhausted within the literal confines of a session of therapy. And on the other hand, such an idea of interpretation is far from well defined outside of those confines. The central issue of this picture of interpretation precisely fits the idea of "reversal" that I have been construing as central to Cavell's model of reading. For the picture is a picture of *turning* us away from one sort of investment in the words of the text and toward another sort.

Cavell takes off from this sense of interpretation:

> The practice suggested to me by turning the picture of interpreting a text into one of being interpreted by it would I think be guided by three principal ideas: first, access to the text is provided not by a mechanism of projection but by that of transference . . . ; second, the pleasures of appreciation are succeeded by the risks of seduction; and third, the risks are worth running because the goal of the encounter is not consummation but freedom. [*Themes Out of School*, 52.]

To place this moment in Cavell's essay, we will have to back up a bit. Those imbued with two decades' worth of literary-theoretical absorption in psychoanalytic texts are unlikely to see the productiveness of this model. For this requires the capacity to locate in psychoanalytic therapy a model of something that many suppose does not, and cannot, exist. Even apart from the usefulness of the model of psychoanalysis, most literary theorists would deny that *any* kind of reading could possess both practical and theoretical effectiveness in the realm of philosophy.

Outside of philosophy, others might deny that a text nowadays could possess such power—or else deny that it *ought* to possess such power. Conversely, those philosophers who are still trying to clear their intellectual palates of the taste of Anglo-American condescension and Wittgensteinian defensiveness toward Freud might find this model a bit too congenial. They may be unwilling to question the methods by which it is to be applied.

Before we can see how this specific version of the reversals of reading helps us to understand the general model, we have to see a little more about where Cavell is taking this idea of a redemptive or a therapeutic reading: "What is this reading, or any reading, for? Freedom from what, to do what?" (ibid., 52). If I am right about the centrality of reading as a model as well as an instance of philosophical method in Cavell's work, he is asking a fairly fundamental question that goes beyond the normal purview of a literary-theoretical account of reading. The question in Cavell becomes tied to a question about freedom, in both its positive and negative dimensions. And this needs to be seen as at least as fundamental to his work as the problematic of skepticism, if not worked out explicitly to the same level of detail.

This discovery of an attachment between reading and freedom, like the discoveries about tragedy and skepticism, is another good reason why it has (apparently) proven so difficult to employ the results of Cavell's obvious brilliance as a critic to some particular set of texts or some particular set of teachable practices of critical illumination. Here, however, he gives us something quite specifically useful to go on:

> In the picture of psychoanalytic therapy, casting ourselves as its patient, its sufferer, its victim (according to the likes of Emerson and of Heidegger, this is the true form of philosophical thinking), the goal is freedom from the person of the author. (So we might see our model in Emerson's "Divinity School Address," which seeks to free us from our attachment to the person of the one who brings the message, an attachment in effect, according to Emerson, of idolatry. . . .) Presumably, we would not require a therapy whose structure partakes of seduction, to undo seduction, unless we were already seduced. [Ibid., 52–53.]

The invocation of Emerson's sense of our tendency to idolize the author who has affected us greatly speaks directly to the question of the Bible and of the nature of inspiration. The question here concerns a certain kind of text as such, and we are unlikely to share Emerson's concern with the texts of scripture. Nor are we as likely as Emerson to mount an argument for the tropological nature of the sacraments and of the Eucharist in particular.[12] If we transpose Emerson's questions into our key, it seems fair to say we are asking about our attachment to what animates the text.

In searching out our attachments to the text, and to what animates the text, we now begin to have a clearer picture of why we have to deal with the animism of the text—or with our fantasies of such animism. We are not, I think, absolutely required to pass through the stage of fantasizing that we are being read by the text that we are currently absorbed in reading. We might get prepared to search out some other path on which to locate our attachments to a text. What we primarily need is a way of exploring our sense of how those attachments are there before us, as if lying in wait for the moment in which we begin to read the text we are already attached to. I think it is clear that we will have to be able to provide a good deal more than a theory that begins with the idea that we project our attachments onto a text.

Here at last we can begin to seek the right level of explanation for the combination of features of reading that the idea of reversal was meant to point to: We must locate the sense of just this particular text waiting for just this particular reader within our ability, such as it is, to depict this encounter of text and reader as representative of human responsiveness as such. This way of reading is to be understood not merely as among the various aids to thinking but as one of its principal modes. Reading is Cavell's version of Emersonian reception, the sort of thing that Emerson has in mind when he writes that " . . . our thinking is a pious reception." But as Cavell makes explicit, we are not able to know whether the piety in question in a given case is a cause or a consequence of our powers of reception.

With the idea of a therapy of reading aimed at the right kind of freedom from the person of the author, we have arrived at yet another warning that the goal of reading Cavell cannot be simply to share in the spirit of his words. At least this cannot be the goal of reading him if sharing in the spirit means *merging* with it. It seems fair enough to say that if the point of this therapy is to gain freedom from the person of the author, then certainly for some authors it is their voice that is most preeminently the subject of idolatry. Emerson is such an author and so, evidently, is Cavell. I do not know how one can pretend to take Cavell seriously as a writer and not feel compelled to struggle with his voice. Whether or not one feels happily anticipated by Cavell's depiction of himself in struggle with Emerson or Wittgenstein, the general invitation is clear enough. So, too, are the methods of reversal by which the invitation can be taken up.

Again, it is in a reading of Emerson that Cavell takes these questions to a higher pitch:

> How can we read his theory of reading in order to learn how to read him? We would already have to understand it in order to understand it. I have elsewhere called this the (apparent) paradox of reading; it might just as well be called the paradox of writing, since of writing meant with such ambitions we can say that only after it has done its work of creating a writer (which may amount to sloughing or shaking off voices) can one know what it is to write. [*Quest*, 115.]

Cavell goes on to identify this work of creating a writer (by writing) with some version of the *cogito*, and this identification gets some commentators tied up into hermeneutical knots. (I examined some of these knots in the introduction and in chapter 2.) Hence it is worth dwelling on the fact that Cavell says that this creation of the writer may involve the sloughing off or shaking off of voices. The real problem in reading Emerson is not how hard it is to take him up in the right spirit, but how hard it is to put him down again in the right spirit.

As we have seen, Cavell has testified that when you "stop struggling with Emerson's words they become insupportable," and surely he is aware that his own words can seem that way. There are, indeed, moments where he seems to suggest that, from time to time, sentences like his and like Emerson's *must* seem insupportable. Moreover, they will seem that way most especially to a reader whose inclinations to the text are fundamentally friendly. Under its somewhat genteel surface, the word *insupportable* suggests a very particular shade of being unbearable or insufferable. Given Cavell's frequent invocation of the realm of the economic in Emerson and Thoreau, we can read Cavell here as suggesting that Emerson's use of these words goes beyond our means of support.

When we are truly paying attention to our sense of being repelled by Emerson's words, we will often find that the words have come to seem too costly for us. They are exorbitant in relation to our daily round of linguistic investment and expenditure. But we have not, in Cavell's sense, shunned these words appropriately if we merely cease to struggle with their exorbitance or extravagance. Not in merely giving up the struggle but in a further reversal of it can we finally learn what there is to learn from these words and from the sentences that contain them. Then perhaps we will also learn how to relinquish them, releasing them from our private holds back into the region of the world from which they came to us.

Elsewhere, he speaks of the shunning of sentences and of voices—for instance, in *The Senses of Walden,* and in *In Quest of the Ordinary* (114). In each of such cases, he is referring to an activity that occurs *within* a particular text, as well as between texts or between people. The shunning of a voice, like the sloughing off or shaking off of a voice, is to be understood as a modification of the text's conversation with itself. This conversation is in turn intended as a kind of working model of how a self learns to rely on itself. It is not by holding fast to one's reading of a situation that one displays resoluteness. Resolution and independence are found rather in the willingness to let go of the apparently legitimate dictation of the past, in the name of one's capacity for rereading.

Cavell's idea of shunning (and sloughing off) is also referring to an exchange that occurs between a moment in a text and a moment in a "prior" text. This shunning and sloughing off of voices may be thought of as bound up in the reversal of the reader of the prior text into the one who is being read. In shunning the voice, we do not entirely reverse the reversal by which we came to be addressed by the prior text, or called upon by it to do something. I am not required to shun a voice because it *failed* to participate in my constitution, or in my conversation with myself. I learn to shun it because its participation in that conversation was successful—indeed, so successful as to be almost unnoticeable. Shunning the voice that helped to create us is an acknowledgment of the self as constituted by the incorporation of voices.[13]

The word *shunning* points in a number of directions, one of which is perilously close to the region of banishment, the very region from which, philosophically speaking, we have been learning to summon the voice in the first place. The painful lesson we begin to learn from such reading is that one's voice is not merely under the *influence* of other voices but constituted by them. We must learn from a text of voices to slough off the voices that inhabit our words. This might teach us something about how close the conditions of autonomy are to the mechanisms of repression. ("It is by a mathematical point only that we are wise.") It is not always so easy to tell the difference between sloughing off or letting go of a voice, and stifling it or stopping one's ears against it.

Cavell has various remedies for these dangers, the most powerful being the model of reading itself, with its inherent powers of reversal. Some of his most interesting remedies are contained in his depiction of a succession of readers at the moment of ceasing to read. Generally speaking, this depiction centers on Thoreau, Emerson, and Cavell himself. Later, the list will include Nietzsche, whose Zarathustra proclaims, "Do nothing more for the reader. Another century of readers and spirit itself will start to stink." Zarathustra, however, can scarcely be depicted as *ceasing* to read, since he is hardly depicted as having any interest in reading in the first place.[14]

Perhaps the most striking of Cavell's depicted relinquishments of reading occurs at the end of *The Senses of Walden*. In that book, however, ceasing to read *Walden* is depicted as closely bound up in the crisis of leaving Walden. Cavell wants us to see that leaving *Walden* and letting go of Thoreau's words is as momentous as leaving Walden was for Thoreau. Indeed, Cavell goes further than even this exchange or merger of identities. Or rather, he turns his reflections about the crisis around, on the axis of the need to call it quits:

> Leaving *Walden*, like leaving Walden, is as hard, is perhaps the same, as entering it. I have implied that the time of crisis depicted in this book is not alone a private one, and not wholly cosmic. . . . The hero of the book—as is typical of his procedures—enacts this fact [of neighboring himself; of warning himself; of self-expression as prophecy] as well as writes it, depicts it in his actions as well as his sentences. Of course the central action of building his house is the general prophecy: the nation, and the nation's people, have yet to be well made. And that the day is at hand for it to depart from its present constructions is amply shown in its hero's beginning and ending his tale with departures from *Walden*. [*Senses*, 116.]

I argued in chapter 3 that Cavell's writing incorporated *Walden*'s sense of its crises about voices. But this is also to argue that Cavell's writing has, to some extent, incorporated *Walden*'s voices. He also took on himself at least the posture of Thoreau's isolation, along with Thoreau's anxiety about the conditions of our public culture and what we might call our popular identity. Here the writer of *Walden* is seen by Cavell to have made something significant—some new construction—out of his departure from Walden. But as Cavell indicates with the present tenses ("leaving *Walden* is hard"), he is in some way identifying the crisis of leaving the pond with the crisis of finishing a book. And at this stage, it is hard to tell which book is in question—*Walden* or the book about Walden. The book that teaches us how to read *Walden* by giving readings of *Walden* is not always at pains to distinguish its own voice from *Walden*'s.

And distinguishing these books is doubly hard, because from almost the beginning Cavell has been insisting that *Walden* is itself a book that is supposed to teach us how to read *Walden*. Now it becomes clear that one of the things he learned from the writer of *Walden* is a peculiar mode of identification and competition between reader and writer. This might be scarcely more than self-aggrandizement, with some book-club sentiments about the encouragement of reading. (It might have to be a somewhat self-conscious and even postmodern book club, but such things are not unheard of.) But given the specific points of identification of Cavell (this reader-as-writer) and Thoreau (this writer-as-reader), some basis for the claim of exchanged identities has been set out. The business of ending a reading (in some sense private) of *Walden* is discovered to be the same as the business of beginning a public reading of it. In both cases, an image of passive acceptance of a need is compounded by a sense of the stern resolve that wise passiveness requires:

> But in *Walden*, reading is not merely the other side of writing, its eventual fate; it is another metaphor of writing itself. The writer cannot invent words as "perpetual suggestions and provocations"; the written word is already "the choicest of relics" (iii, 3, 5). His calling depends on his acceptance of this fact about words, his letting them come to him from their own region, and then taking that occasion for inflecting them one way instead of another then and there, or for refraining from them then and there; as one may inflect the earth toward beans instead of grass, or let it alone as it is before you there. [28.]

We do not just accept the provocation of a writer's acceptance of his own provocations. We must also accept the distance of his words from us, and the words must respect the region of their origin. In Cavell's work, this acceptance turns not so much on accepting his departure from Walden as on accepting the book *Walden* as a book of departures. Each act of writing is already an act of reading—of acceptance—and also a moment of inflection, hence of ceasing to read.

Cavell wants the larger pathos of the departure of *Walden*. But he also wants to prepare us for the smaller crises—and the smaller ecstasies—of reading. His book begins with a departure of its own:

> The very greatest masterpieces, when one is fresh from them, are apt to seem neglected. At such a time one knows without stint, how unspeakably better they are than anything that can be said about them. An essential portion of a teaching of *Walden* is a full account of its all but inevitable neglect. [3.]

He has just finished a reading of *Walden*. And he finds, as is typical of Cavell, a nice thing to say about a treasured author. But suppose we pause for a moment on the idea of a book's being "unspeakably better" than the things one can say about it. Where does one get the stamina to take on the task of reading such a book? An essential part of learning how to write about *Walden* is to learn how to stop reading it, to call it quits. (This is one of Cavell's most encouraging lessons about reading and writing in general.) Calling it quits in this fashion is not a matter of giving up on a writer, and it is not to be taken as an act of ingratitude. One might think of it rather as one of the reversals that gratitude is capable of. As with the reversals of reading, the opposition in question is formed within the deepest of affinities.

L etting myself work through the fantasy of wanting to know what the text knows and forgoing that fantasy for the sake of my better instruction takes me back to Cavell's work on what epistemology calls the problem of other minds, and forward to his most recent work on opera and on the melodramas of the Unknown Woman. From the beginning of his work, Cavell keeps before us the need to give up our demand for a knowledge that would allow us to bypass the necessity of acknowledgment. With the model of reading, we are offered a path on which to acknowledge our seduction by the thing we most wanted to know—in this case a text. Freedom from this seduction comes only by working through the attachments that it fosters.

But what then? In the case of "the other," the point of forgoing knowledge is, after all, to know. Acknowledgment was never a kind of substitute for knowledge—a fancy, intuitive form of it that empirically-minded philosophers could never hope to fathom. Acknowledgment is the home of knowledge, the place in our network of everyday relationships and activities that would allow us to receive a genuine knowledge of others, and also to survive it. (Tragedy, for Cavell, was always a measure of the terrible success of knowledge as much as of its failures.) When we succeed in overcoming the fantasy of knowing what the text knows and of becoming the exclusive auditor of the author's voice, where are we? The books that we care enough about to let go of are, after all, books that we wish to go on possessing and being possessed by. How is that outcome different from the *failure* to conclude one's reading, and from remaining the enchanted prisoner of the voices that created us? In both cases, perhaps, we find ourselves alone in a room, with a book at arm's length.

The price of a knowledge—of persons, or texts, or politics—that wishes to dispense with acknowledgment is a kind of madness or isolation. The price of learning to read, and to think, for yourself is that you must relinquish the voices that have formed you. And what if you discover that, in learning to grow up, you have outgrown the only conversation that you know how to care about? The melodramas of the Unknown

Woman mark out one way of surviving such a fate, preserving a knowledge that is capable of judging the world, despite our isolation within it.
Perhaps our access to the sanity and friendliness of the world, and to the
texts and voices of the world, requires a portion of luck. Those of us who
are hoping for a method less continually threatened by isolation and madness must not hope merely to be rid of the unwelcome voices of the past
or, for that matter, of the present or future. We must rather keep learning
to listen for them and to welcome them. Only then can the conversations
of voice and method resume.

Appendix

STANLEY CAVELL
A Brief Account

(Note: The reader may find it useful to be able to consult a brief ac-
count, addressed to an audience with little or no prior knowledge of
Cavell's writing.)

Stanley Cavell's contributions to aesthetics as an American philosopher and critic must be assessed both within his relation to
specific arts of literature, drama, music, and film and against the central
visions of his writing. Cavell's books are, without exception, anchored in
what he painstakingly characterizes as "readings" of particular works.
He is a practicing critic, whose books have addressed Shakespeare, film
comedy and melodrama, Romantic and modernist poetry, Beethoven,
opera, Poe, Thoreau, and Samuel Beckett. This critical labor is continuous,
or intimately discontinuous, with his readings of Wittgenstein, J. L. Austin, Descartes, Emerson, Nietzsche, John Rawls, and Saul Kripke.

The practices involved in "reading a text" are not easy to delineate
accurately, and the demands of critical attentiveness draw Cavell's work
toward an inveterate particularity of detail and example. This makes his
work nearly impossible to summarize usefully. But his writing also contains a series of unifying poles of investigation, around which his work is
constantly circulating and from which he recurrently takes his bearings.
The two most central of these investigations have been his efforts to
diagnose and to undermine skepticism, and his efforts to delineate a
dimension of existence that he calls moral (or Emersonian) perfectionism. These investigations require a recovery of the voice, both literally
and allegorically, from philosophical or human suppression. *Voice* accordingly becomes a third fundamental term in Cavell's work, bridging the
investigations of perfectionism and of skepticism. This idea of voice, consistently correlated with his practices of reading, is especially suggestive

for contemporary aesthetics. At the same time, the interplay of reading and voice invites comparison with Derrida's early depiction of the suppression of writing by the metaphysical idea of the voice.

"Skepticism" here refers less to an intellectual position concerning the impossibility of knowledge and more to the condition that Cavell diagnoses as underlying that position. For Cavell, skepticism is a contemporary version of the ancient human effort to escape the limitations of the human. Cavell characterizes the wish underlying the theoretical problems of skepticism as an intellectual refinement of a wish to repudiate the world. Descartes' withdrawal from the world of everyday cares and transactions is an emblem for Cavell of the philosopher's determination to remove himself from our ordinary links to the world. Cavell reads the skeptic's sense of the insufficiency of those links as first of all a sense of the catastrophic inadequacy of the ordinary world as a scene of knowledge and, second, as the inadequacy of our position within that world. The skeptic then characterizes his sense of the inadequacy of our position in the ordinary world as a failure of our knowledge of that world.

Cavell depicts skepticism not as a false theory but as a belated interpretation of the situation of human beings as knowers of the world. Skepticism disguises a deeper anxiety about our place in the world. Such anxiety reveals something about the fateful precariousness of our knowledge, which the epistemic constructions of skepticism can never catch up with or domesticate. What philosophy takes as the theoretical problems of establishing the existence of what it calls the "external world" or of "other minds" Cavell diagnoses as maintained within the grip of the very wishes and fears they purport to overcome. The wish to refine the terms in which we ordinarily conceive of and grasp the world is revealed as a wish to repudiate our ordinary grasp of that world. And this wish, in turn, is revealed as a wish to repudiate the world as such.

Cavell relates his diagnosis of skepticism to Wittgenstein's sense of our craving for a totality outside of our forms of life; to Emerson's chagrin at our shamefaced withdrawal of words from their indebtedness to the world; and to Nietzsche's diagnoses of nihilism, nostalgia, and other less nameable revenges against time. The problem is therefore not one of refuting skepticism by, for instance, establishing the mind's capacity to secure a true representation of a world external to us or of other minds. This way of putting the problem already accepts too much of skepticism's self-interpretation. Skepticism believes that it has found a previously overlooked problem for the mind, a gap in our knowledge of what we had all been inclined to take for granted. For Cavell, the task of overcoming skepticism is not to prove the skeptic wrong but rather to undo the ways in which the mind has suppressed its ordinary connections to the world. We are, furthermore, thereby to undo the distortion of the criteria and conditions of a knowledge of objects, events, and people that is otherwise unavoidable, or avoidable only at more obvious costs of isolation and madness. The skeptic accepts the problem of the mind working itself out of a theoretical isolation as a cover—and perhaps as a consolation—for the deeper and less manageable separateness of human beings.

In Cavell's reading, Shakespearean tragedy measures the cost of our extraordinary efforts at once to know and not to know. The connection between the drive to knowledge and the refusal of acknowledgment is already in place in "The Avoidance of Love: A Reading of *King Lear*" (1969, 282–85). Though the links between skepticism and tragedy are only implicit in this essay, and in its predecessor "Knowing and Acknowledging," the drawing out of these links occupies the next two decades of his work. The further effects of this connection of skepticism to its various enactments form the ground of every approach he makes to a work of drama, including film and opera.

The point and scope of these connections have often been misunderstood. Not every tragic denial is analogized in the skeptic's renunciations, and not every skeptical collapse can be tracked in the precipitousness of a tragic fall. The denial and banishment of another in order to prevent the exposure of one's love for that other does not provide a ready-made analogy to the skeptic's renunciations of the world. Before such denials become the stuff of skepticism they must allow the other to represent not only the effects of vulnerability to pain and rejection but also those of our liability to losing the world and the world's intelligibility. The tragic protagonist is seen to be preparing for—and thus to be precipitating—the return of some quite particular forms of chaos, comprehensible in terms of the destruction of that intelligibility.

Cavell's study of perfectionism is a further nodal point of the problematic of the self and its various capacities for transformation and retrogression. Perfectionism is meant to provoke us to a transformation according to an ideal internal to the self's constitution, not one imposed from without. Cavell links the dimension of human self-transformation to Aristotle and Plato as far back as the *Apology*'s "care of the mind." In the modern era, he tracks its primary forms in Emerson and in what Nietzsche made of Emerson. Hence it is not merely an upward path, out of the Platonic cave of imprisonment to a brighter region of more perfect being or to some Arnoldian or Eliotic realm of the cultured. Perfectionism is always equally the demand for the relinquishment of false perfections, including the falseness or constriction of those of our virtues that have outlived themselves. Conformity to a false sense of completion is as much what Emerson averts us from as conformity to the false standards of our neighbors. Showing these conformities to be, or to stem from, the same state would be a task of Emersonian epistemology, one that Cavell attempts in *Conditions Handsome and Unhandsome* (1990).

As with skepticism, the philosophy of perfection is not so much illustrated in works of literature as contested by them. This contesting is essential to Cavell's understanding of the relation of literature to philosophy, where both fields undertake to form themselves from a more primitive and somewhat mythological state of voicelessness and self-stupefaction. The "ancient quarrel" of philosophy and poetry is not over who gets to voice the claims of reason. The quarrel is over which field, at a given moment, is capable of undoing the self-constriction of those claims and of permitting the formation of those voices. The common reliance on voice is as much a cause of the tension between philosophy and literature as it is of the reciprocity.

Such tensions between the voices of philosophy and literature are part of the risks that the perfectionist vision must run. As one risk in the Wittgensteinian response to skepticism is a kind of banal rejoicing in the completeness of the ordinary, so a risk of Emersonian perfectionism is the willingness to accept aesthetic achievement in the place of inner change. It is hard to articulate the relation between perfectionism's exaltation of the voice and skepticism's suppression of it, without slipping into a kind of melodramatic aestheticism. One must do more than measure the philosopher's self-stultification against the thrill of Garbo's looks or the sublimity of an aria.

A principal problem for those who would investigate Cavell's work goes like this: the voice that is suppressed by the skeptic relies on and expresses something like Wittgensteinian criteria and hence the ordinary transactions of our daily lives. The recovery of the voice here signifies the return of just this ordinary world, which is at first the only way the world as such can return to us. What is affirmed in the perfectionist ecstasy of the voice is, among other things, something like the possibility of rising above the second-rateness of this world. These possibilities may, or indeed must, coexist in a single self, but it is not always easy to see how. The voice recovered from the skeptical denials can coincide only for a passing moment or in the space of a breath with the voice that is achieved and memorialized in a perfectionist affirmation.

A crucial corollary follows from the transience of these solutions: In perfectionism, the voice is not figured as an icon of some actual self, glorying in its self-sufficient presence to itself. That may be a reasonable way of characterizing either Hollywood's self-image of its repetitious glamour or reconstruction's vision of the metaphysics of "presence." In Cavell's work, the voice betokens not the self-presence of the actual self but the terrifying proximity of what he calls the *next* self. Hence, the very expressive success of the voice (whether in the soprano's melisma or in the banter of Tracy and Hepburn) alludes to the current self as but "half-expressed" (in Emerson's phrase) and as otherwise suffocated and isolated. That the achievements of perfectionism are temporary is hardly surprising in a vision that emerges from the temporal character of our existence, in particular from the fact of our having begun as children.

Like the work of other philosophers who delineate a field of struggle between philosophy and the specific arts, Cavell's work tends to subvert the very idea of a study of the arts that is essentially separable from the burden of philosophy as a whole. But the study of aesthetics reemerges as an essential dimension of philosophy's knowledge of its own conditions. Cavell isolates a kind of analogy between the conditions of our judgment of a work of art and the conditions under which philosophy seeks to formulate and to communicate its own results. In an early essay, "Aesthetic Problems of Modern Philosophy," he notes Kant's invocation of the idea of a "universal voice" as a means of characterizing the subjective necessity in an aesthetic judgment. He goes on to draw an analogy between such a judgment and the expression of a claim to know what "we ordinarily say" in a given situation.

It is no longer easy to imagine the audience for a comparison between the claim that "The *Hammerklavier* sonata is a perverse work" and the claim that "When we ask 'Do you dress like that voluntarily?' we must be implying that there is something untoward about the way you are dressed." Both remarks can seem to be merely matters of empirical psychology, or perhaps effects of some well-known rhetorical quantities. Moreover, both the aesthetic and the philosophical claim are likely to be taken as *demands* for agreement. But Cavell is arguing that it is truer to the spirit of such claims that they are rather (1) invitations to investigate whether such an agreement in our responses already exists, or (2) part of an effort to make sense of the fact that we go on making such judgments in the likelihood precisely of *disagreement*.

In the case of the philosophical claim (e.g., that there is something fishy about an action), Cavell argues that disagreement is still the beginning of philosophy, not the end of it: It is a datum for investigation. In the case of aesthetics, the controversy in the claim is an invitation to further experience—on the part of those to whom the claim is directed, but also on the part of the one who makes the claim. The practice of making aesthetic claims is absorbed into the practices of reading and into the (self-) critical efforts to disable the mechanisms by which we keep our reading and our experience at arm's length.

Cavell's appeals to experience and to the practices of reading and criticism imply a rigor of attentiveness that is difficult to capture in (further) words. Apart from his ability to evoke a corresponding power of attentiveness and absorption on the side of his reader, his appeals will seem empty. In the absence of such an absorption and such a willingness to follow the movements of his text, Cavell's writing will tend to be seen merely as a series of critical impressions. And his efforts to describe the path of his words and argument will seem to be the expression of a merely personal sensibility, at once refined and extravagant. Such exaggerations have become part of the reception of his work, and the tendency to exaggerate seems to be independent of whether the reception is hostile or sympathetic.

Perhaps partly in response to this situation, Cavell's writing increasingly formulates the explicit wish to create the understanding by which the precise angle of his thought is to be calibrated and the ear by which his tone is to be apprehended. The wish to intervene directly in the formation of the audience for his words—and hence in the reciprocal formation of himself as the "author" of the words—puts his writing in a line of descent from the Romantic responses to Kant. Cavell insists on the capacity of a philosophical text to intervene in the education of a reader's responses, and this education must not be parceled out in advance among the various disciplinary structures that we inhabit. Along with this insistence, Cavell refuses to grant philosophers the possibility that their discourse might be, in principle, both separable from the work it addresses and unmystified in its self-conception as aesthetics.

Nevertheless, we can still say something about Cavell's relation to the subject of aesthetics, more traditionally construed. Cavell's early work in aesthetics shows both his debts to Kant and his departures from a traditional Kantian orientation. In "Music Discomposed," he puts his finger on the sorest point of Kant's avowals of formalism, namely, his apparent reliance on characterizing the state of mind of the beholder as "disinterested." Rather than abandoning the double bind of a formalism that tends to psychologize the audience of fine art, Cavell's work tries to get underneath both sides of the dichotomy. He insists that the "psychology" of the spectator cannot be understood as prior to the formal considerations of the critic or as known apart from the workings of the work in question. And he advances arguments against any consideration of form as existing apart from an audience, evolving as a mere end in itself.

Cavell has presented treatments of such topics as intention (1969), expression (1979), and metaphor and representation (1969). He has consistently monitored the shifting ground between criticism and its objects. More recently, his work on Shakespeare, film, and opera has led him back to a further consideration of the notion of form. As early as his essay "Music Discomposed," Cavell's work mounts a relentless assault on any comfortable isolation of form from content or of "the work itself" from the terms of its address to an audience. Conversely, he insists that we cannot understand the "psychology" of the audience apart from understanding the spirit in which the audience receives a given work. It is an open question how far understanding this spirit entails that we share in it.

Cavell gradually displaces the idea of the "content" as some sort of passive subject matter or neutral fund of material. At the same time, he dismantles the idea of form as the more or less attractive "container" or conduit in which or by which the content is to be delivered to the appropriate audience. Cavell therefore rejects those accounts that give the highest aesthetic ranking to achievements of form, at the price of insulating the form from the pressure of the realities of history and of everyday life. More generally, Cavell objects to whatever renders the work inert in relation to the audience and the audience passive in relation to the work.

Cavell replaces the idea of form as a kind of envelope or container with an idea of form as a kind of medium of knowledge and power. The form of the work is what presents itself as *active* in that work: active in the work's claim on an audience; active in its working out of the implications of a particular "content" or element; and active in its relations with other members of a genre or medium of an art. Thus the concern with the state of mind of the beholder is, in part, transposed toward questions about the implications of form, and about how these implications are to be received by a representative member of the audience. "Form" and the representative apprehender of form must be defined in relation to each other.

Especially beginning in his work on the "comedies of remarriage" (1981), Cavell explores this developing idea of form as a kind of conversation with other members of a genre. Cavell follows Northrop Frye in resisting the intellectual's typical condescension to popular comedy. Both critics resist the idea of the conventions of a genre as constituting a static formula, whose instances are therefore easy to absorb and in that sense "popular." Cavell's essay "Hamlet's Burden of Proof" (1987) explores an idea of form as working out the conditions under which a Shakespearean drama allows us to know a specific content, construed as a scene of knowing. And he explores some related problems about form and significance in music, most recently turning to questions about opera (1994).

Well before the supposed postmodern promotion of critic to performance artist, Cavell characterized the critical responsiveness of the artist as part of the constitution of a work. Accordingly, in the modern period, the experience of criticism may become "internal to the experience of art" ("Music Discomposed," 1969). By the same token, a given work might seek to undo the terms of criticism and reception it anticipates from a given audience. Cavell thus also resists the relegation of the category of "intention" to some place safely within the artist's "psychology." As with the situation of a human being learning to speak, Cavell thinks of the working out of art's significance as produced in the realm where the individual's capacity for meaningfulness meets the resources of a given culture. Each may find the other wanting, and each might try to suppress what the other is seeking to say. But each is made for—and by—the other.

Notes

PREFACE AND ACKNOWLEDGMENTS

1. William Wordsworth, *The Prelude* (1850 version), in *Poetical Works*, ed. Ernest de Selincourt (London: Oxford University Press, 1935 and 1966), book 5, lines 45–49.

2. Published in *Performativity and Performance: Essays from the English Institute*, ed. Eve Sedgwick and Andrew Parker (Routledge, 1995).

CHAPTER ONE

1. Over the past few years, I have presented material on these topics to the American Society for Aesthetics, the North American Nietzsche Society, the American Philosophical Association, the Ohio Shakespeare Conference, the Department of Philosophy of the University of New Mexico, and the departments of English at Duke University and Tulsa University.

2. Some portion of such a tradition stretches back at least to Plato, and perhaps to Heraclitus. We might locate some modern versions in figures such as Nietzsche and Heidegger, and perhaps in Wittgenstein. Freud's writing, which plays an increasingly apparent role in Cavell's work, presents its own problems. It is often addressed explicitly to a professional or quasi-professional audience, which takes its starting points as already established and its results as detachable from the movement of its argument.

One might study the different places at which a group of professionals is inclined to cut off its discussions from their point of origin and allow them to continue as a more truncated set of issues. These newer versions of the issues may well prove to be more tractable and, in some sense, more productive than the versions that gave the initial impetus to the field. Though this idea is similar to certain remarks of Thomas Kuhn's, it is also very different. And a primary difference is the fact that there is nothing in the paradigms analogous to my idea of contact with the initial sources of the issues and problems: Historians of science are interested in the origins of paradigms. Scientists are interested in using them. This suggests an important asymmetry between the understanding of the relation of past and present in the sciences and that in the humanities.

3. *Philosophical Papers*, third ed. (Oxford: Oxford University Press, 1979), 205–19.

4. *Must We Mean What We Say?* 111.

5. Quoted in Richard Rorty, *Consequences of Pragmatism* (Minneapolis: University of Minnesota Press, 1982), 35. I discuss this passage further in "Where the Action Is: Stanley Cavell and the Skeptic's Activity," 111n4, in *The Senses of Stanley Cavell,* ed. Richard Fleming and Michael Payne (Lewisburg: Bucknell University Press, 1989).

6. *Consequences of Pragmatism,* 92.

7. Ibid.

8. In *After the Future,* ed. Gary Shapiro (Albany: SUNY Press, 1989).

9. Consequences of Pragmatism, 93.

10. Ibid. The passage of Cavell he is referring to is found in *The Claim of Reason,* 236.

11. David Hume, *An Enquiry Concerning Human Understanding,* section 12, part 2.

12. William Wordsworth, "Ode: Intimations of Immortality from Recollections of Early Childhood," in *Poetical Works,* ed. Ernest de Selincourt (London: Oxford University Press, 1936 and 1966), lines 126–28.

13. There are large questions and investigations to be pursued about the various tensions of voice and method throughout the history of philosophy. To get a hearing for these connections in Cavell's work on a philosopher who is unreceptive to that work, I would prefer to start by locating his work on a wider spectrum of issues about philosophy and writing. I might start with questions about why Wittgenstein wrote the way he did, or for that matter why Plato wrote the way he did. One might even come to raise a question about why Kant wrote the way he did. These subjects have until recently been pretty much stalled at the perception that Wittgenstein and Plato wrote dialogues and that Kant wrote "badly." There is more discussion of this topic in chapter 4.

14. A good place to learn about the relation of self-knowledge to the method of appealing to criteria is in Steven Affeldt's dissertation, "Constituting Mutuality: Essays on Expression and the Bases of Intelligibility in Rousseau, Wittgenstein, and Freud" (Harvard, 1996). See also Steven Affeldt, "The Ground of Maturity: Criteria, Judgement and Intelligibility in Stephen Mulhall on Stanley Cavell," *European Journal of Philosophy* 6:1 (April 1998), and Mulhall's reply, "The Givenness of Grammar," in the same issue.

15. Stanley Bates and Ted Cohen, "More on What We Say" (*Metaphilosophy* 3 [January 1972]: 1–24). The article is listed in the useful bibliography, compiled by Peter Fasl, that appears in *The Senses of Stanley Cavell.*

16. Michael Fischer, *Stanley Cavell and Literary Skepticism* (Chicago: University of Chicago Press, 1989).

17. Walter Benn Michaels, "*Walden's* False Bottoms," *Glyph* 1 (1977): 132–49. Cf. Stanley Fish, *Is There a Text in This Class?* (Cambridge: Harvard University Press, 1980).

18. Arnold Davidson, "Beginning Cavell," in *The Senses of Stanley Cavell,* 230–41.

19. Stephen Mulhall, *Stanley Cavell: Philosophy's Recounting of the Ordinary* (Oxford: Oxford University Press, 1994).

20. See my review of Stephen Mulhall's *Stanley Cavell: Philosophy's Re-*

counting of the Ordinary, in *Journal of Aesthetics and Art Criticism* 56:1 (Winter 1998), 83–85.

CHAPTER TWO

1. At least once, Cavell was depicted as Franz Liszt. Cf. Mary Mothersill, review in the *Journal of Philosophy* 72 (January 1975): 27–48. But this perception has not been further cultivated.

2. This is one way I can understand how William Rothman arrives at an image of Cavell's *cogito* that possesses the same structure as Cavell's achievement of self-expression and a voice. See below, this chapter.

3. See Ludwig Wittgenstein, *Philosophical Investigations,* third edition, trans. G. E. M. Anscombe (Oxford: Basil Blackwell, 1958), 230. This passage brings the issue of interest to some sort of head:

> If the formation of concepts can be explained by facts of nature, shouldn't we be interested, not in grammar, but rather in that in nature which is the basis of grammar?—Our interest certainly includes the correspondence between concepts and very general facts of nature. (Such facts as mostly do not strike us because of their generality.) But our interest does not fall back upon these possible causes of the formation of concepts; we are not doing natural science; nor yet natural history—since we can also invent fictitious natural history for our purposes.

This passage is well known, but its complexity is not always acknowledged.

4. William Rothman, "*Vertigo:* The Unknown Woman in Hitchcock," in *Images in Our Souls,* 80. This is reprinted in Rothman's *The "I" of the Camera* (Cambridge: Cambridge University Press, 1988), 152–73. These remarks fit in with Rothman's rather Romantic picture of authorship—in particular, a sense of Hitchcock's authorship and of Rothman's unique acknowledgment of it. I will follow out later my suggestion that Rothman separates the specific details of reading, hence of method, from the practices of acknowledgment, and evidently conceives of acknowledgment as something like a single, prior act of recognition—in particular, the recognition of the unique specialness of the author. This recognition is then the means that enables the critic to accomplish the devotion to careful, even minute, viewing, by means of which the "meaning" of the film is revealed to that critic. See William Rothman, *The Murderous Gaze* (Cambridge: Harvard University Press, 1982).

5. Rothman, "Stella's Taste," in *Pursuits of Reason.*

6. Timothy Gould, "Utterance and Theatricality: A Problem for Aesthetics in Mill's Account of Poetry," in *Pursuits of Reason: Essays in Honor of Stanley Cavell,* ed. Ted Cohen, Paul Guyer, and Hilary Putnam (Lubbock: Texas Tech Press, 1994).

7. Michael Payne's comments about Wittgenstein and Cavell would need to be carefully qualified: "Cavell's practice elaborates on Wittgenstein's creation of a philosophical style that operates simultaneously on two levels. One is the level of an imitation of the human voice." See his introduction to *Philosophical Passages* (Blackwell, 1995), 2–3.

8. In *The Claim of Reason,* for instance, he makes some further points about

the differences between "making" and "checking" a confession, as opposed to making and checking a proof. Related reflections can be found in the last chapter of the first version of *The World Viewed.*

CHAPTER THREE

1. Cavell hints at some of these issues in the foreword to *The Claim of Reason.* For his remarks about the need to revise his first account of the notion of a criterion, see page xviii. For his sense of the connection between the mode of writing philosophy that he came to regard as necessary and the need to relinquish a philosophical project, see pages xviii–xix. For his sense that these external matters of composition and revision are not merely external, see pages xv–xvi.

2. A striking instance of this rift occurs in Richard P. Wheeler's "Acknowledging Shakespeare: Cavell and the Claim of the Human," in *The Senses of Stanley Cavell.* In this essay, certainly one of the best on Cavell on Shakespeare, Wheeler insulates his discussion from the entire range of questions suggested by *The Claim of Reason* and the concluding pair of essays in *Must We Mean What We Say?,* the issues about skepticism's enactment of tragedy and of tragedy's allegorizing and condensing of a skeptical problematic. It is worth keeping in mind, however, that Cavell's critical insights can be put to an interesting use by someone not engaged in the skeptical problematic.

3. In a paper presented to the 1996 meetings of the Eastern Division of the American Philosophical Association, I criticized a version of this reading by Richard Fleming in his *The State of Philosophy* (London: Associated University Presses, 1993). Ed Minar was the respondent, and Fleming chaired the session and participated in the discussion. Both contributions have figured in my revisions of this book.

4. These remarks should be taken as extending my comments on the imitation of a previously existing voice. See, e.g., chap. 2, n. 7.

5. Mulhall brings the political discussion closer to the issues of epistemology and ethics in his *Stanley Cavell: Philosophy's Recounting of the Ordinary.* But here too, he leaves it as a matter of "analogous" structures of certain human fields of inquiry or endeavor.

6. Steven Affeldt reinforced my sense of the relevance of this passage to my argument.

7. For those who take themselves to have a firm grasp on what Cavell's elaborateness is in the service of, I would point out that this particular sentence comprises one hundred twenty-three words, as opposed to the two hundred fourteen words of the book's famous first sentence. This later sentence is far less ornate and mannered. It has its own way of folding over on itself, becoming almost literally involuted. But the two sentences are quite different in their mode of address to the reader and in their demands on a reader's attention.

8. In *After the Future,* ed. Gary Shapiro. See chap. 1, n. 8.

9. See my "Where the Action Is" in *The Senses of Stanley Cavell,* ed. Michael Payne and Richard Fleming (Bucknell University Press, 1989).

10. Henry David Thoreau, *Walden and Other Writings,* Modern Library College Edition, ed. William Howarth (New York: Random House, 1981), 296. References to *Walden* are hereafter incorporated in the text.

CHAPTER FOUR

1. This is a topic that deserves some further treatment on its own. Stevei Affeldt addresses this question and a range of related questions in his dissertatio (Harvard, 1996).

2. See Richard Fleming, *The State of Philosophy: An Invitation to a Readin in Three Parts of Stanley Cavell's* The Claim of Reason (University Presses (America, 1993). See also the introduction to *Pursuits of Reason*. So far as I kno this line of interpretation was first isolated and countered by James Conant in "C Bruns, on Cavell," *Critical Inquiry* 17:3 (Spring 1991). Gerald Bruns's respon to Conant, in the same issue, takes the issue away from "living one's skepticisr and toward the "fragility" of our knowledge. This bears comparison to Cave remarks about the "porousness" of our knowledge. This line of thought wo repay further study. See especially *Must We Mean What We Say?* 337; cf. *L owning Knowledge*, 108.

3. I have learned about these and other matters in conversations with Pe Hylton and more recently from his *Russell, Idealism, and the Emergence of A lytic Philosophy* (Oxford: Oxford University Press, 1990). See also David $ livan, "Frege on the Cognition of Objects," in *Philosophical Topics* 19:2 (1991).

4. Other patterns of traditional philosophical interests might also includ interest in the timeless (or at least the long-term) over the temporal (or the sh term); an interest in mathematics and physical science over poetry; an intere the active over the passive; an interest in the meaning or spirit over the letter an interest in mind or spirit over the body. In the modern age, these prefere are not so much displaced as modified. For example, the metaphysical prefei for the mind over the body is transmuted into an interest in mathematical m of the mind. These are models that by definition need not be embodied in thing human or anything with a human voice and that hence circumver traditional difficulties posed for the mind by the human body.

5. One tack toward such a critical enterprise can be found in Ted C "Beauty as a Symbol of Morality," in *Essays in Kant's Aesthetics*, ed. Ted (and Paul Guyer (Chicago: University of Chicago Press, 1982). Another qui ferent tack can be found in Paul Guyer's *Kant and the Experience of Fre* (Cambridge: Cambridge University Press, 1993).

6. See my remarks on Emerson in "Reading On: *Walden's* Labors of S sion," *Thoreau Quarterly* (Winter 1986).

CHAPTER FIVE

1. See chapters 7 and 8 of *Must We Mean What We Say?* At 213–19, is writing in the mode of full-fledged academic dissection and rebuttal— with his own particular flair for it. Already on 219, however, he is tak asymmetry between asking "Is this music?" and asking "Is this (music) the occasion for an investigation of modernism and Romanticism.

2. J. L. Austin, "A Plea for Excuses," in *Philosophical Papers*. Cf. Cavel ments on the issue of Austin's self-description, for instance in *Must W What We Say?* 102 et passim.

3. J. L. Austin, *How to Do Things with Words*, 2d ed., ed. J. O. Urmson and Marina Sbisà (Cambridge: Harvard University Press, 1962 and 1975), 3–4. Austin immediately went on to qualify the importance of such revolutions and perhaps of philosophy itself.

4. Cf. my "Reading On: *Walden*'s Labors of Succession."

5. This is an assumption that Richard Fleming's *State of Philosophy* tends to make. (See chap. 3, n. 3.)

6. This problematic of originality remains a continuing issue for me. Cf. "The Audience of Originality," in *Essays in Kant's Aesthetics*, ed. Paul Guyer and Ted Cohen (Chicago: University of Chicago Press, 1982); "Intensity and Its Audiences," in *Feminism and Tradition in Aesthetics*, ed. Peg Brand and Carolyn Korsmeyer (Penn State Press, 1995); and the article s.v. "Genius" in the *Encyclopedia of Aesthetics*, ed. Michael Kelly (Oxford: Oxford University Press, forthcoming in 1998).

7. Cavell does not, so far as I know, follow out this particular branching of the forest of linguistic symbols that Thoreau explores. Cf. my "Reading On" and my "Repetition, Anxiety and Unintelligibility in Wordsworth and Marx," delivered at the 1990 Bucknell Conference on Revolutionary Romanticism: 1790–1990.

8. *Philosophical Investigations*, #432. The passage continues, "Is life breathed into it there?—Or is the *use* its life?" The question of the life of our words emerges perhaps only after we have "seen" language as a collection of signs. We should not simply identify the use of language as what gives life to our words. For without the threat of the skeptical vision of language as severed signs, we would not normally experience the life of these words. In the normal course of events, when we are speaking to each other, we do not think of our words as alive—any more than we normally think of ourselves as *using* words. We do not normally take ourselves to be talking "in words"—unless perhaps we mean to distinguish this from all the tacit messages we have been sending each other.

9. It is surely relevant that the statue is slightly animated: the robe, for instance, trembles, or at least seems to tremble.

10. Cf. Gould, "Reading On."

11. Cf. Cavell, *In Quest of the Ordinary*, and Barbara Packer, *Emerson's Fall*.

12. On some occasions, Cavell seems to turn this question around and to consider the possibility of the tropological or sacramental nature of all reading. Cf. Austin's use of the idea of the performative to help defeat a view that thinks of statements and descriptions as the "outward sign" of an inward state.

13. I introduced this theme in chapter 3. There remains a question here about the relation of these introjected voices to the introjected pictures that haunt our words. Working out this relation has been a goal of some of Cavell's recent work on psychoanalysis and cinema, for instance, in his essay on *Letter from an Unknown Woman*. It is one of the themes of my essay "Privacy and Its Pictures," a portion of which was delivered to the Gay and Lesbian caucus of the American Philosophical Association in December 1995.

14. Unless you are willing to take something like reading the text of yourself as a form of reading. See my "What Makes the Pale Criminal Pale?" *Soundings* 68:4 (Winter 1985).

Principal Works of Stanley Cavell

Must We Mean What We Say? New York: Scribners, 1969; Cambridge: Cambridge University Press, 1976.

The World Viewed: Reflections on the Ontology of Film. New York: Viking, 1971; enlarged edition, Cambridge: Harvard University Press, 1979.

The Senses of Walden. New York: Viking, 1972; expanded edition, San Francisco: North Point Press, 1981.

The Claim of Reason: Wittgenstein, Skepticism, Morality and Tragedy. Oxford: Oxford University Press, 1979. Trans. Sandra Laugier and Nicole Balso as *Les voix de la raison.* Paris, 1996.

Pursuits of Happiness: The Hollywood Comedy of Remarriage. Cambridge: Harvard University Press, 1981. Trans. Christian Fournier and Sandra Laugier as *A la recherche de bonheur.* Paris, 1993.

Themes Out of School: Effects and Causes. San Francisco: North Point Press, 1984; reprinted Chicago, 1988.

Disowning Knowledge: In Six Plays of Shakespeare. Cambridge: Cambridge University Press, 1987. Trans. Jean-Pierre Marquerlot as *Le deni de savoir.* Paris, 1993.

In Quest of the Ordinary: Lines of Skepticism and Romanticism. Chicago: University of Chicago Press, 1988.

This New Yet Unapproachable America: Lectures after Emerson after Wittgenstein. Albuquerque and Chicago: Living Batch Press, 1989. Trans. Sandra Laugier as *Une nouvelle Amérique encore inapprochable.* Paris: L'Éclat, 1991.

Conditions Handsome and Unhandsome: Constitutions of Emersonian Perfectionism. Carus Lectures. Chicago, 1990. Trans. as *Conditions noble et ignobles.* Paris: L'Éclat, 1993.

Philosophical Passages: Wittgenstein, Emerson, Austin, Derrida. Oxford: Basil Blackwell, 1995. Contains a comprehensive bibliography of Cavell's writing.

A Pitch of Philosophy. Cambridge: Harvard University Press, 1994.

The Cavell Reader. Ed. Stephen Mulhall. Oxford: Basil Blackwell, 1996.

Contesting Tears: The Hollywood Melodrama of the Unknown Woman. Chicago: University of Chicago Press, 1996.

Selected Bibliography

Bates, Stanley, and Ted Cohen. "More on What We Say." *Metaphilosophy* 3 (January 1972): 1–24.

Cantor, Jay. "On Stanley Cavell." *Raritan* 1 (Summer 1981): 48–67.

Cohen, Ted, Paul Guyer, and Hilary Putnam. *Pursuits of Reason*. Lubbock: Texas Tech Press, 1993.

Fischer, Michael. *Stanley Cavell and Literary Skepticism*. Chicago: University of Chicago Press, 1989.

Eldridge, Richard. "A Continuing Task: Cavell and the Truth of Skepticism." In *The Senses of Stanley Cavell*, ed. Richard Fleming and Michael Payne. Lewisburg: Bucknell University Press, 1989.

———. *Leading a Human Life: Wittgenstein, Intentionality, and Romanticism*. Chicago: University of Chicago Press, 1997.

Fleming, Richard. *The State of Philosophy: An Invitation to a Reading in Three Parts of Stanley Cavell's "The Claim of Reason."* Lewisburg: Bucknell University Press, 1993.

Fleming, Richard, and Michael Payne, eds. *The Senses of Stanley Cavell*. Lewisburg: Bucknell University Press, 1989.

Gould, Timothy. "Stanley Cavell." In *A Companion to Aesthetics*. Oxford: Basil Blackwell, 1992.

———. "Stanley Cavell." In *Encyclopedia of Aesthetics*, ed. Michael Kelly. Oxford: Oxford University Press, forthcoming.

Melville, Stephen. *Philosophy Beside Itself: On Deconstruction and Modernism*. Minneapolis: University of Minnesota Press, 1986.

Mulhall, Steven. *Stanley Cavell: Philosophy's Recounting of the Ordinary*. Oxford: Oxford University Press, 1994.

Smith, Joseph, and William Kerrigan. *Images in Our Souls*. Baltimore: Johns Hopkins University Press, 1987.

Index

Prepared in collaboration with Chris Flink

Gould, Timothy: on fantasies of reception, 61; on methods for studying Cavell, iv–xvi, xviii–xix, 3, 6, 28–29, 44; narrative as implying method, xviii–xix; narrative as requiring confirmation, 6; as replacing issues of style with problematic of voice and method, 3, 54–55, 58–61, 70–72; on shift in Cavell's methods, 1, 4, 7, 132–36; tracing emergence of voice, iv–xvi, 1–4, 6–8, 12, 30, 90, 138; *writings cited:* "Aftermaths of the Modern," 107, 216n.8, 218n.8; "The Audience of Originality," 220n.6; "Genius," 220n.6; "Intensity and Its Audiences," 220n.6; "Privacy and Its Pictures," 220n.13; "Reading On," 220nn.4, 7, 10; "Repetition, Anxiety and Unintelligibility in Wordsworth and Marx," 220n.7; review of Stephen Mulhall, *Stanley Cavell*, 216–17n.20; "The Unhappy Performative," xix, 215n.2; "Utterance and Theatricality," 217n.6; "What Makes the Pale Criminal Pale?" 220n.14; "Where the Action Is," 216n.5, 218n.9. *See also* method; reading; reception; voice

Grice, H. P., 102

Guyer, Paul, xx, 217n.6, 219n.5, 220n.6

Heidegger, Martin, xiv, 50 epigraph, 52, 130, 215n.2; and preserving the authentic word, 61; on thinking as suffering and patience, 198

Hitchcock, Alfred, 72–74. *See also* movies; Rothman

Hölderlin, Friedrich, xiv, 165, 192

Hume, David, 10–11, 20, 24, 92–93; *Enquiry Concerning Human Understanding*, 18–19; "Of the Rise and Progress of the Arts and Sciences," 167–68

Husserl, Edmund, 52, 108

Ibsen, Henrik, 165

Joyce, James, 22

Kant, Immanuel, 17, 28; and critique of metaphysics, 107; and discontinuity between nature and freedom, 180; and Romanticism, 130; as source of our anxiety about words, 18, 195; and sublime, 164; and "universal voice," 80–81

Katz, J., 28–29

Kierkegaard, Søren, 24; as transforming reader's sensibility, 34, 171

knowledge: and acknowledgment, 51, 204; disappointment in its success, 143–44; and evidence, 29–30; fantasy of text as possessing, 193–95, 204; Kantian task of, 195; of others, 142–44, 204; of our possibilities, 8, 194–95; porousness of, 219n.2; relinquishing of, 204; and self-knowledge, xii, 71; of voice, 90; of what we say, 2, 8–30

Kripke, Saul, 86, 147, 207

Kuhn, Thomas, 18, 215n.2

Kuklick, Bruce, 171

Lacan, Jacques, 31, 50, 155, 191

limits (limitations), 109, 119; as acceptance of finitude, 39, 89, 144; skepticism as escape from, 208; transgression of, 3–4

Locke, John, 18, 52

madness, 2, 4, 80; and isolation, 79, 118–19, 204–5; and voices, 106–7, 126–27; as unlimited desire for knowledge, 127. *See also* friendship; method; Thoreau; voice

metaphysics: and ideal meaning, 108; overturning inheritances of, 108–9; and voice, 51–56, 79–80; voice as suppression of writing (Derrida), 107–8. *See also* Cavell; Derrida; philosophy; voice

method (methods), 2, 4–6, 25–27, 205; for acquiring self-knowledge, 25–26; Cavell's debt to, 6; as connected to philosophical progress, 4, 68, 75, 133; fervor of, 77; and hearing or listening, 49, 51, 57, 60, 91; inheritance of, 4, 75; and isolation, 205; as not personal, 26, 71–77; scandal of, 26; vs. style and substance, 3, 58–60; as taking representative steps, xviii–xix, 1–2, 66, 67, 71–72, 122, 150–51, 157–59, 188; in Thoreau and Emerson, 13–14. *See also* Cavell; Freud; ordinary language; reading; representative

Michaels, Walter Benn, 31, 216n.17

Mill, John Stuart, 10, 17, 24; *Autobiography*, 45

Monk, Ray (biographer of Wittgenstein), 71, 76